No Mud on the Back Seat:

Memoirs of a Reporter

To Brant Ducey,
with best wishes,
Gerald Clark

Also by Gerald Clark

Impatient Giant: Red China Today
The Coming Explosion in Latin America
Canada: The Uneasy Neighbor
Montreal: The New Cité

Canadian Cataloguing in Publication Data

Clark, Gerald, 1918-

No mud on the back seat : memoirs of a reporter

Autobiography.

ISBN 1-895854-39-3

1. Clark, Gerald, 1918-   .   2. History, Modern - 20th century.
III. Journalists - Quebec(Province) - Montréal - Biography.   I. Title.

PN4913.C42A3 1995   070.92   C95-940425-2

To receive our current catalogue and be kept on our mailing list for
announcements of new titles, send your name and address to:

Robert Davies Publishing,
P.O. Box 702, Outremont, Quebec, Canada H2V 4N6

Gerald Clark

No Mud on the Back Seat:

Memoirs of a Reporter

ROBERT DAVIES PUBLISHING

MONTREAL— TORONTO

This book may be ordered in Canada from

General Distribution Services,
☎1-800-387-0141 / 1-800-387-0172 FAX 1-416-445-5967;

in the U.S.A., from Associated Publishers Group,
1501 County Hospital Road,
Nashville, TN 37218
dial toll-free 1-800-327-5113;

or call the publisher, toll-free throughout North America:
1-800-481-2440, FAX (514)481-9973.

The publisher takes this opportunity to thank the
Canada Council and the *Ministère de la Culture du Québec*
for their continuing support of publishing.

For my grandchildren,
Rose and Clark Sacktor

CONTENTS

Introduction

Back in 1969 Dean Acheson titled his U.S. State Department memoirs *Present at the Creation*. That's one event Gerald Clark did not cover, one of the few. (At least it's not included in these recollections).

Though too modest to confer a title on himself, Gerald Clark can be considered the dean of Canadian journalists with a career that goes back to the Dirty Thirties and doesn't show any signs of winding down after almost six decades. His reports appear often in *Reader's Digest.*

Take a deep breath and consider what this chronicle includes: the Normandy landings; his "liberation" of Paris; the historic link-up of allied and Soviet forces on the Elbe; a vivid eye-witness account of beaten Germans placing their signatures on the unconditional surrender document; the deliverance at Buchenwald. But this is not a chronicle of war. It does include, though, its aftermath: riveting accounts of the trials of the pitiful Marshal Pétain and the monster, Adolf Eichmann. Readers are brought up to today's headlines with a visit to Sarajevo.

There's only peripheral mention of honors bestowed on him by his peers in Canada, but they are especially cherished. There is not a celebrated newspaperman alive who does not want to be known first as a reporter. Gerald Clark is such a reporter.

Shining through these pages are the greatness of David Ben-Gurion who forecast the day when Israel would finally find peace; the brave men who saw Sharpeville not only as a massacre but as a signal that things would never be the same again for South Africa's blacks; the mourning parents of Argentina who to this day hold a vigil for thousands of their children, *los desaparecidos,* victims of the murderous regime that was never brought to justice; the warm and wonderful people of Russia whose endurance is being tested in a different way fifty years after Adolf Hitler was sent to his doom.

A trip to "Red China" as it was called in 1958 won Gerald Clark an Emmy in his appearance with Walter Cronkite in a CBS documentary that led to a book — his first. Network attempts to lessen the impact met a brick wall with this Canadian journalist. At last count Gerald Clark made forty trips to the Middle East where he has spoken to Israel's founders and to its current leaders. One of the most tender episodes in his book tells of his talk with Anwar Sadat and his beautiful wife in Cairo.

Gerald Clark's Canadianism comes through unself-consciously, and I know readers will share his pride without embarrassment. In his long career he rarely has felt it necessary to knock others but he has always reserved his right to criticize anyone, though scolding doesn't come naturally. But he does take time to think — and recall.

I've known Gerald Clark for forty years. During all of this time we were with *The Montreal Star* family, Gerald Clark starting as a staffer with the Cinderella *Standard* that blossomed into a national magazine and I in the 1950s as news editor of *The Herald,* a tabloid that was a victim of corporate euthanasia during its renaissance. For a few years on *The Star* Gerald Clark was my boss as editor, but few knew it: he was almost always somewhere else, interviewing the legendary "Che" Guevara in Havana or tracking down a provocative episode in Laos. One of my favorite recollections is how he came back from India with an account of why a birth control campaign failed; planners had simply failed to anticipate human nature. But enough; let Gerald Clark tell his own stories. As an associate editor I took the bows for putting out the opposite editorial page. But I take no bows for this masterwork.

Edward W. Barrett
Montreal

Preface

IN THE FIVE DECADES SINCE I BEGAN WORK, the world has undergone not only an ideological revolution — the end of the Soviet Union and the decline of communism — but a communications revolution. The newspapers I first knew were community institutions, largely replaced now by network television and an inadequate effort by local broadcasters to do in pictures what the press did in words.

Even the kind of journalists I knew have long since disappeared, apart from death, into offices located in their homes. Newspapers rely increasingly on self-employed reporters — "freelance" was the generic term of the past — who send their stories by modem or fax to editors they rarely meet. Gone is the verbal skirmish in a rest room or the dissection of the day's paper at a nearby bar. Gone is the commiseration among reporters about the stupidity or prejudice of people handling their copy — and reverse comment by copyreaders.

It would be useless to say the old ways were better; I would be branded as fogyish — and rightly so. Some practices of a half century ago — such as pandering to advertisers at the expense of honesty — can't be defended. But if the comparative measure is human contact, and the sheer drive of pleasure in work, I stand by the old ways. One common denominator does link the past with the present — the hunt for the big story, the challenge of getting it. I hope the following pages will show why.

The Montreal Star company drew my early newspaper allegiance. The organization no longer exists, having collapsed in 1979. I am indebted for continued outlet of my reportage to several publications. In particular it is to the Canadian edition of *Reader's Digest* that I express my appreciation for keeping open a world of unbounded horizons.

On a personal level I want to tell Barbara how grateful I am for her patience and sensitivity to my moods and needs. Without her tender encouragement this book would have been much more difficult to write.

Montreal, February 1995   Gerald Clark

1 "He Never Said He Loved Me"

THE WAR IN EUROPE WAS APPROACHING ITS CLIMAX that Sunday afternoon in May of 1944 when I sat in the bar of the Hotel Scribe in Paris. I was waiting for Jacqueline, a lovely young woman I met during the city's liberation. Now I was rewarding myself with a few days of relaxation after covering a great moment in history, the link-up of allied and Soviet forces on the Elbe River in Germany, the allies coming from the beaches of Normandy and the Russians from the banks of the Volga.

Jacqueline was late — as usual. The Scribe was the base in Paris for war correspondents, but few congregated that day in the bar. Most were at the front, where I should have been. I was reflecting with satisfaction on my link-up report when a press officer from Supreme Headquarters burst into the bar. He glanced around, spotted me, and rushed over. "Thank God I've found you!" he exclaimed. "We need a Canadian."

The next thing I knew I was on a bus with sixteen other correspondents — American, British — and then on a plane heading for Reims. There we witnessed the German surrender.

A few years later, back in Montreal, I accepted an invitation to address a group of women students at McGill University. I chose as my theme the lucky breaks in journalism. A corollary was that it didn't always pay to be conscientious. I cited the example of how I happened to be awaiting a date in the bar of the Scribe, when I should have been elsewhere, and as a result was thrust into the greatest story of my life. I went on to talk about newspaper coverage of serious post-war problems. My speech over, I called for questions. A dozen hands shot up, and, before I could respond, a dozen voices chorused, "What happened to the date?"

It was amusing. But frivolous questions disappointed me. I was pretty earnest in those days. Gradually, though, I realized that great world events can be regarded from a variety of perspectives. Even romantic dates can be important. I developed an easy reply to the recurring question. I learned to say, "She was waiting for me in the bar when I got back the next day." But I have yet to figure out the key ingredients to a happy vocation. Devotion and training obviously rank high. But timing and breaks do play a major part.

So does an awareness that truth is not always appreciated. In the early 1950s, when the motion picture industry was beginning to feel the impact of television, I spent a few weeks in Hollywood writing a series of articles. About the first question I heard from men, on returning home, was this: Which actresses did I bed? Apart from fact that I didn't detect anyone grabbing for me, they work hard — up five a.m. to get to the studio, filming sometimes beyond nightfall. These people are tired. I received only disappointed glances in return for the confession that I survived Hollywood chaste.

I was back a year later to do another series. This time I had the answer ready to the inevitable jab in the ribs and query, "How did ya do?" "Not bad," I said. "Not bad at all." Men looked at me with envy, never the wiser, their imaginations soaring to wherever they wanted to take them. It cost me nothing in terms of professional integrity. Cary Grant told me his favorite definition of Hollywood: "A lot of neurotic actors making a lot of neurotic noises for a lot of neurotic listeners." I didn't feel that I was guilty of the same crime, playing down — or writing down or talking down — to people who lacked the opportunity to explore Hollywood or other places.

On the contrary I have never felt any story was trivial or unworthy of attention. Fabrication is unacceptable, but reliance on the reader's own power of deduction can be desirable. Obviously some stories are more meaningful than others, but in all, something, even a little something, can be learned and received with appreciation. On the way back from Hollywood I stopped in Las Vegas — it was a new escape haven in those days. I reported on "Glitter Gulch." The story was summed up for me in one memorable scene at the pool-side of The Desert Inn: a long-legged beauty stretched out on a chaise lounge in a bikini, mink stole around her shoulders. In one hand she held the stem of a martini glass, in the other a book called *How to Fight Fear.*

One of the most difficult challenges in journalism is to find that kind of scene — a simple illumination of a hidden condition. One strives for it, and rarely happens on it. This ties in also with another of my pet beliefs — the importance of serendipity, the unpredictable dividend of travel. In China, in 1958, long before the country opened up to western correspondents, I held a brief, virtual monopoly on the news coming out. The world wondered, as I did, about the rumblings of the sleeping giant.

A big part of the story was the "Great Leap Forward," China's rapid ascent into the Twentieth Century. The country lacked technology but was rich in human energy — at the time generated by eight hundred million people — and ingenuity. How could one translate these forces? I made notes of the dexterity with which craftsmen fashioned lengths of pipes to repair worn ducts in makeshift factories. But nothing I saw came close to ideal imagery — until one day I spotted some children, aged perhaps six or seven, playing in a farm commune. They bobbed up and down on teeter-totters, seesaws. And while they played happily they were unaware they pumped water for irrigation.

Journalism denotes the unusual, either in content or conveyance. That is, the reporter sometimes is placed in the peculiar position of acting not only as public messenger — relaying in print or screen another person's point of view, whether it is theatrical or political — but serving as private courier. In June 1979 I flew to Cairo, my wife with me, for an interview with Anwar Sadat, Egypt's president. The Canadian government was considering moving its embassy in Israel from Tel Aviv to Jerusalem. This would have implied recognition that all Jerusalem, including Arab portions occupied in the 1967 war, rightfully belonged to Israel. On the plane I read an article about Sadat's wife Jehan in Playgirl magazine, in which she complains that he never says, "I love you."

The interview took place at the presidential villa a few hundred metres from the Great Pyramids of Giza. Sadat, as I expected, was both composed and forthcoming. Dressed in navy blue leisure suit with open neck, he paused only to puff his pipe or sip a glass of fruit juice while he condemned Ottawa's thinking. He said that if the embassy move was carried out it would destroy among Arab countries Canada's credibility as a good broker.

After my interview, I asked Sadat a personal question: Would he cooperate in my idea of writing his biography — indeed, a joint biography, the story of what motivated both Sadats. I don't know what possessed me, but I quoted that bit from Playgirl. He laughed and said, "Of course I love her." Then we moved to the terrace, where my wife presented Sadat with a sketch she had just made of the pyramids. His eyes twinkling, he shut both eyelids fleetingly in his celebrated smile. "I have agreed to let your husband write my biography," he announced. Sadat was assassinated before our venture could commence.

From the Pyramids we were driven to the presidential apartment in Cairo for an interview with Mme Jehan Sadat. The lasting impression she conveyed was one of grace and dignified restraint. Her classic English good looks — from her mother's side — blended with dark, lovely Egyptian features. Her beauty was more striking than in any photos I had seen. We talked about her remarkable role as a leading feminist in the Islamic world, of her fight to foster birth control despite religious qualms of her husband.

When the formality of the interview was over, I related my conversation with Anwar Sadat about love. "What did he say?" she asked eagerly. "He said he loves you," I replied. She beamed, the pleasure so clear. Such is the way in which momentous international news becomes overshadowed by yet more momentous personal news.

What is the real role of the reporter? To listen, to observe, to question, and to put together dispassionately collected information by dismissing personal prejudices. It is an impossible task, and anyone who claims total "objectivity" must be inhabiting a computerized module. About the best you can hope for is some clue that will provide an understandable dimension.

In 1990 I attended a reception at the Czechoslovak embassy in Moscow. The host, the Czech ambassador, was Rudolf Slansky — a name from the dark past in the Stalin era of Eastern Europe. His father, Rudolf senior, had reigned as Communist leader in Prague in 1951. Stalin regarded Slansky as not sufficiently subservient, and ordered his execution. Now the son, newly arrived in Moscow, was greeting high Soviet officials. He was, plainly, a bewildered man. What phenomenal changes had caused this topsy-turvy situation? What was the extent of Russia's revolution? Not the old one, of 1917 — rather, the equally profound one of the 1990s?

I stood in the midst of three or four ambassadors, including Slansky, discussing the difficulties assailing Mikhail S. Gorbachev, the Soviet president. "He is taking a middle course," observed the Swedish ambassador, Örjan Berner, "but, as we know, the middle is always flexible." Slansky nodded gravely, "Yes, flexible, but pushing to the right." Added to Gorbachev's problems were the demands for independence from such Soviet republics as Lithuania. West Germany's ambassador, Klaus Blech, criticized the Lithuanians for acting too hastily and contributing to the worries of foreign powers about the Soviet leader's tenure.

"The European dog," said Blech, "will not allow its tail to be wagged by its Lithuanian head."

For me, the reporter, it was the kind of nugget that only occasionally pops to the surface to illuminate an attitude or highlight complex events. But who was to know that in 1991 an attempted coup would nearly finish Gorbachev, and what remained of his power would soon end? And that Europe, rather than restraining Lithuania, would welcome it as a new member of the United Nations?

In 1993 I was back in Moscow, startled by the changes. In 1990 people had money to spend, but shops had little to offer. In 1993 the stores were brimming with food and merchandise, much of it imported from the West. But few Russians could afford anything beyond essentials. Gangsters, exploiting the collapse of authoritarian government and police mechanism, paraded in wealth and ostentation. In one hotel, the new Aerostar, a racketeer strode across the lobby, a bodyguard in front, another behind. The hotel's chief of security, a retired New York cop, said, "I keep asking them to be less obvious."

The story of the former Soviet Union was blighted by lawlessness, bordering on anarchy, but the story of Czechoslovakia, which I also returned to, stood out as a happy and positive example of a tortured country's emergence into democracy and stability.

It was while I was in Moscow in 1955 that my daughter Bette was born in Montreal. I received the cabled news at four a.m. Delighted and excited, I banged on the door of my next door neighbor, Daniel Shorr, who had just opened a CBS news bureau in Moscow. This was at the National, a very Russian hotel — even Lenin lived there at one time — and a sleepy Shorr shared a drink with me.

Five years later I was at the Ashoka Hotel in New Delhi, to cover an impending visit to India of U.S. President Dwight Eisenhower, when I received another pre-dawn cable — from London, where I was then living. It was from a friend, informing me that my wife Rosalie had just undergone serious emergency surgery. Waiting for the first flight back, I tried desperately to contact London. I could not get through on a commercial phone. Again I turned to Dan Schorr, also staying at the Ashoka.

Schorr called me into his room, sat me down and calmed me. He had a phone I could use, he said. Through happenstance, members of the U.S. Signal Corps had been there the day before to install a line to the White House in Washington. Obviously it was in error, but Schorr was not a person to lack appreciation for good fortune and instant communication. I picked up the phone and I heard a relay of American soldiers passing my call through Kabul, Afghanistan to Ankara, Turkey, across Europe, and into London.

Much later I wrote the commanding officer of the White House Army Signal Agency, Lt. Col. George J. McNally, to thank him and his men. In reply, he expressed gratification that his busy personnel had been able to assist "one of our Canadian friends." Today's cellular phones, homing in on satellites, would circumvent a similar problem of contact. But could a cellular phone arouse an immediate, softly spoken response of a colleague, or the magic of hearing the link by link span of distance, or the reminder that Canadians and Americans are always "friends"?

At times I wish I had been a novelist. Bizarre situations can be made so much more believable in fiction than in fact. I've long been haunted by a story told to me by an acquaintance, a Canadian security official who worked in London in the 1950s. A veteran of the Canadian navy, commander of a corvette in the North Atlantic, he recounted how he had spent forty-eight straight hours on the bridge tracking U-boats preying on a convoy of freighters. Survivors of one submarine were picked up, including the captain, who was escorted to the bridge. The German captain started to harangue and insult him. The Canadian, his nerves ragged, hauled out his pistol, and shot and killed the German.

Only a fiction writer could do justice to this shocker, projecting what must have deranged the Canadian's mind and continued forever to torment him. But I am not complaining. I cannot think of a happier or more gratifying profession than the one I chose.

Nor could I have received a more challenging opening to life — born at the end of World War I, educated during the Great Depression, launched into a career at the start of World War II. It was a period of easy decisions: you accepted gratefully such comforts as you could find, without expecting too many more; you worked because there was no choice; you went to war without questioning it. Later generations might resist participation in such horrors as Viet Nam, but few people doubted the justice in confronting Hitler in 1939. Realism and idealism dwelt amicably together.

In a strange way a break, though I only realized it at college, involved my name. It also provides a commentary on the times, the 1930s and after, when anti-Semitism was nasty in Canada. My father was born Shmuel Klughaupt in 1879. An early photo shows him in the uniform of the Austrian army. He looked handsome and daring. But the look is deceptive. He was not a willing soldier. He was a draftee, like most of his contemporaries. If I want to be fashionable, I cite his Austrian background and leave it to the listener to wonder if he came from Vienna.

In fact his home was a small town, Potletch, in Galicia, Poland, part of the Austro-Hungarian empire. As a Jew, his future was limited. His family was poor, his education mainly at a *yeshiva*. He fled the army, a common practice, and migrated to Manchester. There, like so many other immigrants, he worked in a clothing factory. There, too, he met the young woman, Polly Fink, also of Galicia, who was to become my mother. But first Shmuel was determined to get to Canada, and later he would bring Polly for marriage.

Steerage to Montreal on an Allen steamer cost twenty-five dollars. Shmuel disembarked in Montreal in 1903. Immigration formalities were minor, but an official at the bottom of the gangplank asked the names of the newly arrived. When my father said, "Shmuel Klughaupt," the officer said, "You can't come to a new country like Canada with a name like that. What did you do in England?" "I was a clerk," said my father, pronouncing it the English way. There and then, he was renamed Samuel Clark.

I was born with that surname, my given name Jacob. But my older sister Ida decided she preferred Gerald, and that was the way I was brought up. Name changing was routine. Indeed, Ida later became Judith. In my case, who knows what the impact might have been in later years if my by-line had read Jacob Klughaupt? "Klughaupt" in German means "clever head." It might have sounded distinguished, certainly more so than "Clark". More likely, in an age of prejudice it would have bestowed a handicap.

Like other immigrant families we lived in the early years in the area of "The Main," St. Lawrence Boulevard, the border between "English" Montreal and "French" Montreal. We graduated from flats or duplexes on St. Elizabeth Street to Clark Street to Jeanne Mance, to Hutchison, and then came the big jump to Notre Dame de Grace in the West End. There were six of us — my parents, my sisters Ida and Ruth, my brother Harry. I was the youngest, and always felt protected and loved.

I wish I could say there was constant laughter, the sound of music, intensity of debate and intellectual discussion. There was a bit of this, but in general it was a home like most others of the immigrant middle class, preoccupied with toil, survival — and advancement. My father, working as a cutter and buttonhole maker, took a night course in pattern-making. Then he managed to start his own women's garment factory. It boasted the impressive appellation "Smart Style Cloak Company," but it was never a big business. I remember it as a struggle always, my father returning home at eight or nine at night, after fourteen hours of work, a copy of *Forward,* a major Yiddish newspaper from New York, under his arm.

My mother never complained of the hour; such a notion was unheard of; after all, he was trying to provide a decent home for his family. For that matter, my mother was the uncomplaining type. Weren't all mothers in the olden times? I do know that one day, when I was six or seven, my mother, without telling my father, marched off to the dentist to have all her teeth extracted. Then she marched home again. That's the way people functioned. Independence? Self-sufficiency? Feminism? I don't know. It was long before I ever heard of the feminist movement.

While my mother brought him dinner (the children had long since eaten), my father sat at the table scribbling figures in a margin of *Forward.* The sale of a few suits to a department store could determine whether there would be enough money to pay his staff of a dozen or so. When he wasn't immersed in the vital figures, he would quote from an article in *Forward* and tell me if only I read Yiddish I would get so much value from newspapers and books.

In fact, I could read a little Yiddish. But mainly I was studying Hebrew. A so-called *rebbe* — not a rabbi but a teacher — came to the house once or twice a week after my regular school hours. Under his direction I would repeat the Hebrew, usually in a prayer book. But when I asked what it meant, he pulled my chin in irritation. It was none of my business what it meant. It was my obligation just to read in blind faith. I doubt if even he, a refugee from an Eastern Europe *shtetl,* understood the words. That was the style of the age. For me, frustrating.

We had a kosher home and observed the High Holidays, but not much more. Judaism as an attitude was important — always the implicit fear of rejection or persecution by non-Jews — but formal religion was not uppermost. The point, anyway, was that my parents emphasized the value of education, typical of that generation, and were prepared to make any sacrifice to ensure that we received a good one. My mother could think of only one objective — that I would become a doctor. Not only was that the most socially acceptable profession; it meant that a Jewish boy, barred from such fields as engineering and banking, would be guaranteed a decent livelihood.

My father was less dogmatic. He gave me the feeling I would make my own choice, and that would be fine. From him I learned something of pride in quality of work, no matter what the occupation. In his own way he was an artist. Once, he stitched together small branches of fir trees and took my mother to a fancy dress ball dressed as "King and Queen of the Mountain." They won first prize. He was also a perfectionist. I came to appreciate this as a schoolboy when I worked summers in his factory in the Wilder Building on Bleury Street. To this day, whenever I walk into a clothing factory the sounds and the odors send my memory back to early teens and the early 1930s — the not unpleasant sour aroma of animal furs neutralizing human perspiration.

But most of all I can still see my father arguing with a buyer from Holt Renfrew, the high fashion store, who wanted the hemline of a coat two inches longer than he had created it. "This is the way I designed it, this is the way you'll take it," he told her. "Otherwise don't order it." I can't recall the result, except that in my mind it represented integrity. I wasn't aware whether it reflected good or bad business practice. I had problems of my own. Part of my job was to sweep the factory floor, but my father's insistence on the flawless drove him sometimes to check the corners himself. He did the same to buttonholes made by a woman I can place only as Mrs. Blumenthal.

If my father possessed a belief in probity rather than profit, I picked up some hints about the world of real commerce by the time I got to college. I worked at Eaton's, the city's largest department store, a few Saturdays — whenever they called — and during Christmas breaks. My first assignment was as a sales clerk in the sports department. A pile of ice skates clogged counter space. The skates weren't budging at the depression price of $3.19 a pair.

But they vanished in hours after the manager put them "on sale" at $3.49.

My second lesson came when I was assigned to stand on the alert at the bottom of escalators during the Christmas shopping rush. If a woman laden with parcels stumbled I was to leap into action. But since the store's insurance policy covered bodily injury, my instructions were to ignore the customers. My mission, at age seventeen, was to prevent damage to goods by grabbing at flying parcels, not insured.

The need to work was quite simple. You worked if you wanted to go to college — if you could find a job during the depression. One of my closest friends, Jerry Smith, whose father had lost his wealth in the 1929 stock market crash, rose at five o'clock every morning, before going to classes, to deliver *The Gazette.* The newspaper cost five cents in those days, and his take was one cent. Smith was lucky to earn five dollars a week, but it went far toward paying tuition fees of two hundred and fifty dollars a year. Another friend, Monty Berger, turned his stamp-collecting hobby into a very modest mail order stamp business.

Apart from sporadic breaks at Eaton's, I plodded from door to door for Lovell's city directory, assembling names and occupations of residents. Some of the other gatherers would sit in a park scribbling phoney names and information. I was too timid, too conscientious. Once, on Hutchison Street where I had climbed three flights of stairs — two outside, one inside — I asked the usual, "Any boarders?" and when the lady of the house said, "No," I went down to street level, only to have her shout after me, "Does that include roomers?" I struggled up again and said, "Yes." "Oh," said she, "we haven't any roomers either." I'm not yet sure what lesson I absorbed — maybe never to be surprised by answers to questions.

The economics of the period imparted a lasting meaning: the value of pennies. For a few summers I enjoyed a job as counsellor at Camp B'nai Brith. The campers paid nothing for a two weeks' stay — it was a charitable operation. The job yielded ten dollars the first season. On days off, counsellors hitchhiked into Ste. Agathe, seven miles away. Since few cars traveled the unpaved road — or anywhere, for that matter— most of the time we just hiked. Ten of us would gather late at night in Ste. Agathe, at Levine's handy store, to wait for Mr. Levine to let us pile into his taxi — at a fare of ten cents each. Mr. Levine earned one dollar for a return run of fourteen miles.

Not everyone went to college. Of those who did go, I don't recall any of our crowd whose parents could afford the entire cost; we all contributed. Nor did anyone go to college out of town. The goal was McGill University, which stood high in reputation and, located in the centre of Montreal, close in geography.

But apart from the question of money, the first requirement was to win a qualifying score. Matriculation tests totalled one thousand marks. If you received six hundred, you were in — that is, if you weren't Jewish. A Jew needed seven hundred and fifty. The point, as university officials rationalized, was that Jews were so smart it was not unreasonable to expect from them a greater number of points, that without this precondition Jews would flood classrooms.

Nowhere was there an open perception that "smart" students inevitably would outshine those less smart. The Jewish enrolment in McGill's first year in medicine was confined to nine students — ten per cent of the total. But even anti-Semitic patients sought out Jewish doctors, in the simple belief that these had been bred from generation to generation to cure disease, and the quota system sustained this quality. Bigotry, not logic, was the rationale. But I didn't think these things then; I only thought about them years later. When I was accepted by McGill, I was relieved and grateful. The quota system, the discrimination, was not questioned. Challenging it was inconceivable. It was a fact of life.

McGill was comfortable and compact, with only three thousand students (contrasted with forty thousand today). Though a few buildings were cut off from the main campus on Sherbrooke Street, everyone seemed at least to recognize everyone else. The intimate atmosphere was retained in relatively small classes and a variety of campus activities. Jewish students knew there was little point trying to get into the Scarlet Key Society, whose members acted as ushers at important university functions or met and entertained distinguished visitors. The Scarlet Key was almost the exclusive preserve of Gentiles. Nor did Jews feel comfortable about the Players' Club or the Red and White Revue. But there was always *The McGill Daily*.

Since its founding in 1911, the *Daily* had attracted Jewish students to the editorial staff. There was a chance for free expression, seeing one's written words in print. But most of all there was shelter and excitement in the *Daily's* office in the basement of the McGill Union, the building for student activities on Sherbrooke Street. Many students declined or could not afford to accept invitations to join fraternities or sororities. But the *Daily* took pride in its reputation as "the best damn fraternity on the campus."

I loved it, from the moment I stepped through the *Daily's* doorway. And that was, precisely, on my first day of classes — Tuesday, October 1, 1935 — when a sophomore friend, Sydney Cooper, a *Daily* veteran, introduced me to the paper. The walls held photos of early editors, including that of the founder, W. E. Gladstone Murray, who had gone on to head the Canadian Broadcasting Corporation. I gawked at each picture as though it was a sacred icon.

I was in science, taking pre-medical courses without great enthusiasm. In theory my commitment to the *Daily*, like other first-year students, was to spend only one evening a week there, with perhaps an afternoon assignment. Although labs occupied almost every afternoon, somehow I still managed to wander afterward into the *Daily*. I had uncovered a world of endless fascination, and needed nothing more to reinforce this impression than my first big story — an interview with Hazen Sise.

Hazen Sise, the architect son of a wealthy family (his father was president of the Bell Telephone Company), had gone off to fight in the Spanish civil war — on the republican side, of course. Now he was back in Montreal. He spoke in such a low tone I had difficulty catching all his words, but there was no mistaking his idealism. He had served as an ambulance driver with Dr. Norman Bethune, developer of a mobile blood bank.

The Bethune legend had already begun at Montreal's Royal Victoria Hospital where his unorthodox surgical techniques in dealing with chest diseases had earned the scorn of some doctors. But he was much admired by others, and simply as a man — revolutionary, romantic — well known around town. As a child I had seen him in our home, when he had come to examine my sister Ruth, who suffered from tuberculosis. He recommended what was then considered a radical approach to pneumothorax, the collapsing of a lung. I can still see him taking my worried, bewildered mother in his arms, dancing an improvised little waltz, and exclaiming, "She'll be fine, Mrs. Clark, she'll be fine." He was right.

Years later I encountered the Bethune legacy when I went to China on assignment. His plaster bust emerged everywhere, the man idolized in China for his dedication to Mao Tse-tung's troops, a dedication that cost him his life. He died from blood poisoning, incurred after he cut a finger operating on a wounded soldier without surgical gloves — there were no gloves available. Next to Karl Marx and Lenin, Norman Bethune was the best known non-Chinese figure of his day. A practical, political reason underlay his deification. Chinese propaganda fastened on the international aspect of communism. Bethune's nobility and sacrifice were used as an example of how Communists from all lands helped one another.

But now, in 1936, I was concerned only with seeing how my words — my interview with Sise and his experiences with

Bethune — looked in print. There was no by-line — I was too much of a beginner — but there was enormous satisfaction. I don't think I've ever lost the thrill of viewing the transformation that happens to words that progress from draft form to the printed page. You may never be content; you may always believe you could have done better; yet print does impart a glow of its own.

A broadsheet with the format and heading type of *The New York Times* and *The Gazette,* the *Daily* ran four pages of news, sports, features, editorials, and commentaries. To McGill students today, whose paper is a tabloid and not much more than a snappy bulletin board, my generation's *Daily* would be judged as stuffy. To me, it was illustrious and daring. After all, when an elevator crashed in Eaton's, and three people were slightly injured, where was the story in *The Gazette* or *The Star?* Missing — no doubt, we assumed, due to pressure from the store's powerful advertising department. But we carried it! (Eaton's did not advertise in the *Daily).*

In general, however, the paper seldom wandered beyond the campus. A notable exception involved the abdication crisis, when King Edward VIII was about to give up his throne for the woman he loved — Wallis Warfield Simpson — and become the Duke of Windsor. Mrs. Simpson remained in seclusion in Cannes. The press of the world was trying to reach her. Why not *The McGill Daily?* The editor put in a trans-Atlantic phone call and awaited a call back. Of course none came. But another student, hearing of this effort, got his girl friend to disguise her voice as an overseas operator, and found a second accomplice to pose as Mrs. Simpson.

It was a sensational night, the *Daily* staff going wild putting together the exclusive interview in which Mrs. Simpson declared her gratitude to students in far away Montreal for their concern. At midnight, just before copy had to go to the printers, the perpetrator realized the gag had gone far enough. He confessed to the editor. But that wasn't the end. A trans-Atlantic phone call was a pretty big deal in those days. The morning's headline read: "*McGill Daily* Attempts to Reach Mrs. Simpson."

My first out-of-town assignment, in my third year, was in Ottawa to interview John W. Dafoe, editor of the *Winnipeg Free Press* and one of the most distinguished figures in Canadian journalism. He had just been designated honorary editor-in-chief of the newly formed Canadian University Press. I sent my report — by telegraph! — from the Press Gallery in the House of Commons. I was eighteen. Who was to know I would be there four years later as a professional, a regular member of the Gallery? Or that many years later I would hire J.W. Dafoe's grandson, John Dafoe, as an editorial writer for *The Montreal Star?* All I knew at the time was that I had won my first by-line, and it came out wrong — "Donald" instead of "Gerald."

My final year in science was approaching, and I held secret hopes that I might be named news editor of the *Daily*. Instead, the outgoing editor-in-chief, John H. McDonald, called me in to say, "You're the next editor-in-chief." The managing board, with the concurrence of the Students' Executive Council, had appointed me. I was stunned. No Jew had ever reached this height, though many talented young Jews had served on the *Daily*. Leon Edel, well on his way to achieving acclaim as a Henry James scholar, had been a *Daily* figure a decade earlier. In my own time there was the brilliant Philip F. Vineberg, later *bâtonnier* of the Bar of Montreal, who had acted as managing editor.

I was under no delusion. It was no secret that I was Jewish, but my anglicized name on the *Daily*'s masthead would be acceptable. If it had been Vineberg or Klughaupt? Undoubtedly it would have jarred some sensibilities. As it happened, the only instant reaction came from another Jewish member of the staff, who, I discovered, had aspired to the post of editor himself. "You've got to join the YCL," he told me. The Young Communist League? Only then did I realize he was a radical, active in the YCL. I was, in reverse, "safe." Cautious, conservative, responsible. (The Year

Book later tagged me, not glamorously, as Gerald "Responsibility" Clark). But the big personal impact I felt was clear: in a period when I was still floundering about what graduate field to enter, fate had intervened. I told my mother I was heading for a career in journalism. "Do anything you want," she said, "as long as you're a doctor."

The title editor-in-chief carried with it not only work and prestige but living accommodations. I occupied one of the four bedrooms in the McGill Union; three other student executives filled the rest. (The building now houses the McCord Museum). It was heavenly, in effect out-of-town living without the expense. Family and a good home-cooked meal were available at my convenience, only a half hour away with a six-cent bus ticket.

What a glorious education that year as editor gave me! The McGill Union itself was the setting for lively events. The régime of Quebec's autocratic premier Maurice Duplessis, under which we lived, was typified by the Padlock Law. This entitled police to clamp a bolt across the door of any house or building in which "Communist activities" took place. Duplessis provided the definition as it suited him. The Padlock Law was a perfect target for outraged undergraduates. Tim Buck, leader of Canada's Communist party, was invited to address us in the Union. The police would not dare invade the sanctity of a university, but we heard that students from Université de Montréal, hostile to Buck, were preparing to attack. Fire hoses were dragged outside the Union, ready to repel any onslaught.

It never came. It was just another case of bad communications — non-existent communications — that divided Montreal's English and French societies. For the most part we on the *Daily* functioned in blissful isolation, busy with our own activities, sparing little time for the community at large.

One of my most troubling recollections is of a poem we published calling men who served in the Great War, as it was then known, "stupid." This was in 1938, in the wake of the popular

Oxford University movement that proclaimed that under no circumstances would young men again serve King and Country in a war. I was visited by an infuriated group of students whose fathers lay crippled with wounds sustained in the Great War. I can't remember exactly what I said, but I know I was filled with indignation in defence of freedom of expression. I am not so confident now that my defiance was well placed. I saw many Oxford-type pacifists, including classmates, in action in Normandy just a few years later.

On the *Daily* I introduced what I thought would be an intriguing, inspiring series of talks — by graduate old boys and girls to describe how their *Daily* experience led them to bigger and greater levels in journalism. Our first speaker, heralded with appropriate build-up in the *Daily*, was F.I. Ker, publisher of the *Hamilton Spectator*. Ker's attraction was that he graduated from McGill in engineering. Nonetheless, because of his grounding on the *Daily*, he had gone on to professional newspaper work.

Ker gave a most inspiring talk, enough to make undergraduates like me dream on the spot about promises of glory to come. Then Ker had the honesty to say, at the end, that it also happened that he married the boss' daughter, a member of the Southam family that owned the *Spectator*. So much for the rugged road to success in journalism as paved by the *Daily*.

The idea of class reunions doesn't appeal to me. Such devices seem to cater to the past, and that, I believe, implies less than positive thinking. But now, on September 22, 1989, the fiftieth anniversary of the McGill class of '39 was to take place at the Ritz-Carlton Hotel in Montreal. I decided it was indeed a happy milestone. There were six hundred graduates in 1939 from all faculties (contrasted with six thousand today), and one hundred and twenty showed up at the Ritz.

Louis Dudek, the poet and old *Daily* colleague, was there. He said that occasionally he attended reunions, but there was no doubt this one was special. "The emotion will hit later," he said. "We'll feel it when we get home."

He was right. The nostalgia in the brief addresses somehow was appropriate — how our class was worth looking back on, how it was fitting to pay a special tribute to those who did not survive the war. Negatives in university life, most notably quota systems, were long gone. The current generation could not be expected to really understand the prejudices of another era. Who, among the young, would consider startling that a Jew, Bernard Shapiro, would take over as McGill's principal in 1994?

Dudek and I reminisced about the *Daily*, the paper that gave me my start in a field that I have loved ever since. Yet, oddly, I hardly ever mention the *Daily* any more. I do not even include it in my *curriculum vitae*. Ancient history? Probably. In retrospect I think what bothers me the most is my conservatism during that period. Maybe I practised it because I was conscious that as a Jew I was under scrutiny. Jews, in the minds of many people, were either Communists or capitalists Since I was hardly a capitalist it left, according to this kind of logic, one direction only.

By nature, anyhow, I was quite conservative. But as time progressed, I progressed with it. In Peru when I hear *los ricos* talk disparagingly about the "lazy" Quechua peasants who do nothing but chew the coca leaf, I know that radical social reform — revolution — is necessary. The coca leaf, from which cocaine is derived, kills hunger pangs. But the oligarchy, still in place in much of Latin America after hundreds of years, refuses to accept the reality that people's lives are miserable. Today I report on these conditions with the proper emphasis. Today I am what I should have been fifty years ago, a liberal at least.

* * *

I had decided on journalism as a vocation, and I started to hunt for my first full-time job soon after graduation. With the depression still lingering, the outlook was not promising. I was drawn to one ad in the classified section of *The Montreal Star*, calling for a young reporter for an unnamed paper. Good — until the last line. It said, "*McGill Daily* experience not considered." So much for glory.

The Gazette was hiring no one. But at least I had met the executive editor of *The Star*, A.J. West, in my senior year. That was when I wrote for *The Star*, on speculation, an article on a falconry exhibition in the Redpath Library at McGill. West accepted it, but balked at paying, saying a by-line in a metropolitan newspaper was reward enough. I huffed and puffed, claiming I was a professional. He paid me ten dollars.

Now, as I sat before him in his office on St. James Street and asked for a job, he lectured me on the pitfalls of newspaper work — long hours, low wages, hard work. He suggested that I walk across the road and apply to a brokerage firm. My future would be more assured as a stock broker, he said. If he had offered me a chance at anything — as office boy, library assistant, anything — I would have seized it. But I didn't appreciate this kind of counsel. Luckily, an "old boys network" from the *Daily* was operating. Doug Amaron, a former sports editor, now worked for The Canadian Press, the national news agency. He got me a job there on one month's probation. My salary: fifteen dollars a week. I was ecstatic.

The CP's bureau was on Hospital Street, in what is now called Old Montreal. The clatter was a stimulant, a battery of teletype machines whirling out news from all over the world, occasionally punctuated by a rapid, piercing bell to warn of a bulletin coming up. To strangers the bell might have sounded discordant, to me it was melodious. I even thrilled at the requirement of lunch at the desk — twenty minutes (cucumber sandwiches from home) — while still hammering a keyboard.

This was real newspaper stuff, even if I wasn't exactly covering major stories. My task was simply to rewrite, from carbon copies brought over from *The Star,* brief items about accidents or deaths. The terse news agency style followed a rigid formula. It was hardly a challenge and occasionally I tried to veer a bit, only to have my copy brought into line by an editor. But I committed two blunders.

One was to express an opinion. A provincial election campaign was underway, and Gillis Purcell, the CP's general manager, had arrived from the head office in Toronto to supervise coverage. I remember him asking who I thought would win — Duplessis or his Liberal opponent, Adélard Godbout. I'm not sure if I said Godbout, but apparently as a news agency man I should have been non-committal. I probably got away with that gaffe, but the next mistake was unforgivable. In trying to amend what I thought was a dull formula of presenting football scores, I got the wrong team winning.

Purcell, one of the most respected news executives in Canada, did not pick up my "option" at the end of the month. Many years later he attended a dinner in Toronto at which I received a national newspaper award. He made whimsical comments about my disastrous debut. I still felt guilty about my wire service transgression, though grateful I had been cast aside at an early stage.

From Hospital Street I wandered in gloom two blocks to 231 St. James Street, to the fifth floor office of *The Standard,* a sister newspaper of *The Star.* This was a strange old paper, a weekly appearing in Montreal on Saturdays in competition with *The Star,* and other days across Canada in national editions. It was also a paper about to collapse. At least that was what J.W. McConnell, proprietor of *The Star,* believed when he gave it to his son, John G. McConnell, in 1938. Circulation was only 70,000.

J.W. McConnell, one of the wealthiest and most powerful industrialists in the country, was a driven, self-made man. He taunted his three sons, as children, subjecting them to brutal trial. He made them scramble, to see who could pick up the most coins he ejected from a hole deliberately cut in his trousers' pocket.

John G. McConnell was hardly a ruthless, aggressive type. He was, rather, a shy, gentle, withdrawn person — a gifted publisher. He had only been in charge a year, but already *The Standard's* readership was moving upwards (by 1947 circulation had reached 350,000). Davidson Dunton, his friend, was editor. Both were in their twenties, and they had drawn to them a small but dedicated young editorial staff. I was to stay with the organization virtually forever, moving from one company publication to another, until 1979 when the last surviving paper, *The Star,* succumbed tragically to self-inflicted wounds.

But I was not on *The Standard's* staff immediately. Instead, I was "on space" — a euphemism for the garment trade's "piece work." I would be paid for the accumulated bits and pieces I wrote, on the basis of four dollars a column of type — roughly eight hundred words. The length was actually measured in the business office by a ruler or a piece of string, hence the origin of "stringer." My first Saturday on the job I found myself, minutes before deadline, pounding away at a typewriter. But it was not because of urgent news. It was because the sports editor, Len Rountree,was suffering so grievously from a hangover that he could not focus on the keys.

Rountree was a relic of the hard-drinking school, a remnant of the old *Standard* crew. There weren't too many left — just enough to remind me that some stereotypical newspapermen still existed. Next door, at *The Star,* they still talked about Peter Spanjard, a sports editor until the 1930s, who wore his fedora in the office. But he always took it off when speaking to a lady on the phone. Spanjard, an amateur detective, had worked Saturdays on *The Standard* as a police reporter, and was credited with solving a murder mystery.

Basically the weekly staff people were disdainful of *Star* hands, whom they regarded as hoary and dull. Besides, *The Standard* boasted enough of its own characters. There was, for example, Sam Preval, a former undertaker who became *The Standard's* principal photographer. Sam never lost his Yorkshire accent nor his funereal appearance. He dressed always in black, in what looked like the same unpressed suit day after day. Bald and stoop-shouldered, he appeared very solicitous.

Sam, in fact, was a wild man — heavy on drink and low in intellect. But he was friendly. He had contacts everywhere. Early on, when I went with him to the Eastern Townships to do a story on the Mounties raiding a still — illicit liquor manufacturing was still common — I witnessed the value of fellowship. The assignment over, Sam insisted on stopping at a local tavern. He had barely quaffed his first glass of beer before there was a reunion with an old friend who happened to stroll in. The friend asked Sam what he was doing there. Sam told him, and the friend guffawed. That still was a nothing, he said. Now if we wanted to see a real still.....He told us about it, we caught up with the Mounties, led them to the new location, and got a much bigger story.

It was drink, sadly, that cut short Sam's career as an undertaker. He had served his apprenticeship in large funeral parlors, and then decided to start his own business. Not long afterward a woman named Molly, the wife of one of Sam's friends, died. There wasn't enough money for an elaborate final tribute, but Sam was sympathetic and generous. He had just received an expensive casket on consignment. Molly would repose in it during the wake, to be transferred discreetly to an inexpensive pine coffin for burial. Sam partook of the wake with solemn and frequent silent toasts, and then passed out. When he awoke, Molly was gone — and so was the expensive casket. Sam filed for bankruptcy.

Andy O'Brien, who doubled as sports writer and general reporter, was a huge fellow, with a shaft of sentiment matching his size. One night, at the movies, he was deeply moved when Franklin

D. Roosevelt, president of the United States, appeared in the newsreel and spoke inspiringly about the democracies' fight against Hitler. The rest of the audience was moved, too, and burst into applause. Andy wrote Roosevelt to tell him of the boundless respect and affection Canadians held for him.

A couple of weeks later Andy received a reply on White House stationery, thanking him and in effect inviting him to drop into the White House next time he was in Washington. It was signed Franklin D. Roosevelt. Andy, anxious to catch a train to Ottawa to cover a football game the next day, jammed the letter in his breast pocket. On the train, he may have had a drink or two; disastrously, on arrival, he neglected to notice that plate glass doors had just been installed leading from Union Station into the Château Laurier Hotel. The enormous weight of his body sent him and the glass crashing.

Andy woke up in a suite in the Château, bewildered about how he got there, but anxious to leave for the game. When it was time to return to Montreal he made his way carefully to the station, stopping only long enough to talk to a porter. "When I was coming through here yesterday," he said, "I heard a terrible commotion, as though someone had walked through a glass door. What happened?" The porter replied, "Yes, someone did go through a glass door. The police checked his pockets for identification. And you know what?" The porter glanced around furtively and whispered, "He was a personal friend of President Roosevelt. They rushed him right up to a suite."

I worked on all types of stories — interviews, long features, short news items. So productive was I that before long I was turning out six or seven columns of type a week, adding up to a minimum of twenty-four dollars in payment. Dave Dunton called me into his office and congratulated me; from now on I would be on staff! — with wages of twenty dollars a week. After a while I thought I should be paid more, and requested a five-dollar raise. When Dunton was through telling me how lucky I was to hold such a fascinating position, I was almost begging to stay on at any salary.

I still owed McGill fifty dollars for the final instalment of my last year's tuition. There was, I thought, an easy way to earn it. *The Standard* ran a weekly book condensation — usually, for fifty dollars, a syndicated novel, or one churned out on a regular basis by the fiction editor, Ted Fancott. Fancott was of the old school of British authors who could tailor-make, under a variety of pseudonyms, anything to suit anyone.

I spent ten nights batting out fifty thousand words — *The Red Label* — a story based on my "expertise" as a geneticist (I had taken courses at McGill). I told the harrowing tale of how German saboteurs threatened a crucial food source by introducing a strain of insects that could wipe out the entire grain harvest of Brazil. Only by the brilliant detective efforts of a McGill genetics professor, who quickly bred another strain to wipe out the bad strain, was the plot foiled. Fancott accepted it and I received fifty dollars. It was all a neat package: application of my McGill background to remove an obligation to McGill. There was one small flaw, pointed out by Dave Dunton: "You had your characters speaking Spanish. In Brazil they speak Portuguese." I learned a lesson in basic research. I also avoided, in the future, writing about a country unless I had been there.

But life in Montreal at that time was fairly manageable even on a low income. First, no one expected luxury. An evening at a downtown movie (fifty cents a seat), followed by maybe a smoked meat sandwich at Ben's (ten cents), was satisfying. Additionally, no young man or woman even dreamed of an apartment (I still lived with my parents). A suit cost twenty-five dollars, a gallon of gasoline twenty-five cents. But who had a car? Certainly very few journalists. Actually the designation "journalist" was derogatory in those days. It signified an unemployed newspaperman, or, in a sneering definition, "a reporter with a monocle."

One of my tantalizing introductions to journalism was an interview with Quentin Reynolds, who was staying at the Ritz-Carlton Hotel, awaiting a ship to take him to Britain as a war correspondent for *Collier's,* the widely circulated U.S. magazine. Piled high in the entrance hall of his suite were cases of champagne, quite a sight for a young reporter earning twenty dollars a week. Dozens of well wishers barged in to wish him bon voyage. I wondered if this was routine expense account stuff for someone like Reynolds. Not much later I read a comment by Reynolds' editor, "When his (Reynolds') expense account becomes bigger than my salary, he's through." Well, that was incidental. What did strike me was the excitement that even preceded getting in on a major story.

Since breaking out in September 1939, the war engaged most of our attention. I was completing an officers' training course in artillery, and, when a commission came through, dutifully notified my two bosses that I would be quitting. I reported for my medical — and was rejected. High blood pressure. I came back to the office. Again fate, and luck, had presented me with an opportunity. I would have been a miserable soldier, and now I could concentrate on what I was fit to do. Before long, anyway, I was to go overseas in uniform.

Meantime, one big story after another offered itself. There were accounts to write on mobilization, on drilling, on U-boats sighted in the Gulf of St. Lawrence, on Canadian and American lovers separated by a border. (The United States, not yet at war, enforced some travel restrictions between the two countries). Then, on December 7, 1941, Japan bombed Pearl Harbor, and the war took on a new dimension. Not only was the U.S. now involved, but Canada's West Coast was in imminent danger of attack by Japanese warships or bombers — or so we thought. *The Standard* rushed me to Vancouver two days after Pearl Harbor.

I was in my early twenties, and it was the first time I had ever stepped into an airplane. And now I was on a twenty-hour flight in a Trans-Canada Airlines' Lockheed Lodestar. The Lodestar, a twin-engined plane, shot through the heavens at the breathtaking speed of nearly two hundred miles an hour, the propellers pulsating so loudly you could hardly speak to the passenger across the aisle.

There were fourteen of us, fed and cared for by a stewardess who, above all else, was a registered nurse. A traveller simply didn't know what sudden seizures, what perils, might be encountered. Passenger planes did not attempt to conquer the Rockies at night; so we slept in a hotel in Lethbridge, Alberta. And the plane was not pressurized. That meant breathing through an oxygen mask in the rarefied atmosphere high over the Rockies. Air travel was both glamorous and adventurous.

Vancouver was hardly in a state of panic, as we in the East had imagined. But, then, we didn't know too much about each other. I, for one, had never been exposed to the nonchalance of the West Coaster — or the comparative lack of materialist incentives. Blackout curtains were going up — not hurriedly, but at least some people were tacking them into place. A few were even sticking strips of plaster tape over windows to prevent shattered glass from flying. The story called for immediate photos.

But it was a Saturday. One photographer had promised to take the kids on a picnic; another had planned to go sailing. I received authorization to spend as much as fifty dollars. That was an absolute fortune — more than a photographer, even back in the decadent and rich East, earned in a week. And this would have been for only an afternoon's effort. But I never did find a cameraman willing to forego other obligations simply for the money. I'm not convinced that values have much changed. The leisurely pace of the West Coast of the 1940s remains in the 1990s.

Indeed, I noted this in the spring of 1990 during a stay at the Empress Hotel in Victoria. The hotel had been completely refurbished, at considerable cost, and yet had miraculously pre-served much of its old character and charm. The ladies still indulged in the ritual of afternoon tea in the lounge, with the same unchanging menu of strawberries and cream, half a crumpet laced with honey and butter, a dainty watercress sandwich, an equally delicate cucumber sandwich, scones and jam, and two kinds of tarts.

But nothing can quite restore the haunting image of Billy Tickle and his trio — war or no war, Japanese threat or no threat — playing steadfastly at five o'clock, every day except Sunday. Nor could there ever be a return to 1942, when I came back from a reporting voyage on a mine-sweeper (a tiny, converted fishing boat whose ceaseless bobbing up and down gave me my first and only case of seasickness) to discover that my room in the Empress was in the "alcoholic ward." That was the name Royal Canadian Navy types, fresh from action and with lust blazing in their eyes, gave the section of the hotel allocated for their raucous use so as not to disturb the dowagers who maintained year-round living quarters elsewhere in the hotel.

I retain clear recollections of the contrast to Montreal in 1942. Someone on *The Standard* — maybe it was Dunton, maybe Glenn Gilbert, the managing editor — hit on the idea of assigning a reporter to look into the quality of schools for wartime welders. Several such schools had sprung up, luring men and women eager to apply quickly learned skills as highly paid welders in aircraft factories. There were rumors that these instant graduates did dangerously flawed work. A reporter named Fergus was assigned to take a course in a welding school, get a job on the assembly line at Canadair, the big Montreal-based airplane manufacturer, and then write an article exposing the menace to our fliers.

Weeks passed, and Gilbert suddenly remembered Fergus. Where was he? There had been no word from him. Gilbert reached him at home at night and said, "When are you coming back to the office?" "What office?" Fergus replied. "I'm making sixty-five dollars a week as a welder."

During this period I discovered that people believe what they want to believe. The office assigned me to follow a so-called miracle man, J.A. Desfosses, who claimed to be the seventh son of a seventh son of a seventh son — and therefore thrice blessed.

Desfosses rented space in a half-dozen cities and showed up in each for four hours every week. The line-ups of people waiting to see him stretched for blocks. He was happy to have me sit with him while one person after another recounted details of his or her ailment.

Desfosses, looking attentive, merely nodded and said, "I will do that for you." Nothing more, nothing less — except each visitor, on the way out, was eligible to pick up in the waiting room a copy of Desfosses' memoirs — and make a contribution, the sum unspecified. Desfosses' revenue was huge.

The Quebec College of Physicians and Surgeons had taken Desfosses to court several times on charges of false practice. But it could not make a case. At no time did Desfosses claim to perform any miracles or medical services. Nor did he directly ask for fees. But it was obvious that people, hearing him promise to "do that for you," inferred that a miraculous cure was underway. And they wanted to ensure the miracle by buying his book.

Some doctors told me that in those situations where the disease was imaginary Desfosses probably did some good. But the awful fear was that many people, suffering from grave illnesses that required medical or urgent surgical treatment, ignored it in favor of a Desfosses phenomenon. I wrote a great exposé, pointing out the perils he presented to everyday society. We received hundreds of letters. All but a few said, "How do we get in touch with him?"

Not long after my introduction to aviation I travelled by train to Dartmouth, Nova Scotia, and there boarded a Canso Catalina, a big, ungainly flying boat of the RCAF, to write about an anti-submarine patrol. There were no submarines, but there was a huge steak cooked by a crew member over a galley stove. Such are the minutiae of memory.

Over the years I have somehow identified any new aircraft in my life with an experience, usually trivial, or some exposure to the exotic. Soon after the war, the Boeing Stratocruiser, a converted bomber, came into civilian use. On the first leg of a slow flight over the Atlantic I made my way down the stairs into the bar — formerly the bomb bay — for drinks. Then I climbed back to the passenger deck for a lavish dinner, and before long my berth was ready. I slept in pyjamas the remainder of the trip to London.

By contrast, not long after that delight, I was subjected to the frolics of a Russian pilot keeping his Ilyushin 14 to a height no greater than a couple of hundred feet. The fuselage shuddered, and a samovar of hot tea skidded down the aisle. I am sure the bushes below bowed as we pulsated past. Hedge-hopping from Leningrad to Moscow is an encounter one does not easily forget. It was not dissimilar to a wartime excursion I made over the battlefield near Falaise, Normandy, where an entire German army was fighting to escape encirclement.

I had talked a British artillery regiment into allowing me to go aloft in a spotter plane, an Auster. The midget Auster, with a single engine and two open cockpits, the fuselage covered in fabric, looked and felt like a leftover from a World War I movie. And the pilot, very English with handlebar moustache, might have come straight from *Dawn Patrol,* except he was a gunnery, rather than air force, officer. I sat in the cockpit behind him, and we took off from a pasture next to an apple orchard.

The scene below me on this clear July day was dramatic, shells dropping into enemy positions as he radioed back directions. I kept gaping over the side, figuring the heavy draft was normal in an open cockpit. We landed, and when the propeller sound had faded, the artilleryman turned to me. His face looked ashen and he said, "I say, old chap, you were a bit heavier than I expected. We clipped a tree on takeoff." I peered directly beneath my seat. An entire length of fabric had been ripped out, leaving a hole between me and the ground. I doubt if my heart would have lasted if I'd detected the source of the draft earlier.

A more light-hearted snag occurred during the 1950s on the inaugural flight of a Britannia from London to New York. Soon after we departed the roof began to leak — condensation, explained a stewardess. Just a small problem, she added. Then she distributed "brollies," and for the rest of the ten hours over the Atlantic passengers held unfurled umbrellas above their heads.

The ultimate in speed came in the late 1970s when my wife and I travelled on a Concorde from New York to London in little more than three and a half hours. With everyone else seated and waiting, Henry Kissinger rushed in seconds before take-off. Kissinger had recently completed his celebrated shuttle diplomacy, as American secretary of state, between Egypt and Israel. My wife was bursting to ask him a question. "Send him a note," I said. She scribbled one and gave it to a flight attendant. Soon Kissinger came alongside. "You have a question?" he said to her. "How do you feel," she asked, "when people criticize you." "Oh," said he, "do people criticize me?" That was the end of the conversation. Kissinger made no history in our company. He swung around and marched away.

Over the decades I have met scores of interesting, and sometimes challenging, fellow travellers on all types of airplanes. In 1958, for example, there was the Swedish businessman on a Soviet TU-104 from Moscow to Peking. He insisted that no matter how exhausted we were on arrival, a visit to a restaurant, which he knew from a previous trip, was mandatory. It specialized in Peking duck. Thus, weary, unshaven, bedraggled after a journey across two continents, we did go to Restaurant No. 1, next door to the main railway station. Our duck, hanging upright over a fire so juices could penetrate one end and depart the other, was cut by a master carver into small pieces, then reassembled under skin browned to the consistency of crinkly tissue paper. It proved the taste sensation of my stay.

Thirty-five years later, food was an element, of a different sort, when I stepped aboard a Canadian forces' Hercules C-130 transport in Zagreb, Croatia. I was on assignment for *Reader's Digest,* heading for the besieged Bosnian city of Sarajevo. Relief supplies were in urgent demand, and I found myself aloft in a flying warehouse, squeezed in beside crates of Greek feta cheese — the cheese made in Denmark and packaged in Iran — flour and vegetable oil. The load totalled 18.7 tons.

This was no commercial plane with fancy decor. Bare metal girders, unshielded from view, held no soundproofing to protect the interior from the roar of four mighty jet-prop motors. The Hercules is a massive, bulky, ponderous, marvelous machine. The men who fly the Hercules love it, even though it resembles a faithful draft horse rather than a sleek thoroughbred. Compelled to wear a flak jacket, I sat on hard nylon webbing that folded down from the wall, thinking: What was I doing in this set-up at my age? The last time I occupied a bucket seat, albeit a metal one, was when the war ended in 1945 — almost a half century ago. Still, in 1992, it felt good to be alive.

Yet nothing compares in glamor or adventure with my first flight across Canada on that little Lodestar. I thought about it recently when I embarked in Montreal on one of Air Canada's big, modern jets, an Airbus 320, for Vancouver. I was heading there to do a magazine piece, not on the possibility of a Japanese attack but on the influx of wealthy Hong Kong Chinese. After dinner I was offered a choice of liqueurs, and automatically selected Drambuie. It is a kind of reflex on any long flight, in memory of the man who introduced me to Drambuie, Rod MacInnis, the airline's public relations chief back in the days when it was called TCA.

I mentioned this to the flight attendant who poured the drink. He was awed by the reference to TCA (nomenclature long forgotten), and even more enthralled when I described my initial flight over the Rockies and the way everyone, including crew, inhaled from an oxygen tank. But maybe it was my sentiment about Drambuie and a TCA pioneer that got to him. A little later he reappeared at my side with a bottle of Drambuie and the warm words, "Compliments of the purser."

I hope I run into the same flight attendant again; I'll tell him why TCA stopped treating the press to inaugural flights. It did so when jets were introduced on the Montreal-Paris run, and some enterprising reporters, staying at the Hôtel George V as airline guests, called room service and ordered buckets of champagne. But the bubbly went to their heads, and they decided to order call girls into the bargain — all on TCA's account.

The licentiousness of the press owed part of its origin to poor wages — and accompanying indignity. Early on, when I was covering the courts in Montreal, a lawyer tried to hand me fifty cents because I had used his name in a story. The gesture, startling as it was to me, was not surprising. I heard that a father and son team from the now defunct daily *Le Canada,* earning twenty-five dollars a week between them, depended on handouts.

It was also the custom of metropolitan newspapers to carry long obituaries and lists of mourners at a prominent person's funeral. For a while, people waiting their turn at a funeral home to give their names to a reporter, noticed that the first man in line slipped him a two-dollar bill. After that, each respectfully did the same. No one realized it was a conniving duo from *La Presse* at work. The practice ended the day an editor found himself accosted.

It didn't take long before I appreciated that larceny was not merely something that you wrote about. Various forms of it surfaced in newspaper offices, whether it involved acceptance of movie passes or discounts in the restaurant of the legislature in Quebec City — or cash bribes. This disturbed me, but not enough to allow it to dilute my feeling that journalism was a great profession, and *The Standard* a great paper to grow with it.

We were small in number — a score or so on the editorial side — with some of conspicuous talent, including Mavis Gallant, who emerged as an admired fiction writer. We retained a crusading approach to our mission. That mission, as far as I was concerned, was to help enlighten the public about important developments, and, while gathering information, to keep learning myself.

A while ago I read that Elspeth Cameron, the biographer of Hugh MacLennan and Irving Layton, said that she always searches for the moment in the life of her subject when he begins to turn into himself. There were a couple such moments for me. One was on the *McGill Daily*, the other *The Standard*. On *The Standard* the immersion was not only in reporting but in actually producing the paper. We all filled in making up pages and doing layouts. This meant sublime periods in the composing room with its aroma of ink, the sight and sound of steam hissing in pots of lead, and the intense clacking of the Linotype machines. It also meant witnessing the highest order of quality and dedication.

Men and women, who had served years in apprenticeship, caressed keyboards of the Linotype machines in an even rhythm, and one after another lines of type fell into place in the trays beside them. Master craftsmen like Jimmy McKee would carry the trays to "the stone," the large steel table and frame of the page into which would go the columns of hot type. McKee always wore a clean starched collar, despite the uncontrollable stains from the frames and fumes from the pots.

McKee, a Scotsman in his fifties, had never lost his Old Country accent or courtesy. He growled about the stupidity of reporters trying to act like make-up men, but he always saved us from ourselves. I can't imagine composing room people ever letting their editorial colleagues down, anywhere, at any time. Somehow I sensed there was a continuity between the McKees of the 1940s and printers of past ages, maybe going all the way back to Gutenberg and moveable type, their loyalty and pride of accomplishment setting them apart.

The similarity ended only in the 1970s when "hot" type gave way to computerized "cold" type, and old artisans were forced by technology into the humiliation of pasting printed strips of paper down on page layouts. In that sense I prefer to ignore modernity and cling to the past. I have never ceased to marvel at the miracle of how deadlines were always met, even when bottomless pots of hot metal had to be transformed into newspapers.

2 Ottawa and Normandy

IN OCTOBER 1942 I BECAME *THE STANDARD'S* Ottawa correspondent. It was a challenging post for a young reporter. This was the capital, immersed in wartime decision-making, and a magnet for some of the best brains from all parts of the country. The city, normally undisturbed in its civil service habits, suddenly became animated and exciting. I rejoiced for every moment of my stay. I could even afford to share an apartment with an old family friend on Somerset Street, within walking distance of Parliament Hill. Price of a car was still far beyond reach.

There wasn't a better place for a newspaperman to be, short of overseas. I found enough of a sample of the foreign element to satisfy a longing for broader exposure to the world. There were missions of several governments in exile — French, Dutch, among them — and soon our new allies, the Russians, would arrive in numbers. Although I was interested in political affairs, provincial or federal, but not overwhelmingly so, my gravitation — as I sensed back in the earlier days on *The McGill Daily*, when I met Hazen Sise fresh from the Spanish civil war — tended to pull in the direction of news of foreign events.

Still, my mandate was to cover primarily the domestic side of the war effort, and I had no complaints. I was even entitled to use the Press Gallery in the House of Commons. The Gallery was beginning to show symptoms of overcrowding, with desks in what was normally the news room overflowing into the corridors. Nonetheless, correspondents from the major papers — radio, represented by the Canadian Broadcasting Corporation, was the only other medium — congregated there, without the need for the National Press Building that exists today. There were some marvelous, venerable types, notably Charles (later Senator) Bishop, who had sat at the same desk for nearly a half century, dressed in black vested suit with high, starched shirt collar, writing his dispatches to *The Montreal Star* by pen, never by typewriter. There was also Jim Oastler of *The Star,* who never deviated in his choice of tie — the plaid colors of his clan.

These were civilized men, helpful to me. But not all members of the Gallery were so inclined. On almost my first day, a hardened type from a Toronto paper stood beside me while I struggled with a feature story. "Don't forget the blacks," he muttered. "Huh?" I said. "Don't forget the blacks," he repeated. I had no idea what he meant. I mumbled an innocuous response.

Later I asked Jim Oastler if he knew what this was all about. Oastler explained that "blacks" stood for carbon copies — carbons of stories that I was expected to distribute to others in the Gallery. Oastler knew I had no intention of joining any club on those terms. I worked for a weekly, and if I developed a story, I wasn't going to give it to a daily to print first. Oastler said, "Just ignore them. Play it your own way." That's what I did. I still survived in the Gallery, with camaraderie offered by a few, and disdain by the others.

Standing apart from this petty insularity was P.J. Philip, the correspondent of *The New York Times*. Philip was a recent arrival, having served as *The Times'* correspondent in Paris for many years, escaping before the Germans could pick him up. He was a courtly, older man who added an elegant, cosmopolitan touch to the Gallery. His reminiscences about Paris between the wars provided insights into a fascinating period I had only read about. Long before Prime Minister Mackenzie King's spiritualism attracted public awareness, Philip wrote a piece that became a classic — an "interview" with King's ghost whom he met while sitting on a park bench.

Others above Gallery intrigue were the two Tass men — the first Soviet correspondents in Ottawa. Both bore the given name of Nikolai, one promptly dubbed "Little Nick," the other "Big Nick." "Little Nick," a former locomotive engineer, was a cheerful, gregarious type. "Big Nick" was so named not because of his size but because he was reclusive and restrained, thus presumed to be the NKVD (forerunner of the KGB) officer giving orders.

Ottawa was a compact city, physically easy to cover. Most of the domestic news was generated in buildings that faced Parliament Hill: the Commons, the Senate, the East Block, which housed the prime minister's office and the Department of External Affairs. Around the corner from the East Block, no more than a few hundred yards, stood the Château Laurier. Flanked by the Rideau Canal, this majestic hotel was the gathering place for the élite of Ottawa society, which meant the upper civil servants.

Almost any noon one could identify, standing in line in the cafeteria, people like Lester Pearson, who was assistant under-secretary of state for external affairs. Perhaps next to him would be Princess (later Queen) Juliana, of the Netherlands. A corner of Ottawa's Civic Hospital was declared Dutch territory when Juliana gave birth there to her third child, Margriet. Dutch exiles were touched when their flag was hoisted over the building. Such was the cosiness of the city that it conveyed no obvious signs of a capital at war — no blackouts, no troops marching off to the front. But there was a sharpness in the air, as though everyone strove to make moments count.

One of my pleasant tasks was to write about the bright people. "Man of the Week," a profile of an interesting personality, appeared every Saturday on the editorial page, complete with portrait by a gifted but little known photographer, Yousuf Karsh (before he became famous by snatching Churchill's cigar from his mouth, and capturing with it Churchill's bulldog pugnacity). Some women were chosen, but no one thought it necessary that the title of "Man of the Week" should take this into account.

The range ran from generals to professors to industrialists. But to me, John Grierson, the documentary pioneer who established the National Film Board in Ottawa, was the outstanding subject. Grierson had brought with him from his native Scotland a novel theory about documentary movies, a theory he liked to explain to anyone who would listen — and he had a compelling way of making people listen. I remember his definition: "A documentary is a pattern of thought and feelings." Grierson didn't string pictures together simply as a series of facts. He linked them in a carefully thought-out pattern — to analyze, to show the relationship of world events to our everyday lives. Is there a television producer, anywhere today, who does not try to emulate the Grierson technique of the 1940s?

Ottawa's news stories almost invariably dealt with how the country was accelerating its war activity. The biggest news event, however, took place not in Ottawa but in Quebec City. Winston Churchill and Franklin D. Roosevelt met there in August 1943 to consider grand strategy for the invasion of Europe, and in particular to choose a commander to lead that joint operation. Since Mackenzie King was their host, we of the Press Gallery were among the hundreds of allied reporters who congregated in Quebec.

In practical terms we might just as well have remained in Ottawa. Roosevelt and Churchill stayed tightly isolated inside a secured Château Frontenac Hotel, and we were given only a glimpse or two of them when they posed for group photographs. Otherwise the press was segregated in the Clarendon Hotel, where my former editor, Dave Dunton, now head of the Wartime Information Board, gave an occasional briefing. Because of the need for secrecy, the news content was practically non-existent. Some writers simply turned on their imaginations.

Others put two and two together, hoping for an answer approximately close to the truth. Don Iddon of London's *Daily Mail* heard that an American officer named Eisenhower had arrived in Quebec City, and this could mean only one thing: he would be named supreme commander. The moment it appeared in Fleet Street, the dispatch was picked up by the agencies and flashed back to Quebec, where it created a sensation. There was one flaw. The Eisenhower whom Iddon had stumbled on was an expert in psychological war, Milton Eisenhower, not his older brother Dwight D., who did indeed become supreme commander — later.

Despite the dearth of hard news, the Quebec Conference was perceived, accurately, to be an historic event. Even on the fringes, one felt the drama of the coming together of the two great leaders, with their principal military and political advisors, to map the big attack on Hitler. My publisher, John McConnell, a quiet but inquiring man, was intrigued by the major-league atmosphere of Quebec and decided to visit us.

McConnell arrived at the Clarendon around eleven in the morning, and I met him in the lobby. He said he would welcome a drink. The bar was not yet open, and I knew that by-laws dictated that beer only could be ordered — in bedrooms. We went upstairs, and McConnell, sipping a bottle or two, listened intently to the small tit-bits I could report to him about the conference.

I had already detected a popular suspicion about newspapers: People are never quite convinced they are getting the whole story in print; they feel that in some way the writer is holding in reserve fascinating revelations for a private audience. I doubt if there is a reporter alive who has never heard a friend say, "I read what you wrote in the paper yesterday. Now, tell me, what's *really* going on." McConnell wanted the really, but I'm not sure I satisfied him.

There was a follow-up to this little interlude. Weeks later, when I was in Montreal on a visit from Ottawa, McConnell called me into his office in great embarrassment. It appeared that the business department was questioning my expense account for the Quebec Conference. It was hardly an extravagant expense account — no Quentin Reynolds' champagne — just meals and a modest room at the Clarendon for eight days. I'm not usually quick about these things, but I said, "Don't forget, it includes the beer." McConnell shrugged submissively, and that was the end of that episode.

It was not nearly as good an expense account yarn as the one told around the newsroom of *The Montreal Star* involving a crafty old reporter named Gérard Dery. Dery came back from an out-of-town assignment with a huge bill, on the last line of which he had appended, "one pair of shoelaces, ten cents." He was summoned into the office of the irate executive editor, A.J. West, who bellowed about the hundreds of dollars of extravagance on a hotel suite, lavish entertainment, and then spluttered, "And you expect me to pay for new shoelaces?"

"My shoelaces broke when I was on the job, Mr. West," said Dery. "I had to buy another pair."

"I will not pay for your shoelaces," shouted West, slashing off that item and automatically initialing approval of the rest of the account.

In my case the nearest I came to expense-account immortality was years later, 1958, when I returned to my base in London from a trip to China. I lacked hotel receipts, because the Chinese did not routinely issue such things. I received a query from an office accountant in Montreal asking me if I could, for the sake of the federal and provincial tax departments, produce even a trifling bit of paper as evidence that I had incurred hotel costs in China. I was befuddled — until I thought of the Chinese laundry around the corner, on Finchley Road, where I took my shirts every week. I dropped by, got the owner to scratch a long list of meaningless items in Chinese ideograms, and sent this documentation to Montreal. I was not confronted again.

There was a small, mournful postscript to the Quebec Conference involving Canadian censorship, which was a haphazardly applied wartime tool. An industrious and competent Gallery member, Austin Cross, whose staff job was with *The Montreal Star,* sent occasional "stringer" reports to *The Daily Express* in London. He filed a cable in clear language, before the Quebec Conference, saying Churchill and Roosevelt were going to meet. Censors automatically killed it. Cross tried again, this time engaging in euphemisms, like "bosses," which any sub-editor, or enemy agent, could interpret immediately. Again the dispatch was killed, but now it was considered a grave security breach. Word went as high as Mackenzie King's office.

The scene shifts to Quebec City. Mackenzie King is host at a dinner party for the important visitors. Very few outsiders are invited. Cross suffers the bad luck that one of these is J.W. McConnell, proprietor of *The Montreal Star*. King apparently makes a nasty comment to McConnell about the kind of people in his employ. Details are provided. From then on, Austin Cross becomes a full time "stringer."

Several times I had asked the office to send me overseas as a war correspondent. *The Standard* kept a man covering the campaign in Italy but no one standing by in Britain for the inevitable opening of the second front. The Quebec Conference spurred me even more, to no avail. So I plodded on in Ottawa. Then, one October day in 1943, I received a phone call from Montreal. I was to apply for accreditation as a war correspondent and leave for London! Two weeks later I was on my way.

My departure, from Central Station in Montreal, was on a military boat train to Halifax. My father, pacing nervously on the platform, obviously pondering what to say, pulled me aside from the rest of the family, thrust a flask of brandy and a bag of grapes in my hand, and said, "You will meet many strange women. Be careful." That was the sum total of any conversation we ever had about the facts of life.

It was the best of two worlds. I was in uniform, I was in civilian clothes — whichever suited the occasion or the mood. Accreditation meant that a correspondent held the honorary rank of captain; if captured he was to be treated as an officer. But correspondents received no military training, and were prohibited from carrying weapons. The job was still with the newspaper, which continued to pay salary and expenses. (In later wars — Korea or Viet Nam or the Gulf — reporters could not claim this duality; armies granted them neither uniforms nor honorary status).

Hotels in London were jammed, and it was usually more fruitful to try for a reservation as an officer rather than as a civilian. (The telegram to the first hotel I stayed in, the Park Lane, was garbled, and my name came out "General Clark." Confirmation was immediate). But if anyone in the army tried any bullying tactics, the response was to stare wide-eyed and say, "You can't do this to me. I'm a civilian."

In fact, there was little manipulating one way or the other. You were a Canadian, you were at war — there was no doubt about the justice or obligation to fight this war — and you felt lucky to be performing the task you were best suited to do. This was the assignment of a lifetime. And this was London, the greatest city in the world, made even more exciting by the sense of sharing both dangers and privations. One rule said that, in order to conserve energy, people should not take a hot-water bath deeper than five inches. I was sure that even the King of England observed the restriction.

Idealism was not absolute. I knew of restaurants that circumvented the decree that a meal must not cost more than five shillings; waiters, in writing their bills, simply doubled the number of diners and the price. But in general British fair play dominated. (My admittedly pro-British bias has some of its origin in the fact that Manchester had offered my parents a warm haven before their migration to Canada). I thrived on the challenge of the times and the experience of living abroad.

Before long I even enjoyed the comfort of a small apartment of my own. A colleague, Clifford Sifton of *The Winnipeg Free Press*, returned to Canada and I inherited his service flat at 56 Welbeck Street. The London I had read about was all around me — Baker Street and Sherlock Holmes two or three blocks away, the Barretts of Wimpole Street even closer. If I wanted the real essence of my

London, there was Fleet Street on a No. 9 bus, Fleet Street not only with its seductive imagery of journalism but bearing memories from my youth.

Fleet Street was London E.C.4, the postal code for all the free samples — ventriloquists' secrets, itching powder — one obtained through *Gem* and *Magnet,* the weekly boys' magazines. (The effect of English romance or exploit was obvious among Canadians of earlier generations. On a trip to the Far East that I took in the 1950s with Lester Pearson, then external affairs minister, we had to make a detour to Peshawar, in Pakistan's northwest frontier region. Pearson insisted on visiting the Khyber Pass, home of Pathan tribesmen and scene of action books written by one of his boyhood favorites, G.A. Henty). Perhaps best of all, the Fleet Street of 1943 still led to the narrow Wine Office Court of Samuel Johnson and one of his cherished taverns, Ye Olde Cheshire Cheese.

The centre of activity was Trafalgar Square and Canada House, and next to it C.M.H.Q. — Canadian Military Headquarters. That was where we checked in whenever we wanted to make work trips to air force or army bases. And that was where we awaited indication of how long it might be before we would be briefed on the invasion. In the meanwhile we were free to wander around, write about the training, the "Baby Blitz" (German bombers made a short series of raids on London in 1943), civilian morale, or everyday life.

I did a piece on understandable British ignorance of distances in Canada. It was pegged to a story about the evacuation of British children to Canada a couple of years earlier. One woman, whose ten-year-old daughter had sailed from Southampton for Halifax, cabled a cousin in Vancouver to meet the child. The cousin cabled back: "You meet her, you're nearer." I did another piece on Petticoat Lane, in Whitechapel, where pushcart merchants sang out in Cockney Yiddish, "Hyse buygels," hot bagels.

* * *

On May 16,1944 Field Marshal Bernard Law Montgomery, commander of the British, Canadian, and American troops who would land in Normandy, summoned us, the correspondents, to a special briefing in London. I must have been impressed, because I retained my notes, and through a small miracle found them recently. Great security accompanied that briefing. Even in the typing of my notes, I referred to Montgomery as X, so no enemy agent would know, should I receive an unsolicited visitor, to whom I was referring. (A little ego is permissible in journalism; in reality I am not aware of any war correspondent who was sought out by enemy agents).

After the war I scribbled in pencil the identification of X as "Monty." I described him "in battle dress, a few rows of ribbons on tunic, the picture of a warrior, though his build, slight and almost frail-like, belies his apparent stamina and physical fitness." And here he was, telling us, with remarkable candor, that the Germans possessed "excellent" equipment. "Technically," said Montgomery, "he, the German, knows how to use his weapons superbly. Technically, he is admirably trained, perhaps better than our own men."

None of this was publishable — at least then, on the eve of our men going into action. I felt, at the time, that Montgomery was preparing us for possible disaster, and should it come, we would then write with an understanding of how we — the allies — were indeed amateurs. We comprised a bunch of civilians thrust into war, into hasty, though well intentioned, training — handicapped by the the casualness of democracy's life patterns.

But Montgomery also said something that I treasure now in reliving my notes. I can almost hear him — his clipped tones, his habit of repeating key phrases. The German? "He knows how to use ground most effectively. This stems from his Teuton background. Yes, Teuton. The Germans are a military race. We are militant, but they are military." In his childhood — Monty went on — the German played at military games. The German fought battles in the playing field. Yes, in the playing field. He learned the value of cover. He learned how to use ground, and today that ability remains. Yes. He is probably better in the employment of ground than our men. Montgomery, speaking in 1944, is also saying, "Our men have learned to laugh at misfortune." And so, the battle will be turned by these amateur soldiers, able to accept limitations. Monty's ego was famous — and contagious. That, of course, was the point: it was intended to inspire men engaged in war.

Days passed, and then came the signal we, the correspondents, had awaited, in common with millions of troops. The invasion was imminent. The sign was imprecise but unmistakable. We were told to vacate our apartments and move into hotels. This would make it harder for enemy agents, who might be keeping an eye on correspondents, to be alerted by a last-minute mass quitting of flats or apartments. It was one of those well thought out little details that helped to confound the Germans; they never did learn exactly when or where the main landings would take place.

I was in the English Channel, aboard HMCS Prince David, formerly a Canadian National small luxury liner that had once sailed serenely along the coast of British Columbia. Then she had been converted into an armed merchant cruiser for the rough North Atlantic. Now she was, in navy language, a "mother ship," laden with landing craft and the soldiers who would occupy them in assaulting the beaches of Normandy. Included were city-bred graduates from the universities and streets of Regina and Fredericton, and sinewy recruits of Le Régiment de la Chaudière — lumberjacks and farmers from the woods and fields of Quebec.

Royal Marines and Free French partisans augmented the cosmopolitan mix of infantrymen, engineers, gunners, military police. A lesson had been underscored during the disastrous Canadian raid on Dieppe two years earlier: Do not assign all the men of one unit to the same ship. Split them among several ships, so that if one vessel goes under, the soldiers on the others will still be able to function. The arrangement was just another detail in the most mammoth military operation of all time.

It was overwhelming — the sight of the vessels around us, as far as the eye could take us. The crunch of heavy bombardment of the coast and drone of airplanes never seemed to stop. On the scene were four thousand landing craft, five thousand large ships, more than eleven thousand aircraft. We knew none of the statistics, of course — only the sensation they created. Nor did we know that the choppy seas and heavy weather would cause a twenty-four-hour delay, postponing the landing to June 6.

The captain of the Prince David, Commander Thomas Kelly of Vancouver, summoned officers. After three days aboard ship, isolated in secrecy, almost stationary in the middle of the English Channel, he was able to tell us, "Gentlemen, in twenty minutes we lift anchor. H-Hour is seven forty-five in the morning." Then he removed sealed maps from the safe and distributed them. Lieutenant Tony Ladas, twenty-four years old, of Ottawa walked slowly into the mess deck where his Chaudières were gathered.

"We attack in the morning," he announced straight out. There was a spontaneous cheer and a common expression swept everyone's face: joy. But was it really joy? Or was it protective coating camouflaging another emotion? Who could be certain? Who could know that Tony Ladas was soon to die? I mentioned Ladas in a story and later received a poignant letter from his parents. They asked: What had he said? What had he done in those final moments?

What do people say before they enter battle? How do they behave while they are waiting? What do they think? These are questions as old as man himself. If there were common answers aboard the Prince David I could not find them. Everyone felt fear or apprehension. That generality was not difficult to establish, but the rest were distinctive, individual fragments of reaction. The men talked about families or jobs. Did they philosophize about the justice of fighting this war, the need to stop Hitler? Maybe in years to come, when memories and motives mellowed, these proclamations would ring out. But now, with only hours to spare, each person was alone with his thoughts — the soldier who cleaned his finger nails with a bayonet, the Chaudière who said, "We have the advantage over other soldiers. We speak French." I heard only mundane concerns. Pte. Lionel Langlois, a former shop clerk in the Gaspé, murmured, "I wonder what slit trench I'll be lying in tomorrow night."

Some read the army's little booklet that said, "Don't, even if food is offered you, eat the French out of house and home. If you do, someone may starve." Some counted the two hundred francs (worth about $4.50) they had been given, and gambled in card games. A last fling? A thought of winning for the future? Others watched a movie, *No Time For Love,* and inevitably shouted in chorus, "You can say that again." That was jocularity, or was it more? Favorite songs, *Mairzy Doats* and *Melancholy Baby,* played through the ship's loudspeakers. The speakers also warned, " Clean clothing will be worn." The men knew what that meant. They took hot showers and put on fresh socks and underwear; you go into battle as immaculately as possible, to minimize danger of infection from wounds.

A chaplain, Leo Gillard, a Newfoundlander, said, "I've heard men curse God many times. These same men, when they're faced with the reality of life, pray to God." In another way of supporting spirits Lionel Langlois and other Chaudières sang a popular French-Canadian ballad, *Partons, la mer est belle,* as they clambered down nets on the side of the Prince David to bound into landing craft. "The sea is nice," they sang. "Let's get into our boats, fishermen...."

Major Charles MacLean, twenty-seven years old, not long before a textile salesman in Montreal, also would be touching down early to conduct traffic at an "exit," leading away from the beaches.

He hoped he could match together pieces of the various units converging from different directions.

It is an awesome scene. All along the beach, on hastily laid mesh wire roadways, convoys of vehicles and troops move forward. Signs marked "tank exit" or "troop exit" tell you precisely what path you are supposed to take. And to make certain that you follow directions, a voice comes booming over the loud speaker system, "LCI 269, come in now. LCI 269, come in now." And then follow more detailed instructions to Landing Craft Infantry 269. The voice I hear amplified smacks of a good, healthy Canadian accent, so I scurry over to the green placard that reads "MLO," which stands for Military Landing Officer.

The voice does not belong to Major MacLean — this would be too much of a coincidence in a beachfront that stretches fifty miles or more. It belongs to a captain from Sudbury, Arthur Cressey. I ask for directions to the press camp, and then I ask how the fighting is going. "I don't know," he says. "The main fighting's a couple of miles inland. Have you just arrived?"

"Yes."

"Then you tell me what's new."

This is a fine start. I am here to gather information, not spread it. I tell Cressey what I have heard on the BBC this morning, and he is appreciative. I move along the beach, past smashed concrete gun emplacements in Hitler's so-called West Wall. Then I come across one emplacement that is intact, the bombs and the shells having missed it. Its sides of steel and concrete are four feet thick to protect a 75-mm gun and four machine guns. Inside are two rooms with nine bunks, the bunks covered with comfortable spring mattresses bearing French trade names. The electric light and air-conditioning systems still work.

The Germans have obviously left in a hurry, because there is still some uncooked food on the stove and five eggs ready to be cracked for breakfast. The present occupants, four British soldiers who haven't seen fresh eggs in months, are about to devour them. They have also found Camembert cheese and Calvados, products of Normandy, and a couple hundred tins of German sausage that they do not like. They will feed the sausage to an Alsatian dog, now snoozing in a corner. Scattered on a table are copies of a Berlin newspaper dated two days before D-Day, and an unfinished letter which starts, "Liebe Marlene."

One does not require a demonstration that war is deadly, and this war is still raging, with no end in sight. The bodies of fallen Germans lie on the roadside, though the bodies of allied soldiers are already buried or taken away; it is demoralizing for others to see them. Still, it is astonishing how quickly life returns. Here is Courseulles-sur-Mer. Its decimated buildings illustrate incisively the fury of our bombardment. Yet here and there stand out symbols of normality: an intact gasoline pump proclaiming the value of Esso, the cheery ochre front of the Hôtel des Gourmets, an advertisement outside a tobacco shop that advises, *"Le Petit Parisien* en vente ici."

Villagers are returning to their homes. They are still dazed. Some survived the shells and bombs by taking shelter in their basements, others by moving to the sanctuary of friends farther inland. Now they trundle their belongings in pushcarts. Tanks and jeeps crawl by in the opposite direction. There is no cheering, no crying of thanks for liberation. Maybe the joyful shouts flow when you are untouched physically — or later, when you have recovered from panic and shock. It is not yet time. One old woman stops for a moment to concede she is happy to see the soldiers in khaki. "But they took so long in coming, didn't they?" she says. Still bewildered and wary, she won't talk to me about life under German occupation. Who knows whether the soldiers in grey will be back?

At a casualty clearing station British and Canadian wounded rest side by side on stretchers. Those who are able to, want to speak about the speed and valor of stretcher bearers. Others about the heroism of fallen comrades. A British captain relates what two German prisoners told him: "We were on sentry duty on the beach when we saw the armada of assault ships approaching. We ran back to our officer who was asleep and woke him. He accused us of drinking, and told us to go back. 'No one can invade in weather like this,' he told us."

There would be, as the war progressed and advances developed, a variety of press camps, ranging from tent accommodation to deserted châteaux. My first billet in Normandy was a farm house room I shared with H.D. "Zed" Ziman, a literary editor of London's *Daily Telegraph,* an "old" man in his forties covering the Canadians. Ziman wore an immense moustache, and his very English accent filtered through it with mumbled difficulty. He was gutsy and gallant. Our farmer landlord and his wife were terribly worried about their young daughter at boarding school in Caen. Just a few miles away, Caen was target of an enormous allied air attack. The Germans were still being cleared from Caen when Ziman volunteered to go in search of the girl. He found her, alive and well in the ruins, and triumphantly brought her home.

The press camps varied in population, with anywhere from a dozen to several dozen members, including the military. The most important figure was a batman named Brayton. Ross Munro, highly respected dean of the Canadian correspondents, took first claim on Brayton's services, but the rest of us also benefitted. Brayton brought hot water to our billets for shaving, washed shirts (when we were long enough in one spot), but mainly he retained a cool, no nonsense Saskatchewan farm manner when drama unfolded around him.

Lionel Shapiro, of North American Newspaper Alliance and the best writer among us, enjoyed a flair for theatrics. He had honed it while working as a columnist in New York for *The Gazette* of Montreal. Walter Winchell, the feared chronicler of Manhattan nightlife and theatre gossip, befriended Shapiro, who accompanied him on his rounds. Now, "Somewhere in France," where a half dozen of us spread our bedrolls in the same room, Shapiro woke one morning and decided he was dying.

"Brayton," he cried out in a voice of anguish, "bring me my water bottle." Brayton glanced at the inert figure, hesitated, but finally reacted when Shapiro repeated the plea

It might have been a dugout scene from *Journey's End,* R.C. Sherriff's celebrated play about World War I. With flickering candle for illumination, Brayton lifted Shapiro's head while he placed the water bottle gently to his lips. Just then a press officer marched into the room and proclaimed, "General Crerar is giving a briefing in twenty minutes." Since H.D.G. Crerar was commander of the First Canadian Army, this was no time to dally. Shapiro almost knocked over Brayton in his rush to scramble. His fatal disability had vanished.

There were some stirring reports from the press camp — long, absorbing accounts of life and hardship endured by soldiers who were, primarily, civilians propelled into an alien environment and set of conditions. Ralph Allen, of *The Globe and Mail,* covered an action in which two Hitler Jugend, the fanatic young generation brought up to believe utterly in the fuehrer, held up a Canadian advance. One was killed by gunfire. The other still held out, until the Canadians hurled a grenade that tore off an arm; but still the German resisted. He caught a second grenade and threw it back. It took a third to kill him. Allen described the combatants as "little boys who never had the chance to become the little boys they might have been."

Possibly the most original pieces were written by J.A.M. "Jam" Cook of *The Winnipeg Free Press.* Many of Cook's readers were prairie farmers. Cook wrote about the wheat fields of Normandy in a way that told the people back home something of the terror endured by troops seeking cover under shelling. He was inspired by the allied breakout from Normandy into other ancient provinces. Taking his cue from a romantic hit song of World War I, still popular in the 1940s, he sent a one-line story: "Roses are blooming in Picardy." It appeared that way, under his by-line, in a prominent position on the front page of *The Winnipeg Free Press*.

Me? One evening in September 1990, putting together some wartime notes, I called Jack Donoghue in Calgary. The last time I had seen Donoghue was when he was a captain and a conducting officer in Normandy and beyond, one of those fearless and peerless men who dealt daily with demanding and temperamental correspondents wanting to go to impossible places. A long, long time had elapsed, and Donoghue was in a mood to reminisce. Suddenly he said, "I can remember one thing when I conducted you — you never put your muddy boots on the back seat of my jeep." I said, "How I wish that you remembered me because I had."

But maybe that was it, just like the commentary in the McGill annual attesting to my sense of "responsibility." Getting mud on the back seat of a jeep meant that you climbed in over a clutter of water bottles and weapons, and stepped anywhere you found a gap. I must have been tidy and steady and selective. No heroics, no drama. It's a lousy non-label. Still, Donoghue did remember something about me after forty-five years.

This is what I wrote in July 1944:

The old man with the large white moustache and black beret lit the Canadian cigarette and said in French, "Des ruines et des collaborateurs." Then he went on to explain: "Monsieur, when a city like Caen has been liberated there are two big jobs — to clear the debris and pick out the collaborators."

Today as you go through Caen you see what the old man with the large white moustache means. Caen is a dead city struggling to life. It is a horrible example of what can happen in France when a town or city or village lies in the path of a determined attacker and an equally determined defender. Its eyes are sore from the sight of twisted steel. Its nose is overwhelmed by the smell of death that hovers over it. Its ears are tired of the whisperings: "Georges Durand, he should be punished. He worked with the Gestapo," or "Pierre Bertrand, he should be punished. He sold all his produce to German soldiers."

Take a walk with me through the streets of Caen. They bear the imprint of the most devastating air and artillery bombardment any city has endured. Bulldozers, many of them driven by Canadians, push through roadways to clear rubble that has blocked traffic. Bombing the enemy sometimes creates a boomerang effect. It may trap him and prevent him from bringing in reinforcements, but it also slows up the advance of our own troops.

There is not a street in Caen that escaped untouched. On some streets nothing remains standing. The famous University of Caen, founded in 1432, has disintegrated. Other ancient landmarks have vanished. Here and there amidst desolation are preserved such historic buildings as Abbaye aux Hommes, built by William the Conqueror nine hundred years ago. Men and women who survived there in terror during the bombardment still squat in discomfort on its cold stone floor. A baby lies on straw in a corner near the pews while her mother tries to lull her to sleep. In contrast, a blonde girl, with a bowl of cold water in front of her, tries to freshen her face and put on mascara so she can greet Canadian and British soldiers swarming into the city.

Some of those who took refuge in the Abbaye aux Hommes and other shelters are plodding through the rubble trying to salvage what is left of their homes. They stand atop a mound of stone that is punctuated by a piece of dirty cloth that once was a bright living room curtain, or a piece of tile from what was once a modern bathroom. For Caen, the old, also possessed many modern buildings. Its chief city architect, Brillaud de Laujardière, shakes his head sadly and says, "It will be a city of the future. It will need to be completely rebuilt. Plans? We never had any big plans. We liked our city as it was."

Caen counted a normal population of sixty thousand. Half were evacuated before the allied assault began. Of the rest, one thousand, nine hundred were killed and one thousand, one hundred injured. The wounded have been removed to hospitals in Bayeux, which through a strange fate of war escaped untouched. Hundreds of Caen's citizens remain unaccounted for, and many bodies are believed to be lying in the rubble. Others, homeless, are sent to rear areas to special camps or billets. Today about seven thousand still exist in the ruins. And others are straggling back, though they are not supposed to. "When you have a home, monsieur," the old man with the white moustache says, "you try to go back, no matter what is left or what anyone says."

They came back from battle, weary after ten sleepless nights, dirty after all those days in mud and dust — and worried. Not about themselves, but about the major and his men. "Is there any word?" they asked, and when they were told there was none, they held their heads low, slipped away and said nothing. This was like the last war in one way. You fought for a certain period, perhaps five days, perhaps ten. Then when you were so battered that you could fight no longer, you were pulled out, and others took your place in the line.

That was as far as the similarity went. The line was not static, as it had been in World War I. In the past, the soldiers fought from fixed trenches, and when they were relieved they could walk down those trenches and along dirt roads through their own positions to where they could rest properly. Now, in World War II, the soldiers fought from trenches, too, but of a different kind — the kind you dug in an hour, just big enough for you and a companion.

You might stay in that slit trench for a couple of hours, then advance to a new position, and dig another. And when you were pulled out of the line, you travelled over roads in what you liked to call "our" positions, but the enemy tried to make these his positions, too. He was constantly infiltrating through orchards and wheat fields, sometimes with powerful and well camouflaged Tiger and Panther tanks.

It was especially sad to see them come back this time, I said in my report. I was writing about the Black Watch of Montreal, a Highland battalion with a distinguished record from World War I. What they had just undergone, plunging ahead despite redoubtable opposition and bungled support, resulted in the virtual annihilation of the regiment. This might have happened in World War I, but was it supposed to happen in a modern war featuring rapid deployment and communications?

A foretaste of what was to come, a sample of confusion in battle, was experienced on the night of July 23 when men of the Black Watch waited in slit trenches at a place called Hill 67, near the Norman village of Ifs. "Hill" was an imaginative way of describing what was not much more than a gentle slope with some scarred trees atop it. It was a black night, so dark that a German patrol stumbled accidentally into Black Watch positions. Rifle fire flashed in the darkness and it was almost impossible to judge who was shooting at whom.

A Black Watch corporal, Jack Miller, awakened from deep sleep in his slit trench to discover that someone had landed beside him. The next thing Miller knew, the intruder began jabbering in German. "Like a fool," Miller later confessed, "I had left my rifle on the ground above, and the German was about to blast me when Otto jumped in." Otto (surname Bulow) was a Dane who had left Denmark in 1939 to work as a houseman for a wealthy Montreal family. He did not like Germans after what they had done to his country. He grappled with the enemy soldier. Miller managed to climb out and clasp his rifle and bayonet: "I tossed it in and Otto caught it and stuck the German — but stuck him good."

Otto then sank back and relaxed for a moment. Other Germans had hidden in the tall grass, and Otto stood up and shouted in German, "German soldiers, come in. We won't shoot you." At first a few came in hesitatingly, and when the others heard there was no firing they gave themselves up too. The total bag: eighteen dead Germans, thirty-six prisoners. The Black Watch suffered casualties as well.

Nonetheless, that was a minor engagement — nothing that could presage the disaster that followed in less than forty-eight hours, on July 25, 1944, a date that has entered military books on tactics. The Black Watch, as part of a brigade attack, was given the objective of routing Germans from the village of Fontenay-le-Marmion. The attack ran sour from the start. Two support battalions that were to clear the Black Watch's "start line" in the neighboring villages of St. André-sur-Orne and St. Martin-de-Fontenay, were unsuccessful, pushed back by the Germans. The Black Watch, instead of taking off for Fontenay-le-Marmion through territory in friendly Canadian hands, now had to fight their way to the start line.

The battalion came to a crossroads outside St. André, and the commanding officer, Lt.-Col. S.S.T. Cantlie, set out to reconnoitre. He was caught in crossfire of German machine guns, and died on the way to a casualty clearing station. Penetrating into St. André, three other senior officers were killed or wounded. On the slim shoulders of a major, Philip Griffin, fell the responsibility of leading the four rifle companies.

They'd always spoken of the major with awe and respect. One of the youngest majors in the Canadian army at age twenty-five, he was also one of its most brilliant. Before he enlisted, Griffin was completing studies for a PhD degree at Macdonald College, the McGill University agricultural school in Ste. Anne de Bellevue, Que. His men and fellow officers — those who were left — continued to speak highly of him. But the reality was that this was an inexperienced battalion, which had arrived in France only two weeks earlier.

So many officers met death or injury that several platoons were commanded by corporals. And they still needed to clear one thousand metres before reaching the start line. There was some question whether they should simply stay in St. André, since the original plan had been ruined by the failure of other units to clear the way. "We will go on," the major decided, and in the morning they went on — a couple of hundred of them. They battled their way through cabbage fields into orchards, digging between walls, advancing a few yards at a time, always in line of mortar and machine gun fire. On the way they killed some Germans and took some prisoners.

Griffin penetrated a hundred metres beyond the start line when the wireless set in his jeep was shot out. Three forward artillery observation officers, equipped with their own transmitters, had been assigned to the unit so they could bring down buttressing fire. But in one case, a set broke down, in another it was demolished, and in the third the signaller was wounded. The Black Watch in effect were bereft of artillery or tank support. Griffin led about sixty soldiers, who could still fight, on to the broad crest of the slope before Fontenay-le-Marmion. They came under direct fire from a half dozen dug-in Panther and Tiger tanks. German 88-mm guns, concealed in haystacks, hit them over open sights.

It was slaughter, but still Griffin pressed on. As one of the few survivors told me, "Major Griffin was at the head, and the last I heard him say was, 'Forward, men. We've got to keep going.'" On August 8, when other Canadians finally succeeded in occupying the crest of the ridge, Griffin's body was found lying among those of his men. The total casualties of the Black Watch on July 25 came to three hundred and twenty-four. One hundred and twenty lost their lives; others were captives, in German hospitals or prison camps.

One day an official army historian would write: "Except for the Dieppe operation, there is no other instance in the Second World War where a Canadian battalion had so many casualties in a single day."

In military colleges through the years debates would follow on whether to plunge ahead when original planning goes awry. But for the men of the Black Watch in that grim period in Normandy there was no time or inclination to analyze the action. Forty who did not normally engage in combat — batmen, cooks, drivers — held off Germans who surrounded them in St. André, held them off so their comrades could come back that way should they have to retreat. They didn't retreat, and the others knew they were either dead or prisoners. When the batmen and cooks returned to the rear, after a night and morning under German attack, they asked about the major and his men in the hope that they had found another route of escape. Told that none had come back, they dropped their heads in silence.

There were survivors, but not many. Fifteen soldiers of the rifle companies eventually managed to reach our lines. A few others I came upon by chance a month later during the liberation of Paris. Seriously wounded, they lay in a hospital nursed by French nuns. I took their names and personal messages and gave them to the commanding officer of our press contingent for relay home. There was not much else one could do or say to comfort these victims of war in which officers still said, even though the text books would not have said it, "We've got to keep going."

3   The Road to Paris

WHILE THE EMPHASIS OF MY *STANDARD* ASSIGNMENT was to report on Canadian soldiers, I felt free to move to wherever I believed the main story was developing. The invasion had taken place; and after fierce fighting in Normandy the allies were now advancing rapidly inland. In immediate terms, no road ahead that was more enticing than the road to Paris. Militarily, it might not have made a prime objective; emotionally, it was matchless. Eisenhower decided that the main allied armies would by-pass it. But Charles de Gaulle's Free French, largely for political design and to aid the resistance fighters who had risen in Paris, were pressing toward it.

I shared a jeep with Maurice "Moe" Desjardins, correspondent for the French-language service of The Canadian Press. Moe was a handsome, dashing fellow. A more spirited companion, especially on a story like this, the entry into Paris, one could not imagine. The cathedral town of Chartres was our first objective. We stopped only once on the outskirts, to push aside a jerry can. Otherwise the macadam road was clear of any debris or obstruction.

In Normandy, where people still suffered the effects of the bombing and shelling, there was little cheering for the liberators. But now, on the unscathed path nearing the capital, the crowds — exuberant, uninhibited — went wild. People lined the cobbled streets of Chartres, and cried out, "Vive les Américains, vive les alliés." It was only when we stopped at the Mairie, the town hall, that we received recognition as Canadians.

German prisoners shuffled uneasily under the guard of French civilians who wore over their shabby suits armbands with the initials FFI (French Forces of the Interior). Some were short, fat men who carried half their weight in rifles and sub-machine guns. Some were stoop-shouldered with white hair, hand grenades strung in belts around their waists like medieval charms. Some were clean-shaven boys with the tired eyes of adults. "A bas les Boches," screamed a woman as she spat at a German. The inhibitions, the fears of Normandy that the enemy might return, did not exist here.

As this procession passed slowly by, there came into view, in the courtyard of the Mairie, a line of twenty women, their faces pressing the grey stones of the old building. Other women — and men — held the captives' heads and sheared their locks while the crowd uttered curses of approval. "It is not very pretty is it," said a woman, who, glancing at our shoulder flashes, added, "In Canada, perhaps they will not understand." I had no comment, but she persisted, "These women sold themselves to *les Boches*. What more must you know?"

The woman, in her early thirties, was herself a resistance fighter, dressed in a blue Red Cross uniform but with the revealing emblem of de Gaulle, a tiny Cross of Lorraine, fixed on a tunic pocket. She was dark-skinned and attractive, and eager to describe what had befallen the French under the Germans. We made our way to a twisting street, rue du Soleil d'Or, and there to a tiny café. We sat and drank brandy and ate fried potatoes. But the woman could not stay long. She intended to start, before nightfall, on the journey to her home in Paris.

I looked at her in astonishment and said, "But there are still Germans between here and Paris."

"I am going by bicycle," she said. "I know the side roads. The Germans are running. They will not stop a woman."

I wanted more of her story, and now there was no time. She anticipated my question, "When you arrive in Paris, call me." She wrote in my notebook her name — a countess, no less — and phone number, Elysées 34.28. It was so casual a gesture, as though this was peacetime and a gracious woman was inviting a dumb-founded visitor for cocktails. We said our farewells, I never expecting to see her again.

The next day Chartres was full of rumors. Within fifteen minutes a half dozen people stopped me to ask the latest news or relay the latest gossip. I could believe none of it, not even radio reports. One minute the Americans were in Paris, the next they were only a few kilometres away, in Versailles. And then they were not in Versailles, they were by-passing Paris to leave the FFI to annihilation. I hailed a jeep load of U.S. officers to ask what information they possessed, whether American troops really had entered Paris. No one knew.

"We probably won't announce it," cracked a lieutenant, "until Mrs. Roosevelt makes an appearance." It was an everyday condescending reference to the president's peripatetic columnist wife, Eleanor.

In fact, as we confirmed later, none of the major allied armies was going anywhere near Paris. Only a French armored division, with a token American escort, would enter. But the confusion prevailed. To add to it, we were accosted by a young French couple who requested a lift in our jeep. They had been married in Chartres while street fighting flared, and now were off on their honeymoon. Where to? "Paris, monsieur," they said in a tone that suggested mine was a dim-witted question. What if there were no trains? What if a war was being fought, if there was skirmishing all around? More cogent than all these questions, however, was another: What French couple had ever heard of spending a honeymoon anywhere but in Paris?

That night the road was clear and we gave the honeymooners a ride to Rambouillet, which was not far from the destination for all of us. The road signs read: Paris 50 km. Moe Desjardins and I went to the préfecture in Rambouillet to find a place to sleep. The police filled out a "billet de logement" for a home at 16 rue du Hasard. As though the last few days had not been bizarre enough, the requisition permit quoted the law of May 23, 1792. If French emotions were great in those moments of revolution, I could not imagine them greater than in these moments of liberation.

75

* * *

In the morning Rambouillet gave us a send-off. The people threw flowers and called out, "Bonne chance, bonne chance." We travelled through open countryside, pure and fresh in the August sunshine. Only a few slit trenches on the side of the road marred the scenery, and I caught sight of a lone German body, bloated, the arms upright, lying under a chestnut tree. The sign posts brought us nearer and nearer: Paris 25 km., Paris 10 km. Then Moe said, "Nous sommes arrivés." We were, indeed, in Paris!

I said nothing. I was intent on taking in the buildings on either side, as though sanity had returned — the first modern buildings we had seen in Europe, with the green canopies shading the windows, and the flower boxes, and the wide boulevard. Only it was wide no longer. Hundreds of people, a million people, pressed forward from the sidewalk and closed in on the jeep. "Merci, merci," they shouted, and I looked as quickly as my head could turn, from one face to another. I saw young women in front, laughing joyously, their cheeks flushed, their eyes sparkling. And I saw old women in the back, waving weakly, the tears flowing.

This progressed for blocks, and always the buildings grew more magnificent and the crowd more thunderous. All we could do was hold out an arm and flick the hands of the people as we passed, like a card flapping the spokes of a bicycle wheel. "We will never forget you, we have waited so long," sobbed an old man, the medals dangling from his chest. And still the old women at the back waved us on, weeping all the while. And still the wide boulevards were not wide enough, because the people massed into the roadway and the jeep could hardly move.

Then we halted. Two or three American half tracks had preceded us, but they disappeared, and now we were alone, except of course for the ever-surging multitude. The pause was enough. Within a minute the back of the jeep was laden with champagne bottles, and friendly hands were clenching glasses. "Drink," a man commanded. "Drink with us." The man handed glasses to the other bystanders and everyone drank. I wanted to push on to the Hôtel Scribe, the planned rendezvous of correspondents. There the transmitters would be set up. There I could send my story. But a woman edged forward, hugged and kissed me — and others followed. "I'm sorry if I scraped your face," I said. "I didn't have time to shave this morning." Everyone laughed again, and in the rear an old woman still wept.

There was the sound of rifle and machine gun fire — and the dull *broomph* of tank cannon. The shots grew louder, and to them was added the din of blaring horns. A dilapidated car, with Tricolor draped on its hood, a dozen armed men positioned on the running boards, honked its way through the throng. The riders wore the helmets of the French army and the armbands of the FFI. A man leaped off and kissed me on both cheeks.

"Welcome," he said, beaming. "You've come at last." I asked about the gun fire. There was a battle, a tank fight, just ahead, in the Jardin du Luxembourg, he said. And the Germans held the top of the street we were on. But the man knew of other routes to the Scribe, on the far side of the Seine. "Wait here a few minutes," he instructed. "I will check which streets are safest."

Then, the champagne corks flying, I had a sudden thought. I must phone the countess we had met in Chartres. Why at that precise instant, I did not exactly know. It was a fantastic idea that fitted the atmosphere. "Are the telephones working?" I asked no one in particular. "Yes," answered several voices together. "Where can I find one?" A man, with apron around his waist, pushed forward, "In my shop. Come with me." In seconds I discovered myself in a grocery, the shelves bare except for a sign, "Pas de ravitaillement aujourd'hui." No rations today.

I thumbed through my notebook, gave the shopkeeper the number, he dialed and handed me the phone. The signal was not the same as at home. Here two quick rings, two quick rings, two quick rings. A woman answered, and moments later the countess came on the line. She sounded hardly surprised. She was brimming with news about what was happening to her and others in Paris' liberation, and agreed, if the streets were passable, to meet me tomorrow morning at the Scribe. I put down the phone and could scarcely believe myself. I had spoken to someone at the other end of Paris as I might have spoken to someone in Montreal. Yet between our phones a tank battle raged. "It is a crazy war," I said to the shopkeeper. He said, "It is a cruel war."

The FFI car guided us across the Seine. Who could mistake those stone bridges? I searched for street signs and saw avenue de l'Opéra and boulevard des Capucines. There were newspaper kiosks at the corners, and *vespasiennes,* and then rue Scribe and a fine six-storey building, "Hôtel Scribe" — across the road a store, "Old England," the name in large letters untouched by Germans.

The jeep pulled alongside the hotel, and the inevitable crowd surged forward to greet us. I manouevred my way through the revolving door into the lobby. To the left was a reception desk, and straight ahead a porter stood smiling behind a longer desk. The lounge, opening into the center of the lobby, was dark, but civilized and luxurious with its potted ferns, its settees, its armchairs. A tall, grey haired man strode up and grasped my hand. "I am Louis Régamey, agent general of the CNR," he said. "Welcome to the Scribe."

This, it transpired, was another unanticipated oddity of war. The Scribe's proprietor was Canadian National Railways, and, knowing this, Col. Richard Malone, chief of our press contingent, had requisitioned it for Canadian war correspondents. Malone, on a different route into the city, was as surprised as I was to find the phones functioning. He got through to the hotel and was transferred to Régamey. Now this CNR agent, who had managed to survive the German occupation because he was a French citizen, was on hand to greet us individually. He escorted me to the desk, where I registered. This was not 1944 but 1934, and I was a young tourist on my first visit to Paris.

"Perhaps you would like to see the last registration card that was signed?" said Régamey. I examined it — Joachim Hugo Klapper, *Obersturmbannführer,* lieutenant-colonel of the Gestapo. The Gestapo had taken over the Scribe in 1940, and the Canadian government, as owner of the CNR, received payment for four years' rental in a roundabout way. Now Gestapo officers had checked out hours before we checked in.

The American and British press groups had learned of the Canadian windfall, and the Scribe became the official billet for all allied reporters. Soon the lobby was filled with men and women waiting for rooms. But meantime they propped their typewriters on the reception desk, on tables, on any available surface where they could work. The clicking of keyboards was rivalled by the hissing and popping of champagne corks. Régamey took it upon himself to help waiters haul case after case into the lobby. More than one writer succumbed to the emotion and celebration.

I heard my name called, and an Australian colleague weaved his shaky way toward me, and mumbled, "What a piece I wrote, mate, what a piece. Wanna hear it?" Before I could answer, he read it aloud in its entirety: "Begin story. The story of Paris' liberation cannot be told in words. End story." It was probably the most intelligible account to come out of Paris that momentous day.

That night, after sending off a story, I set out in search of a late meal. The Scribe dining room was not functioning, and the only restaurant that appeared open was a short way down the blacked out street. I entered and found about a dozen and a half men and women there. The owner, it turned out much later, was a notorious collaborator. But right now he sought to endear himself to the liberators.

The only "liberators" in uniform were an American sergeant and a private, and myself. I never did learn who the male civilians were, but after much toasting we were seated at a long table and fed sumptuously. Our host gave a little speech in English — he said he had lived for a while in California — and then walked around the table, to whisper to each woman. There were smiles and nods in response. He sat down for a moment, and rose again to repeat this performance with the men. Arriving next to me, he bent low, motioned with his eyes to the blonde next to me, and murmured, "It's all right. She'll sleep with you tonight."

Such overwhelming hospitality matched the city's mood of gratitude. But first we were expected to go on to a night club. We piled into two jeeps, provided by the Americans, but before we could proceed farther than a couple of blocks, air raid sirens began to howl. German planes were overhead, uttering a rude last gasp to the Parisians. Our drivers, the American soldiers, wanted to stop and take to shelters — and so did I — but the mad French insisted we accelerate. They had never experienced an air raid. Anyway, I decided I should return on foot to the Scribe and complete another story. "Pauvre Canadien," said the blonde, shaking her head in bewilderment.

My second lesson in French romantic values, as contrasted with a Canadian's excessive work compulsion, came the next morning. The countess arrived at the Scribe at eleven, a submachine gun slung over her shoulder. She had helped ferret out a few Germans still resisting in the city outskirts. I wanted her story more than ever. With no bar or dining room yet operational, the only place we could talk quietly was my room. She sat in an easy chair; I perched on the edge of the bed, a notebook in hand. Within less than fifteen minutes the door opened, a chambermaid viewed the scene, excused herself and backed out.

An hour later, the countess was leaning forward in her chair, animatedly giving me details about French resistance against the Germans, and I was scribbling away steadily. The door opened again. The same chambermaid, carrying a load of towels, started to enter. She paused. "Monsieur," she cried, flinging the towels in the air, "you are still talking?"

* * *

It was not all ecstasy. No people on earth could have burst out of four years of captivity under a hated foe more passionately than Parisians. That was the joyous, laughing side that played a large part in first impressions. The other side was not so pleasant. The cost of living had soared tenfold since the occupation, reflected in *le marché noir,* the black market. Everyone talked about *le marché noir* with disgust and loathing, yet everyone at one time or another dealt in it. There was nothing else to do if you wanted to eat or dress properly.

The staple food was bread, and that came to three hundred grams a day under the legal system of rationing. The allotment of meat for each adult was eighty-five grams weekly, along with eighty-five grams of spaghetti, a small pat of butter, and eighty-five grams of jam whenever it was available. There was no jam in July, nor in August, when we arrived.

The black market continued to operate long after the German departure. But Gallic verve still surfaced. One of the first press conferences given by a French government official, which I covered, dealt with the food crisis. He explained that Paris must continue to accept acute shortages though there was an abundance of produce in Normandy. A lack of transport created the obstacle. It was like — and he groped for an analogy — "Like a woman's brassiere. Only a thin fabric separates the two important halves, but it is vital."

I revisited the Scribe many times in later years, but in 1984 it was for a special occasion, to write a magazine article about the fortieth anniversary of Paris' liberation. I sat in the bar of the Scribe, my thoughts on some sights and sounds of four decades ago. I could even imagine hearing the rhythmic clatter on the sidewalks of wooden-soled shoes — the footwear worn by women because there was no leather. But now the tone was of low voices of well-dressed men and women enjoying cocktails.

Still, one voice prevailed — that of *The Montreal Star's* Sholto Watt, an eccentric and a linguist, who, on an August evening in 1944, established himself at the end of the Scribe bar. Gripping a snifter of brandy in one hand, he picked up the phone with the other. When the switchboard operator responded, Watt said in French: "I would like to place a call to Brussels." The chatter of other imbibers faded. There was a war on. Hundreds of thousands of German soldiers occupied the territory between Paris and Brussels, as well as the Belgian capital itself. Did Watt think the telephone lines would still be connected?

A series of clicks sputtered on the line and a female voice said in French, "This is Brussels."

Watt took a sip of brandy and said, "I would like to speak to the German field commander." Another series of clicks. Another voice — this time male, German. Watt said in German: "Give me the field commander, please." All the bar waited in awe and silence. More clicks and then a new voice — the field commander himself. Watt drank deeply and finally said, "This is Sholto Watt of *The Montreal Star*. The jig is up. You might as well quit." He put down the phone and concentrated on the brandy.

Inevitably, with the horde of new arrivals in the days after liberation, the cognac at the Scribe ran out — and so did most of the liquor supply in Paris. But, as I remembered it, Greg Clark of *The Toronto Star,* on a reconnaissance of his own, touched down at the Ritz bar. There he heard a bartender describe some strange alcoholic beverage that was pushed aside in the cellar. The Germans scorned it. It did not taste like any *schnapps* they were familiar with; certainly it bore no resemblance to scotch. Clark decided to look— and to his delight discovered case upon case of Seagram's V.O. He confined the secret to a few Canadian comrades, but the Americans also tumbled to it — and that oasis, too, soon dried up.

I thought back to Moe Desjardins, who spent less time in the bar than he did in the "journalism school" he set up in the Scribe. Desjardins, on frugal Canadian Press expenses, found the nominal cost of a Scribe room too high. But he managed to persuade Louis Régamey that the CN should subsidize a sister Canadian agency, CP. In return for free accommodation, Moe said he would teach young French students something about journalism. Thenceforth, when Moe came to Paris on leave, he would toss his bedroll on the floor of a complimentary storage room, enjoy hotel services, entertain aspiring female students — and forget journalism.

I thought, too, of my own sojourns away from the front, particularly the epic afternoon when I was summoned to the German surrender. The bar had been transformed in forty years. In 1984 the room was called Le Saint-Laurent, with lithographs of old Quebec City and the river adorning the walls. The supply of V.O. and other spirits was abundant. The building was still owned by the Canadian National, the hotel itself operated by a French company.

I had often wondered about the odd wartime arrangement whereby the Germans, meticulous and correct, had paid the hotel in occupation francs or scrip for its running expenses, and some of this went toward the rent. Régamey managed to invest the revenue in Suez Canal bonds, returning a profit that awaited the CN when the Germans were driven from France. Thus, at least indirectly, the Germans subsidized the Canadian enemy.

I reflected on the communications in the hours following Paris' liberation, when everyone was so breathless to get out the thrilling news. Before transmitters could be set up at the Scribe, a press officer thought of landing a light plane on the Champs Elysées to ferry out dispatches. But nothing came of it. Much more practical was the route of some reporters who discovered that radio signals could be sent from the Eiffel Tower to London, for re-transmission to Canada or anywhere else in the world.

The original version of the mahogany bar in the Scribe is still there. In 1984 I tried to visualize the ring left by Sholto Watt's brandy glass. But too many coats of varnish had covered the years since 1944. Worse still, in 1994, when I was back in preparation for the fiftieth anniversary of Paris' liberation, I found the top now hidden by black marble, part of altered, Greek décor. Nonetheless, my memories remained.

Scarcely ten days after Paris, the capital of Belgium fell to the allies, this time the British. The entry into Brussels was marked by the same kind of euphoria that had swept Paris. But there was no ambiguity. The French undoubtedly appreciated the allied liberators, but their joy was tinged with the bitter memory of the collapse in 1940 of their own forces, whom they considered superior to Americans and British in the art of warfare. It was one reason why Eisenhower had sent in a French division to help the FFI in Paris.

The Belgians, old hands at surviving occupation, had fewer illusions to haunt them. Many men and women still recalled the Huns on their streets in World War I. The Germans, returning a quarter century later, were more lenient — or shrewder — than the first time. They did not denude the country. They paid well for goods and services. They allowed the Belgians to retain much of their manufactured goods for their own use. As a result, Brussels department stores displayed consumer goods in far greater abundance than Paris shops.

There was another reason. "When you have lived through one occupation, and you see another war coming, you know what to do." It was a sixty-year-old woman who spoke these words as we sat next to her table in an outdoor café on the boulevard Adolphe Max. I had met, by chance, a fellow Montrealer, an army corporal named Miller, and we watched and listened. All Brussels was promenading down the wide avenue, spilling onto the roadway and impeding enthusiastically the army vehicles trying to pass. "We have learned one thing," the woman went on. "We have learned to think of the future and keep large supplies."

That was a practical explanation, but there needed to be more. The Belgians had suffered spiritually, and, in loss of freedom, at least as much as the French. But the individual resistance retained a quality all its own, and I saw an example of it that I had not seen anywhere before. Miller and I understood there had been a round-up of Jews (though, in common with most people, we were utterly unaware of the extent of concentration camps or the existence of the extermination machinery known as the Final Solution). We were anxious to determine what remnants of Jewry remained. Had any synagogue, for instance, reopened?

The timing was appropriate, for the High Holidays were underway. The concierge at my hotel located a synagogue. When we arrived there, midway through the Yom Kippur service, we counted about forty men and women, all terribly wan and shabby. As soon as the service ended, Miller and I — the only ones in uniform — were surrounded by virtually the whole congregation. Some simply touched our arms, some just gazed at us with moistened eyes. One after another they had episodes to relate of four agonizing years of survival. Several had been concealed by Christians. Many women were alone, their husbands long ago shipped off to German labor or concentration camps; the women were not even sure which kind of camp or whether their men still lived.

We were besieged with invitations to break the fast with worshippers. We declined at first, for we realized we would be depriving them of scarce food. Then we understood that the *mitzvah,* the joy of giving without expecting reward, would be specially memorable to them. Finally we did accept, and two couples took us to the home in which they had been hidden. The two men quietly slipped away just before the meal, and we knew we were taking their portions. Still, the sharing was precious — to all of us. The poignancy was overwhelming, for we represented to these people their first link with the outside world.

Yet they had never completely lost touch, either with happenings abroad or events close by. Word of mouth was the principal method of communications. Within days of Brussels' liberation a newspaper in Yiddish made its appearance — typewritten and mimeographed on ten pages of legal-sized paper. My knowledge of Yiddish was too rudimentary for me to understand much beyond the date and name — *Unser Wort* (Our Word). But I knew someone who would appreciate it — my father. I sent him the paper, and received back a letter of intense emotion. After his death several years later, I found *Unser Wort* carefully preserved among his most precious belongings.

There was a satisfying, a pleasing feel to it when I typed the dateline: "With American Forces Inside Germany." Soldiers of the U.S. First Army, assaulting the most heavily fortified position in Hitler's Siegfried Line, were over the border, inside Aachen — known earlier as Aix-la-Chapelle, home and capital of Charlemagne. The contrast, a mere month after Brussels, was stark. Civilians huddled as refugees on the outskirts — pushed out from the centre, they said, by their own German soldiers lest they hinder operations. There was no greeting of liberators.

I can still turn to my original notes, and see in the wreckage of the first house I entered a gaunt cat biting at a morsel of dried meat and some flaky potatoes beside the overturned plate on the floor. Blue drapes flapped against the shattered windowpanes. There was no other sound. Then the cat licked the last specks and moved off, brushing against a table that was supported by two legs and the wall. The table toppled, and a picture fell with a loud crash. Adolf Hitler lay in a broken frame amid the grey plaster that splattered from the ceiling like tears of regret.

This was symbolism in its purest form. Aachen, the first German city to yield to the conquerors, was dead. Its buildings, now twisted into rubble, whispered through the October wind: "We have paid the price. Must all Germany share our fate?" Many of its people could not speak. They rested beneath the ruins, lifeless memorials of a system they had nurtured for twelve years. "When war comes to Germany," I wrote, "it comes with no less fury than in Normandy or in Flanders or in the dike lands of Holland. I have seen Caen and now I have seen the death of Aachen. It suffered a more horrible death than Caen — slower in its strangling, more devastating in its finality."

American troops were clearing the last couple of snipers from one of the few existing rooftops when I went deeper into the city. "We've given them hell, haven't we?" said Capt. David Haight, twenty-eight years old, a slim company commander. I nodded. No other agreement was necessary. This was Germany now. This was an enemy city beaten out of recognition, its ancient and modern buildings left with little more than their misshapen outer walls. Aachen did not die only because the Americans besieged it for six weeks. It encountered four years of hell when the Royal Air Force raided it more than eighty times. At least three-quarters of its damage dated back to that strategic bombing.

I walked along the once grand Wilhelmstrasse and could detect not a single building intact. On the side streets, piles of stones and bricks lined the roadways next to the shells of what had been stately homes. A sign, half submerged in bits of masonry, caught my eye: *Palast Hotel Quellenhof.* The Blue Guide book that I'd bought in Brussels informed me on page 264: "230 beds, 52 Monsheims Allee, a palatial house of the first class with thermal and other baths." Now the chairs, which once must have been richly upholstered, lay in tatters. Rats crawled over shreds of dirty tablecloths, gnawing at pieces of shrunken fruit.

I stepped into the office of the newspaper *Politisches Tegeblatt.* Its presses on the main floor were studded with machine gun bullets, mementoes of the street fighting between the Americans and the last defenders of the city. Strewn on the floor were copies of the final edition. An editorial pledged: "We will never retreat from this venerable city."

I entered more homes, to note the solemn evidence of hasty departures: food half cooked on a now cold stove, children's clothing hung nearby to dry, dresser drawers open, with snapshots, shaving kits, hot water bottles — a hundred items — tossed on the floor. On one unmade bed I saw a tuxedo, and beside it a mauve evening dress. I was about to move into the next room when I noticed the Paris label, and speculated whether the gown had been the gift, or a trophy, of a Nazi occupier of Paris.

On the street again, I wondered where all the people had fled. Aachen's population once stood at a hundred and fifty thousand, yet I had seen no one besides American infantrymen. Then I heard footsteps, almost echoing my own, and swung around to glimpse two old men, carrying bundles and walking perhaps twenty yards behind me. They just walked, apparently aimlessly, their footsteps bouncing with an unearthly resonance from one mound of rubble to another. I felt no pity for them. They were guilty of causing the war, were they not? And yet were they? It was odd, I was incapable of making a judgment, at least at that stage and about these old, dejected men.

What is there about the commonality of survival and death in war, the alikeness of civilians wherever they are trapped? Only four months ago it was Caen, its people caught on the anvil of battle. Now it was Aachen — an enemy city. I could see no physical difference; rubble looks the same wherever it is heaped. But I could feel an enormous difference emotionally — empathy in the case of the French of Caen; coldness — or at least indifference — in the case of Germans of Aachen.

"Why did you stay?" I asked a sixty-year-old woman who plodded through the tiny Shutzen Strasse with a suitcase in one hand and the hand of her eight-year-old grandson clasped in the other. "Why did I stay?" she said. "This is my home. I have lived here all my life, and not even the SS could make me leave." How often had I heard the same refrain in Britain and France? Everywhere, people said: "This is my home. No matter how much of it is destroyed, no matter what the dangers, I will stay on." It was the arch British enemy of the Germans, Winston Churchill, who spoke of the universality of survival: "Death and sorrow will be the companions of our journey; hardship our garment; constancy and valor our only shield."

No part of the war that now swept across Germany could have been as horrifying or unimaginable as the entry into the death camps. The existence of these camps — Buchenwald, Auschwitz, Dachau, many others — was known to allied officials, but hardly publicized. I do not think I was alone among the correspondents to come across Buchenwald in utter shock and disbelief. The image of crawling skeletons, covered only with loose skin, registers forever in the mind's eye, along with the sight of similar, but literally dead, humans stacked in grotesque heaps. The eye still sees them, yet what also clings to my mind is the endurance, or determination, of the human spirit. The spirit was tested, but it was there nonetheless.

Europe's most unusual underground movement began operating on the surface by the time I reached Buchenwald. Seventeen thousand of the men, women and children who were liberated by the Americans continued to live in their old huts until they gained enough strength for transport to proper refugee centres. They ran their own affairs, under leadership of the same men who, behind barbed wire and despite the scrutiny of SS guards, succeeded in forming an armed resistance network.

I was told details by one of the organizers, a young Dutch journalist named Pieters, who spent six years in the camp. As in Brussels, men and women, who were freshly released from darkness, introduced light with a rapidly produced newspaper. Pieters worked on it, a mimeographed sheet published in six languages. During captivity, he and his comrades ran an oral news service for Buchenwald's inmates. One can speculate about the question of hunger for information surpassing almost the question of hunger for food. If there is an answer it might be found in places like Buchenwald. Certainly the ultimate lesson in survival is to be found there.

Ingenuity was the companion of desperation. When Buchenwald prisoners left their enclosure to work in munitions plants in nearby Weimar, they were forced to help the Germans. But at the same time they helped themselves. At the end of each shift, men carried in their pockets parts of machine guns and rifles, and stuffed powder for ammunition under their fingernails. If they feared spot examination, they swallowed the bits and pieces, for later retrieval. At night they assembled the components in a half dozen illegal workshops in tunnels and caves they had dug throughout the vast grounds.

Though the SS guards suspected strange activity, not once did they uncover any of these subterranean lairs. For one thing, they rarely entered the enclosure itself, relying on the prisoners themselves to move each morning the bodies of those who had died overnight of starvation or disease. Buchenwald's secret committee also conducted trials of people they suspected of spying for the SS. "They were quick trials," Pieters said. "When we found a man guilty, it was the end. His body was hauled away. We simply told the guards he was another typhus victim."

Among Buchenwald's scientists and professors were several military veterans and experts. These men formulated a plan of attack to rescue at least some of the remaining women and children from wholesale massacre by crazed guards as the Americans drew nearer. They knew the SS had laid demolition charges at several points in the camp with the intention of setting off explosions at the last moment.

Those inmates with even a particle of energy were assigned to handle the homemade machine guns and rifles. Some would watch the SS, to strike when they were about to activate the charges. Others would storm two points in the enclosure, one group to cut the electrified fence. But the main thrust would be to form flank and rear protection for the mass of unarmed men, women and children — and shoot at any SS who got in the way. "At least a few of us would be saved," said Pieters.

The plan was never put into effect. SS guards, without unleashing their demolition plungers, fled before the Americans arrived. Armed inmates even proceeded into the woods to help the U.S. infantry round up their former tormentors. When I was there, German civilians from Weimar shuffled on a compulsory tour of the camp, to view the crematoria and the ovens, and the remaining piles of human ashes and bones. They denied any knowledge of Buchenwald's purpose, though the stench of burning flesh permeated the entire area.

The scene must now shift abruptly in time and place. In May 1993 I visited the new and overpowering Holocaust Memorial Museum in Washington. Since its opening a month earlier, capacity crowds lined up for entry. Every day three thousand, five hundred people — young, old, Americans, foreigners — filed past exhibit after exhibit of German barbarism. The silence from such a multitude was incredible; they walked slowly, stood and stared at carpets of shoes of the dead, at walls, three storeys high, covered with photographs of inhabitants of a Jewish community that simply disappeared. They did not even whisper to one another, the overall impact was so shattering. Unlike the citizens of Weimar, forty-eight years ago, they were not compelled to make this pilgrimage. Nor did they deny any knowledge of the Holocaust. They wanted to know more.

So did I. An archivist, Dr. Robert Kesting, dug for me from the museum's files a copy of the report by the first U.S. soldiers, who, on reconnaissance, April 11, 1945, stumbled upon Buchenwald. These men, according to the typewritten account, were members of Combat Team 9 (9th Armored Infantry Battalion of the 6th Armored Division). They had no idea Buchenwald even existed, until some escaped prisoners told them of "a large camp in the woods" slightly to the south. "There is reason to believe," said the report, "that the prompt arrival of CT9 saved many hundreds and perhaps thousands of lives." The Americans saw "some of the SS guards, who were securely staked down to the ground." Their fate remained unreported, probably deliberately.

All I could remember of that April experience was this: If you were a Briton or an American or a Canadian, you walked away from Buchenwald with sweat on your forehead and a curse on your lips.

It was a few minutes before five on the Sunday afternoon of May sixth 1945. We were flying at a level of about a thousand feet. Below, farm fields in their spring greenery were dissected by the highways. Above, the clouds parted, revealing a clear blue sky. I sat on a bucket seat near the front of the C-47. All the occupants were quiet. Then, from the centre of the plane, Brig.-Gen. Frank Allen, chief of public relations at Supreme Headquarters Allied Expeditionary Forces (Shaef), unbuckled his seat belt and motioned to the correspondents. Some of us kneeled on the metal floor so we could hear. Allen cleared his throat and above the throb of the engines said in his Virginia drawl, "We are going on a mission to cover the signing of peace."

The end had appeared imminent — the Russians and the Americans had met on the Elbe, Hitler was dead — but now that it had really come, it was such a simple announcement. My hands felt clammy.

"Yesterday," Allen continued, "emissaries of the German government met Shaef and Soviet officials to discuss the terms of unconditional surrender. Certain conditions were laid down, the results of which were communicated to the German government. Instead of replying to that communication, a representative of the German government will arrive for further consultation, and presumably for acceptance of the conditions, at Shaef's forward headquarters in Reims."

Allen paused, and I am sure we all feared he would never go on.

"This group," Allen finally said, "will represent the press of the world. The story is entirely off the record until the representative heads of government have announced the facts to the world. I therefore pledge each and every one of you on your honor not to divulge the results of this conference or even of its existence until it is released by Supreme headquarters."

I found myself nodding automatically. It was obvious that premature disclosure might mean that some of our men would lay down their arms before enemy soldiers were informed: death due to instant communication. At five-thirty — forty minutes after take-off from Paris — the C-47 landed at Reims' airport. A reporter commented, "It was near here, not so long ago, that Hitler danced a jig of joy when he learned France was asking for peace." Such trite thoughts were not only permissible; they seemed necessary to offset the awesome dimension of the story. I thought it appropriate that Reims, the champagne centre of France, would be toasted around the world.

We drove in a line of cars for ten minutes toward General Eisenhower's advance headquarters. German prisoners, in work gangs, trudged along the edge of the road — guarded by black American soldiers. On the streets, men and women strolled arm in arm. I wondered if they had any idea what was happening in their midst. There was no indication of it. Military police, neat in their white helmets and white belts, saluted the cars as we passed through gates that bore the lettering *École Professionelle*. Modern red brick buildings formed three sides of a quadrangle. In the main corridor of this commercial academy a bronze plaque paid homage to France's fallen in the last war.

General Allen led us to a room on the ground floor, and we took positions around a conference table. I stared idly at the maps on the wall. "I'll give you the picture up to the moment...." It was a new voice speaking, and I looked up. A colonel, who wore the flaming sword insignia of Supreme headquarters, went on speaking. "Yesterday, Admiral von Friedeburg, commander of the German navy, came down from Montgomery's headquarters after negotiating the earlier capitulation in the north......" I removed the creased note paper I carried in my tunic pocket and made notes..... "von Friedeburg desired to surrender directly to the allies in the west and to skip the Russians. General Smith turned it down. He said he wasn't prepared to talk about anything but unconditional and simultaneous surrender in the east and west."

It sounded so ludicrous — bargaining, negotiating at this stage. But that's the way it was done, according to the unwritten rule book. It was obvious that von Friedeburg couldn't accept allied terms on his own authority; he was told to dispatch a message by wireless to Admiral Karl Doenitz, whom Hitler had chosen to succeed him as head of the German government. Von Friedeburg was to request that he be given the authority or that Doenitz send his chief of staff with the necessary approval.

"That reply," said the colonel, "came at eight minutes past five this afternoon, just a short while before you gentlemen arrived. It was carried by General Gustav Jodl, the German chief of staff. I don't know what was in the reply. Jodl went into conference with General Smith a few minutes ago."

"What is General Eisenhower doing in this?" a reporter asked. "Is he entering directly into the negotiations?"

"No," said the colonel. "According to military protocol that's all done by his chief of staff, General Walter Bedell Smith. General Eisenhower is informed at every stage, of course, but he won't see the Germans until it's all over."

"Will the signing come tonight?" someone else asked.

"They're still talking. It may take hours."

"How did von Friedeburg act? What sort of man is he?"

"Well, he's about sixty — tall and aristocratic. He flew from Montgomery's headquarters at Luneburg, accompanied by his aide, Colonel Fritz Poleck, and two British officers. From what I've been told, he slept in the plane, apologizing that he hadn't had any sleep in ten days. The weather closed in and the plane was forced down at Brussels. The party had a couple of sandwiches at an RAF snack bar, and some beer, and came the rest of the way by car. That took about four hours, and von Friedeburg slept again."

"Yes, but how did he take it? Was he very nervous?"

The end of my pencil broke. I snatched another from my pocket.

"He didn't seem particularly upset. When he arrived he asked if he could go somewhere to wash up before meeting General Smith. He hummed to himself as he changed his collar and washed. Poleck was nervous, though, and didn't seem to know what it was all about."

"Where did von Friedeburg sleep last night?" The questions now were coming from all parts of the conference table.

"Not far from here — in a seven-room house. He was guarded by a half dozen M.P.s. At about a quarter to eleven he and Poleck and a couple of our officers had supper. They didn't do too badly — pork chops and red wine. Von Friedeburg commented on the meal and the fine table linen. He sat up until midnight, listening to the radio. This morning he was up at seven."

"And Jodl? What's he like?"

"When he arrived at the airport here, he saluted our people. But when he met von Friedeburg in his billet there was no saluting. He just said 'aha,' like a man who was glad to see someone else in the same predicament. Von Friedeburg sat down to drink coffee, but Jodl marched up and down the room impatiently. He's short, bald and ruddy. In his fifties, I'd say."

"Did Jodl have anyone with him when he arrived?"

"Yes," said the colonel, "Major Wilhelm Oxenius, an interpreter."

"You say they're in conference now with General Smith?"

"That's right. They're all upstairs. I'll keep you in touch with developments — as soon as I receive them." He quit the room.

It was six-thirty. The door opened, and General Allen came in. "Here's something that might break the tension," he announced with a smile, holding two pens forward. "They'll be used in the signing. I'll pass them around." I fondled one. The top was gold, and the barrel khaki colored plastic. It was not the old-fashioned type of dip pen one would have imagined for a formal treaty as extraordinary as this one. It was a modern, streamlined pocket fountain pen. Perhaps to symbolize modern warfare? I had never seen this model before. Allen explained it was new — the Parker 51. Eisenhower bought a batch of the pens to give his officers at the end of the North African campaign; these were two he had kept for himself.

The door opened again. The colonel was back. "Here's another bit of news," he said. "The letter which Jodl carried authorized him to sign unconditional surrender. But, in talking to General Smith, he brought up the point that while the German High Command could agree to the surrender to the Russians as well as the western allies, there was no guarantee that German troops in the field would do so. He's obviously haggling for time. Every hour the negotiations continue means another hour for the Germans to move closer to the allied positions and escape from the Russians."

"What happens now?" I asked.

"I don't know. General Smith is conferring with General Eisenhower. They've called in General Ivan Susloparoff, who's been empowered by the Soviet High Command to sign on their behalf. I'll go upstairs. I'll report the latest in a few minutes."

A few minutes? Why couldn't they get this business over? I arranged my notes in some sort of sequence, and tried to think of a lead for the story, but quickly gave up. What was the use? Some new development might change everything. That was a poor rationale, of course, but it served to delay facing the real hardship of newspaper work: making the most important, the most complex, story come out the simplest, the clearest.

It was an hour before the colonel reappeared: "Gentlemen, here's the situation up to the minute. General Smith has told the envoys that unless they can guarantee that all German forces stay in their present positions, whether they are near the western allies or not, we will continue the war. Jodl knows there's no point in debating any longer. A few minutes ago he wrote a message to Doenitz. There'll be a delay of at least three-quarters of an hour. I suggest you have something to eat. You'll find a canteen at the end of the hall."

I doubt if anyone ate. I know that I didn't. I imagine we all peered out the window at the scores of colleagues who had streamed in from all sectors of the front. Their noses were pressed, at least figuratively, against the glass. But they were restricted to remote control rumor and unofficial information. Only seventeen of us were privileged to share this first-hand writing of history. Ironically one of the first persons I was able to pick out in the exterior darkness was a frustrated Matthew Halton of the Canadian Broadcasting Corporation. My commitment, as Canadian representative in the eyewitness group, included doing a broadcast for the CBC.

At two in the morning — Monday, May 7, 1945 — General Allen reappeared and said in a room suddenly still, "Well, gentlemen, I think this is it."

Now, after an anxious watch of more than eight hours, I did not feel any flush of excitement. At least I do not remember any. Perhaps, finally, it was all taking place too quickly. We mounted a flight of stairs to a door marked "War Room" and saw at a glance that it was not a large room — about forty feet long and thirty feet wide. But it was impressive. Spotlights shone from the whitewashed ceiling onto the maps that covered the walls — maps the Germans would have sacrificed divisions to have examined earlier in the war. These were huge maps that disclosed the position of allied armies and supply dumps. One of the maps specified air activities, but I could see that no bombing targets had been entered on it for two weeks. The last mission stood out in bold black letters, "Food supplies to Holland."

Even the land operational maps appeared antiquated. Blue and red contours, showing the progress of battles, had not been moved in days. The German lines were still drawn in northwest Germany, as these had existed before the capitulation to Montgomery. Obviously, planners at Shaef had been too busy considering the final steps to peace to worry about the last statistics of war.

I was excited now, perhaps because of the sight of these sacred maps in this shielded room; perhaps because of the realization that this was no surrealistic setting. It was not a railway carriage in the forest of Compiègne, where the armistice was signed in 1918. This was a room, with four walls, in the red-brick building of a technical school, and this was no mere armistice. It was total, unconditional surrender.

There were now about forty people in the room — army personnel, reporters, still photographers, newsreel men. The newsreel operators — this was several years before television — adjusted their three cameras while floodlights glowed. I heard a colleague whisper, "Look at the map on the left. The Pacific theatre. It's odd, isn't it, to think of another war in progress?"

But where were the signatories, the men from both sides who would subscribe their names to peace? The answer came at two-thirty a.m., with an abrupt silence. Allied officers began to enter the room. First, there was Maj.-Gen. H.R. Bull, allied chief of operations. Bull moved across the red carpet, no trace of emotion on his face. He stared ahead, and it was the same for the others who followed — British and American and French officers, and a Russian. This must be Susloparoff. He was big and well built.

The cameras clicked, and I watched the allied chiefs as they shuffled from chair to chair to find their names on the place cards around the conference table at the end of the room. The table, about twenty feet long and eight feet wide, might have come from the office of bank directors. On one side were eight chairs for the allies, and on the other were two chairs, probably for the Germans, and at the ends extra chairs. Not long ago allied strategists planned their campaigns at this table.

The officers talked in low voices as they stood there, and I could not hear what they were saying. Only once or twice could I catch a trace of what I took to be a nervous smile. Susloparoff snuffed out a cigarette in a glass ashtray atop the table. A white pad of paper lay on the table before each chair. A fountain pen and a microphone broke up the otherwise bare centre. Then General Smith came into the room. It was two thirty-four a.m. The room was hushed. Where were the Germans? Then, clear and sharp, I heard the quick military steps outside. A Shaef officer appeared. Behind him, in uniform, were three Germans who halted at the doorway. I knew who the first two were from the earlier descriptions — General Jodl and Admiral von Friedeburg. The third must be Major Oxenius, their interpreter. The Shaef officer shoved another chair beside the two that faced the allied chiefs. He went back for the Germans.

They marched in — erectly, briskly, with their hats off. Jodl looked haggard, his face heavily lined. Von Friedeburg was taller and more distinguished in appearance. Did they seem bewildered, as though they did not comprehend the circumstances? I could not decide. They reached their chairs and bowed slightly. General Smith sat down, and so did the other allied representatives. Then the Germans sat down, opposite them. Major Oxenius took the high-crowned hat that Jodl had lain on the table, and put it on the floor to give him more space. I counted. Thirteen men now sat at the long table.

There was no delay. General Smith told the Germans where to sign. They followed his instructions, and removed white documents from the plain manila folders before them. At two forty-one a.m., with the gold-topped fountain pen, Jodl signed the declaration of unconditional surrender of all German land, sea and air forces. I thought I saw his hand trembling. General Smith signed, and then the Soviet General Susloparoff.

It was all over in five minutes. Jodl got to his feet. "I want to say a few words," he said in English. His voice was hardly above a whisper, but distinct in the stillness of the room. "General," said Jodl, "with this signature, the German people and the German armed forces for better or worse are delivered into the victors' hands. In this war, which has lasted more than five years, both have achieved and suffered more than perhaps any other people in the world. In this hour I can only express the hope that the victor will treat them with generosity."

General Smith stared at Jodl, coldly, dispassionately. Only on the broad face of Susloparoff was there any semblance of a look of triumph. The Germans, with their hats in their hands, walked from the room. It was a mechanical motion. I wanted to shout, or do something, to disrupt the terrible stillness inside me and in the room. At last, I heard General Smith say to his associates, "Thank you, gentlemen." There was no cheering, no handshaking. I could almost sense what was in their minds: a terrible war has ended, this is no time for gloating.

Jodl and von Friedeburg marched seventy-five feet along the cement corridor leading to General Eisenhower's office. The supreme commander and his deputy, Air Chief Marshal Sir Arthur Tedder, were waiting for them. Eisenhower's blue eyes were glacial as he regarded the Germans who stood before his desk. In one sentence he demanded whether they understood and agreed to carry out the terms of surrender they had just signed. Jodl said, "Yes."

They left Eisenhower's office, their heads cast down, the reflection of a defeated Germany.

4   Back to the 18th Century

"MILITARY HISTORY," SAID U.S. CIVIL WAR GENERAL William Tecumseh Sherman, "is to die in battle and have your name spelled wrong in the newspapers." For a correspondent in World War II, it was sending your story from the front, and not having it arrive. I was unaware of such a disaster until long after the event.

My office faithfully mailed me clippings of my pieces. It was only when the war was over, and I was clearing out from our last press camp — in Holland — that I noticed a gap. There was no clipping of a story I wrote about the very early days of the battle for Aachen. I remembered some circumstances. The army had established a new, flexible system of communications. Instead of returning to the nearest press camp to file, you could rely on any divisional headquarters to transmit your copy to the War Office in London. From there, forwarding was automatic to your paper — in theory.

I followed this routine when I raced to be among the first reporters to describe what it was like to enter a German city. After seeing the story off by British dispatch rider, I felt free to concentrate on a follow-up, a long feature piece. But that first account never reached Montreal. Only with peace, did curiosity impel me to ask our London bureau to put a tracer on it. After some delay, word came back. The dispatch rider had not gone aground or defected. He had indeed arrived at divisional headquarters, and the story had been transmitted, as arranged, to the War Office in London.

There was one flaw, not untypical of wartime operations. The higher command had neglected to notify men and women on the lower rungs about the new press arrangement. Apparently, a junior officer who was on duty when my message landed on his desk in London, glanced at it, and said to his clerk, "Hmmm, useful intelligence report." The clerk dutifully sent it over to the intelligence branch. As far as I know, it may still be there, if the original filing cabinets remain. I've wondered ever since whether to be flattered or affronted by the designation.

Mine was a communications difficulty that did not confront an Associated Press reporter, Edward Kennedy, one of the select group who witnessed the German surrender. Kennedy decided unilaterally and arbitrarily to ignore the news embargo to which we had been pledged on the flight from Paris. On our return to Paris, he bypassed normal censorship, got on a phone line to London and dictated his story. London censors thought it had been cleared in Paris. Thus did the world learn of the end of European hostilities — before allied leaders could make the announcement, before preparations to alert, and protect, the armed forces. It was a time of high controversy for Kennedy, but hardly a shining moment for journalism.

I was not a combat soldier. When a battle situation became too rough, I could pull out — and frequently did. I operated by a simple rule: I was no good to anyone — my editors, readers, and, most important of all, to myself — as a casualty. So, to me,"soldiering on" became an easy exercise. It lacked the hardship and the subservience that would have been demanded of me if I had been accepted as an artillery officer.

Nonetheless, the job of a correspondent involved some peril and rough living. Even surviving a jeep ride over unpaved terrain, and then facing inedible rations, meant austerity. Yet, at the end of it all, I came away without the elevated blood pressure that had kept me from military service. My blood pressure rose again periodically in later years. I suppose the moral is that, if you are happy and fulfilled, your health will reflect it.

I also suppose that the most glamorous history of foreign corresponding involved horses — sending hand-written dispatches by swift riders to the first ship to leave the Crimea for England, or, in the case of the American Civil War, to the nearest telegraph station. A British motorcycle rider brought me as close as I came to that era. But I still romanticize about it, especially with the advent and reliance on digital magic and laptop computers.

I write now on a computer, with built-in dictionary, thesaurus, spell checker, and encyclopedia, and appreciate that it saves considerable time. But does it match the personality of my old Hermes portable typewriter? I know all about the practicalities of fax transmission, but where is the allure compared with the "old" ways of transmission? Almost everyone uses fax in Tokyo today; nothing else will do — not even a phone call, except in extreme circumstances.

On a visit to Tokyo in 1990, I employed a fax machine at my hotel to confirm with a man at the *Asahi Shimbun* newspaper, a few blocks away, details of appointments he was arranging. But he didn't receive the message (four days later he told me it had landed on the wrong desk). I thought back to the days of Telex: for instance, in Saigon 1971, sending a long account to Montreal from the teletype shack — thirteen thousand kilometres apart — and the instant clattered response from my office, "RCD MTL." Nothing will compare with the joyful reassurance that what you sent had arrived where it was intended.

Still, to be fair, not all the old ways worked perfectly everywhere. Once, I reached India fresh from the Soviet Union with a story I had not wished to submit to censors there. I rushed to the cable office in New Delhi, handed in the several sheets of copy, moved into my hotel, showered, relaxed for an hour, then enjoyed a leisurely dinner as a guest at the Canadian High Commission. On the way back to my hotel I decided to pause at the cable office to check on the time my story had cleared. There, standing at the counter, was the clerk to whom I had handed it. He was still counting the words.

Immediacy in journalism is no longer a novelty. Live television coverage of news events makes us blasé about technology. But maybe not everyone. I still find it thrilling to see in print something I wrote only hours earlier. The late 1950s provided a highlight. Based in London for *The Montreal Star,* I was due to fly to Montreal for an office meeting. I covered a morning session of a NATO foreign ministers' conference, and barely managed to catch a flight to New York. There I switched to another plane for the hour's hop to Montreal. And on that plane I read in *The Star* my London report on NATO. It seemed like wizardry.

I yearn even for the mystique when a long-distance phone call, especially to or from cut-off places, meant adventure. Bureaucracy and censorship were stringent in Moscow in 1955. But when I was there that October, and my daughter Bette was born in Montreal, Russians — very sentimental about children — broke red tape and records to expedite a call for me. It was to my wife Rosalie in the Herbert Reddy Hospital in Montreal. I was excited enough at my end, but apparently there was bedlam at the other end. A hospital switchboard operator, rather than chance a broken line, raced up several flights of stairs to Rosalie's room, shouting, "A phone call from Moscow, a phone call from Moscow."

Ten years earlier, the Russians were not far from my thoughts, though for other reasons. The main event after Reims was our entry into Berlin in July 1945. The Russians had taken the city in May, but they required time to denude it of usable machinery or material before admitting the western allies. I had first encountered Soviet troops in April, when armies from east and west converged on the Elbe River, effectively chopping Germany in two. I retain several memorable images of that link-up.

Perhaps uppermost is the way Russians spoke of the enemy, with intense ideological hatred. If you asked our men — Canadians or Americans — why they were fighting, you heard embarrassed, awkward answers. Usually there were vague, inarticulate points about saving democracy or defending freedom. The Russians? Their answer was unswerving: "We are eliminating fascism." The Soviet soldier never referred to "Germans." His mission was to kill "fascists." The political commissars had done an effective job, at least with that generation.

The second point that struck me was the large number of uniformed women at the front. Young Soviet women shared all the dangers of their brothers in arms. None were used directly in infantry engagements. Most served as signallers and traffic police. But, in fluid situations, they often confronted Germans, and in battle won the same medals as the men. The women I met were not always the rugged, masculine types I had seen in photographs. Instead, many were youthful and pretty. The only unfeminine features were their Red Army battle gear and sub-machine guns that resembled Chicago-gangster tommy guns.

Overall, there was a cheery atmosphere when Americans joined the Russians on the Elbe, a camaraderie laced with vodka and balalaika music. A high level of affability remained in Berlin three months later. I even received a personally escorted tour through Hitler's former apartment and offices in the remains of the Reich Chancellery. My guide was a Red Army infantry sergeant-major, Peter Dorokov, one of the first to reach this final location of Nazi resistance. Past mounds of rubble, and up a dozen steps, we came to a reception room in which chosen guests once awaited the order to proceed to Hitler's office.

The reception room was no longer fit for guests. Like the rest of the complex, it had been destroyed by U.S. and British bombers and shells fired by Soviet gunners during the siege of Berlin. What must have been a magnificent glass roof was now a series of twisted frames of window panes. Dust and powdered masonry covered the red marble walls. In the centre of this vast mausoleum, which measured about a hundred by three hundred feet, a Soviet army artist sat before his easel serenely painting the scene.

We side-stepped a crater that dropped at least a hundred feet, and Dorokov said, "Now we'll see something interesting." He led the way along a central corridor, off which lay the gutted openings of five doors. In front of one, he stopped and said simply, "Look." Over the doorway, inscribed in stone, was the name "Adolf Hitler." Inside, a massive marble table lay overturned in the midst of splinters of furniture and fragments of upholstery — all that remained of Hitler's private office.

From then on the tour became repetitive — into the dining hall with two giant chandeliers dangling a few inches from the floor, into upstairs offices where broken desks and bomb holes made walking treacherous. Rain fell through gaps in the roof, onto a mound of cardboard cartons. The Russians had cleared most of the valuables and papers for examination, but there were still enough souvenirs waiting for plucking. We went into one room after another strewn with sodden cases of medals. With appropriate ceremony, Dorokov laughingly presented me with some of Hitler's most prized rewards. I still own a collection of about thirty different medals from these stores. If I wore them I would be recognized as a brave German soldier: *Ehrenkreuz*, the Iron Cross, first class; or an efficient war worker — *Verdiens Kreuz*, first class; or a productive mother — *Mutters Medaille*, for bearing ten children for the Third Reich.

Stuck among the cartons were a few sheets of badly stained blank stationery — Hitler's own. By this time the sight of massive wreckage was so commonplace that this wasted expanse, harboring the ghost of Hitler, did not make any particular impression. I suppose the significance of an overturned marble table was too obscure. Even my trove of Nazi medals carried little impact; there were so many of them. But the note paper was different. It bore only the printed words "Adolf Hitler, Berlin W8, Kanzlei des Führers." Its very blankness reflected the elimination of the deadliest scourge of our time. I retrieved one clean sheet, which I sent to my father. I have it today.

We headed for the shelter — or bunker, as the Germans called it — a vast system of underground concrete rooms, a hundred metres from the Chancellery by tunnel. Amid crumpled tables and bits of cement we kicked at bottles of sedatives that the fuhrer may have administered to himself in anxious moments. "Is this where Hitler died?" I asked. "Hitler dead?" said Dorokov. "We don't know if he's dead." At that stage in history, the Russians were still speculating that Hitler might be alive, at large in Spain or Japan (still at war). But not much later it was established that it was here, in this bunker, that Hitler did indeed commit suicide after taking the life of his bride, Eva Braun.

I was billeted in a large home in Zehlendorf, a residential suburb, much of which escaped the devastation of commercial areas. There I was introduced to a stall shower lined with several vertical spray faucets — a revelation to a person brought up on a simple overhead unit. What must it have been like for Russians from villages where they had never seen indoor plumbing? I didn't doubt the stories that many, spying a flush toilet for the first time, thought it was to wash feet, and used it accordingly.

Berlin — or what remained of it — was the most ravaged city in Europe. I filed this account:

"Berlin today is a city whose mothers and fathers are waiting for the gas to be turned on so they can lead their children into suicide. It is the onetime capital where no government buildings remain standing, and where a few men and women who look to the future are forming new political parties. It is a city where a girl will sell her body for a chocolate bar, and where people forget their hunger and misery in a night club, *Femina,* that exists incongruously in a basin of rubble. The destruction is such that no man in his wildest nightmare could ever have visualized the fury of modern warfare. You can measure some of it if you think of the city of Montreal as totally destroyed, with homes and stores and offices marked only by the corners of four walls or by a pile of stones. One-quarter of Berlin — the central area which equals Montreal in size — lingers in this grotesque condition and must be completely rebuilt."

I went on to say that another half of the city was so heavily damaged that it would take five years just to clear the debris. I was very wrong about my forecast. Within five years, not only was the debris gone, but new buildings were beginning to sprout everywhere. I was perhaps closer to reality in sizing up the early stages of East-West tensions. These showed themselves in the simplest form. In the night club *Femina* I heard a Soviet woman in uniform trying to wheedle, in passable English, information from two American soldiers. What was the make-up of their units? How long did they expect to stay in Berlin? It was primitive espionage, and the Americans weren't going for it. They were plainly irritated.

It is hard to believe that mutual distrust, built up steadily over the next forty-five years, would vanish without anyone really expecting it; that the Russians and the Americans were allies again in 1990, both condemning Iraq's Saddam Hussein for his invasion of Kuwait. It is even harder to believe that the lines which divided Germany in 1945 were wiped out in 1990 — and a vibrant Berlin again could proclaim itself as the spiritual capital.

I never cease to be struck by the way the wealthy retain a special attitude towards money, which people of modest income will never be able to emulate. John McConnell, the publisher of *The Standard,* was about to take his first Atlantic flight, weeks after the end of the war — in a military plane, unheated, unpressurized. He sent his secretary, Marge Morris, to Morgan's, a Montreal department store, to buy a pair of Stanfield's warm, "long john" underwear. A day or two later he noticed in *The Star* an

Eaton's ad: the same brand on sale at $4.98. And he had paid $5.49!
He dispatched Marge Morris back to Morgan's, by cab, to get a
refund and walk the block for another pair at Eaton's. Never mind
the cost of the taxi, or the time expended. There was a principle
at stake that only a rich person could properly understand.

Anyway, McConnell arrived in Paris in reasonably sound
shape. Promptly he set out to buy a gift for his wife, preferably a
Paris gown, a luxury that hadn't been seen in Canada in several
years. But prices, at the official rate of exchange, were crazily high,
and here is where a car of mine fell into place.

Late in the war, in Germany, I had stumbled by chance on
an acquaintance from the Prince David, Major Charles MacLean.
He was leading a convoy of armored reconnaissance vehicles of his
regiment (17th Duke of York's Royal Canadian Hussars). But,
instead of military equipment, he was driving a Hanomag, a German
sedan that he had found "abandoned," a euphemism for any number
of unofficial bits of trophy collecting. MacLean told me that
practicality was forcing him to give it up. He was also short of
cigarettes. I had an extra carton. Thus was consummated a
quintessential wartime barter deal. I drove off in the Hanomag —
the first car I ever owned — only to have it emit a horrible stench
that signified the clutch was burning out. The car shuddered to a
halt after a few miles.

In one of those rare bits of good fortune — my thesis still
held about getting the breaks — a garage, taken over by the army,
was within pushing distance. I left the car in the care of military
mechanics, and not many days later in Hanover located the plant
where the Hanomag was manufactured. Only its skeleton remained.
But, an added break on a break, the spare parts depot still
functioned. I bought a new clutch as nonchalantly as though this
were a supply store at home in normal times. The army mechanics
installed it, and I headed for Paris, to claim a parking space outside
the Scribe. Because of the rampant thievery in Paris I also prudently
rented, for night use, an indoor garage around the corner.

Now the plot darkened. Lionel Shapiro, my correspondent colleague who had miraculously climbed from his death bed in Normandy, was also aiming for Paris in a liberated car. He was in a mood to celebrate. Lionel had run into an old friend, Erika Mann, daughter of novelist Thomas Mann, who quit Germany in 1933 in protest against Nazism. Erika Mann had come over from the U.S. to do an article for *Liberty* magazine on the attempt on Hitler's life by a group of high-ranking Wehrmacht officers on July 20, 1944. She knew many prominent Germans, and was able to obtain the first authoritative account of that dramatic event.

Shapiro accompanied her, and apparently she had no objection to his filing the story — one of the great post-war stories — to his news agency, well ahead of her own publication. Euphoric, Shapiro may not have been concentrating on driving. Pulling into the Scribe, he dented a fender on my Hanomag. All was forgiven that evening over drinks, which he paid for, in the Scribe bar.

Now McConnell enters the scene. He still wants to get that dress for his wife but not at an exorbitant price. He suggests I sell my Hanomag to get enough cheap francs for the dress. He'll pay me a thousand dollars. I am indignant. I need the car for my work. Besides, such commerce would involve the black market. How could he even think of such a thing? The indignation grows with the martinis. That night I decide I should not try to manoeuvre the Hanomag to its indoor sanctuary. I leave it outside the Scribe. The next morning it is gone.

McConnell never purchased the dress. Nor, of course, did I ever collect a thousand dollars or see my little Hanomag again. I am sure the four tires alone — jeep tires scrounged from the army — brought the French liberators a healthy retirement fund.

If 1945 was the year of peace, it was also the year of retribution. The initiation of a long series of trials of people accused of crimes related to the war took place almost immediately. A onetime French hero, Marshal Henri Philippe Pétain, was in the dock in Paris. The Germans would soon have their turn at Nuremberg. As late as 1961, in Jerusalem, I would be drawn into coverage of proceedings against a principal architect of Hitler's extermination program — Adolf Eichmann.

But Pétain was the first notable. This old man had enjoyed celebrity in France and much of the world, the general who distinguished himself by holding Verdun against the German army in 1916. He was called out of retirement by his country again. But this time — in 1940 — he served as chief of the government that signed the French surrender to Hitler. Now France, and much of the world, labelled him a defeatist. In reality, France itself, striving to expunge grubby pages from history, was on trial.

The setting was appropriately historic, the Palais de Justice, where Louis XVI was found guilty in 1793 of treason and crimes against the new revolutionary government. He was guillotined. While the prosecutor called for the death penalty for Pétain, few expected it would be carried out, in view of his age and the controversy around him. Old timers recalled that the Dreyfus trial, a half century earlier, split France into two. Now there were supporters of Pétain who believed he had acted in France's best interests. But they stayed prudently silent.

It was my first experience of the elaborate preparations of a people— it might have applied to the people of any country — demanding vengeance and the attention of the world. No more than a handful of the public were allowed into the Paris courtroom with a seating capacity of three hundred. Almost all the space was allotted to judges, jurors, witnesses, lawyers, diplomatic representatives — and the press.

Originally only twenty foreign correspondents were to be admitted; but with more than two hundred applications the figure was boosted to forty, in addition to fifty French journalists. Officials decided they could squeeze in the extra reporters by allowing each twenty inches of hip space. I managed with the ration. (I can barely remember it, but an old newspaper photo shows me in a very tight squeeze).

The officials, particularly resistance leaders, made certain that nothing would happen to their prisoner before judgment. Six hundred police, in seven cordons in and around the court, stood watch day and night in case some impatient patriot decided to shoot Pétain. His doctor, who said Pétain, then eighty-nine, was as strong as a man of sixty, sat behind him constantly, while two stretcher bearers remained close by for any emergency. Experts even pried open small windows just beneath the roof, to let in fresh summer air. The windows had been closed since the days of Louis XVI.

I could almost imagine myself back in the atmosphere of that eighteenth-century upheaval, the citizens dispensing justice. Here, in July and August 1945, sat a jury of twenty-four persons. They were hardly impartial, since twelve were men who voted against Pétain's elevation to power in 1940. The other twelve were members of resistance groups whose colleagues suffered torture and death at the hands of Pétain's police. Three judges, the highest in the land, sat in vivid attendance in their scarlet robes and ermine capes.

It all felt anachronistic. Six hundred pages of close handwriting formed the basis of the prosecution by André Mornet, "the procurator of the Republic." Here he was at age seventy-five, white-bearded and fiery, yet one could only visualize him as a younger man prosecuting Mata Hari during World War I. He had argued passionately for the death of the Dutch dancer, accused of spying for the Germans, and he had won — both the case and lasting fame.

And now there was the new accused one, Marshal Pétain, proud and deaf, sitting in his impeccable tan uniform, fingering the silky white hair that bordered his bald head, or clutching his kid gloves — all the while blinking incessantly as though he could hardly keep his eyes open. Was this the same man lionized as "le vainqueur de Verdun," the man whose rallying cry, "Ils ne passeront pas," once stopped the giant German offensive and saved the nation?

It was not Pétain who stopped the Germans in 1916, declared one of Mornet's witnesses, Paul Reynaud, the former French premier. "That is a sheer myth," he said, and quoted the memoirs of General Joseph Jacques Césaire Joffre, commander in chief of the French army in 1916. Pétain's attitude at Verdun was so defeatist, said Reynaud, "that Joffre had to promote him to higher rank in order to remove him. The real hero of Verdun was not Pétain but his successor, General Nivelle." And so began the process of pulverizing a legend that in 1917 served the purpose of restoring morale in mutinous French forces.

One after another, famous figures rose against him. There was Léon Blum, the first Jew to become premier of France — freed from a German concentration camp only three months ago. There were ex-premier Edouard Daladier and others whose appeasement, weakness, lack of preparation, or own defeatism, contributed to France's collapse in 1940. Michel Clemenceau, son of Georges "Tiger" Clemenceau, premier of a victorious France in 1918, turned toward Pétain and spat angrily: "If my father lived today he would bitterly regret having conferred on you the title and dignity of Marshal of France."

Pétain stared into distance, his eyes flickering no distinct message. Only once did he speak in his defence, and that was at the opening of the trial. Standing in front of rows of French reporters, many of whom had worked in the underground press during the German occupation, Pétain said in a loud and sharp voice: "I will not answer any questions. I did a necessary act to save France and to help allied victory by proclaiming armistice. If you condemn me, you will be condemning an innocent man."

The formal accusation was clear and simple: Marshal Pétain was charged with being an enemy of Republicanism, of surrendering to the Germans to seize power, and of maintaining intelligence with Hitler. Much evidence was introduced by the prosecution:

Pétain's refusal, while he governed from Vichy, to keep France's fleet and colonies at war; his telegram to Hitler in 1942, after the Canadian raid on Dieppe, urging arms for France to withstand further invasions; his authorization of transfer of French guns and supplies in Tunisia to help Rommel fight off a British offensive.

Defence lawyers sought to prove that Pétain was playing a double game by pretending to collaborate with the Germans when in reality he was fighting for time. Frenchmen sympathetic to Pétain's age but bitter about the past that he represented, saw in one sentence of his statement a touch of his old vanity: "My life matters little. I have made France the gift of my person." His death sentence was commuted to life imprisonment by the new French leader, Charles de Gaulle, who had served under Pétain in World War I — the same Pétain who was godfather to de Gaulle's son Philippe, a pilot in World War II. Thus was the cycle completed.

Pétain died in 1951 in his ninety-sixth year. I remember at the time of the trial thinking how hypocritical it had all seemed, a people taking a man they had drafted in a moment of disgrace and panic, and then using him to expiate their own shame of defeat and surrender. But I was yet to learn how vengeance was an irreversible force.

It was a grey November day in 1945 in Nuremberg, contrasting with the sunshine of Paris less than four months earlier. A few curious young boys stood by as army cars drew up and men in the uniforms of the United States, Britain, France and the Soviet Union stepped out. Two white-helmeted military police at the gate of the court house snapped to attention, and the boys imitated them. "You are too slow, Alfred," one of them shouted. "Your mother could do better." They all laughed, then scampered off in search of cigarette butts.

Across the road, three old men walked slowly, carrying bundles of bed sheets for the billets that had been turned over to the Americans. I wondered what these Germans were thinking, whether history enfolding around them made any impact. Probably they were no longer interested in history. The mundane present was too important. Who would clear the rubble around them? When would this ancient city — site of Hitler's most spectacular rallies — be rebuilt? Nine-tenths of it lay in ruins; nearly three hundred thousand people struggled for shelter in the ruins.

Or maybe the three old men were just thinking, as many Germans were thinking, "We lost the war. What is the use of going through all this ceremony now? If Goering and the others are guilty, punish them. Do not waste time with words." That was what one German had told me a fortnight earlier. Since then, others said the same. I had yet to meet a single German who admitted he or she shared responsibility, that he or she had ever joined the Nazi party. To hear them, you would believe that almost every "good German" sheltered or saved a half dozen Jews. It was astonishing how all the Nazis had vanished.

There were men inside the court house who had another idea. The pick of allied legal brains, they were intent on establishing fairly and clearly the guilt of twenty-two of Germany's most important leaders. That was for the record and for the sake of future historians. But for the sake of the world their mission was greater. With the millions of words they were speaking and presenting in writing, they hoped to establish in international law that any war of aggression was a criminal act — and the individuals who caused it would be held personally responsible. Nor would men and women guilty of crimes against humanity — the slaughter, for instance, of civilians — find escape in arguing they were merely, as good soldiers, obeying orders of a superior officer.

As I walked into the court house my eye caught the inscription above the doorway — the Ten Commandments. The courtroom itself had sustained severe damage in air raids. But the Americans, with assistance from SS prisoners, had done a good job of restoration; the walls of dark panelling bore few scars. Behind the judges' bench awaited eight chairs in red upholstery. Deep green drapes shielded daylight from the broad windows. Instead, fluorescent lights opened up from the high ceiling. Batteries of floodlights for cameramen added further brilliance, setting off stone figures over the wide marble doorway through which the defendants would parade. The figures represented Justice and flanked a carved scene of history's first recorded wrongdoing — Eve tempting Adam.

I think all the journalists in that room must have manipulated at the same moment the switch that allowed headphones to unscramble translations in Russian, English, French or German. When I look back today at my old clippings I see that I noted that I was aware that this was "a moment for posterity." Such was the level of platitude in dealing with it. The reporter, though, could forget emotion and start scribbling notes the instant the marble doors swung open and in marched a half dozen military police, their white helmets and white belts almost luminous. And then came the defendants — Hermann Goering, Rudolf Hess and Joachim von Ribbentrop, right down to the youngest, Baldur von Schirach, thirty-eight, head of the Hitler Jugend. The drama of the moment was lost in an inane thought. I wondered whether they knew that the beige carpet they trod on cost the U.S. government $25,000 in the German black market.

Twenty defendants were in the dock. Twenty-four had been indicted. But Gustav Krupp, Germany's foremost munitions maker, was in hospital suffering from a brain disorder. Robert Ley, slave labor expert, had called it quits by stripping a towel and knotting his neck to a toilet pipe in his cell. No one was sure whether Martin Bormann, Hitler's deputy, was alive, but he was being tried in absentia. Ernst Kaltenbrunner, head of the SD, the dreaded *Sicherheitsdienst* security service, whom allied psychiatrists labelled as the bully type — "strong and hard when on top, cringing and crying when not" — on the eve of the trial burst a blood vessel in the back of his head. In hospital he apologized to his guards, saying, "I'm very sorry I cannot be in court."

The others said nothing memorable. They comprised a mixed lot — generals who mapped campaigns in violation of treaties, diplomats who engineered bloodless coups, economists who exploited occupied lands. Now they were in court, looking more stoical than one might expect. Prison doctors broke Goering of his habit of swallowing four tranquilizers a day. He was thinner than I had anticipated — until I realized that imprisonment had cost him fifty pounds. Flabby pouches drooped under his chin. Jet black hair combed well back did not hint of his age, fifty-two — until I detected lines that burrowed deep in his forehead. There was no definable expression in his eyes. He peered straight ahead.

Over the weeks Goering was to relax and vary his expression, sometimes glancing at the press section, with a part-sneer, part-smile, or hint of inquisitiveness. Sometimes he laughed aloud to ridicule a prosecution statement. Otherwise he might stroke his chin thoughtfully. If only Hitler hadn't insisted on attacking the Russians! Or was it something else he pondered? Intricate checks, daily medical examinations were held, there was constant surveillance of cells, to ensure that none of the accused would emulate Ley's suicide. But who was to guess that at the end Goering would outwit his captors with a smuggled poison capsule?

In the meanwhile he was the centre of attention, the leading survivor of the Nazi regime. Most of the time he just sat there with his hands folded, looking neat in a light grey Luftwaffe uniform he had designed for his exclusive use. Only two other men were in uniform — Wilhelm Keitel, chief of the High Command, and Alfred Jodl, chief of staff of the Wehrmacht, whom I had last seen in May in Reims. After he signed Germany's surrender Jodl appealed for mercy for his country. Now he did so on his own behalf, saying, "For what I have done or had to do, I have a pure conscience." Jodl's uniform in Reims was covered with insignia and battle ribbons. Now it was bare, with no trace of rank. The German armed forces existed no longer.

Defence lawyers, dressed in black gowns, wore the distinctive velvet hats of German courts. Prosecution counsels nearly filled the rest of the room. They were Robert H. Jackson of the United States Supreme Court, Sir Hartley Shawcross, youthful attorney-general in the Attlee government of Britain, François de Menthon of France, General R.A. Rudenko of the Soviet Union, and many assistants from the four nations. The statistics were overwhelming: sixty buildings in the neighborhood restored to livable state to house one thousand, four hundred lawyers, experts and clerks. The Soviet delegation numbered more than two hundred, the American seven hundred. Among the Americans were two hundred civilian female secretaries from Washington, so heavily dated socially that bids became mandatory a fortnight in advance. German women were available, but women from home were more acceptable.

Everyone rose when the judges entered. Sir Geoffrey Lawrence, Britain's Lord Justice of Appeal, moved to the centre of the long bench to take the presiding judge's chair. There were equally distinguished jurists from the other countries — including former attorney-general Francis Biddle of the United States. American, Soviet, British and French flags were draped in the background. This was called the International Military Tribunal more for convenience than for accuracy, since most of the judges and their deputies were civilians.

The whole of the formation was unusual, for the tribunal lacked any established precedent to draw on. There was only agreement, arrived at three months earlier, to assemble articles from the criminal codes of the four allies, laying the foundation for international procedure in war crime trials. Some provisions came from the Anglo-Saxon side — the assumption, for instance, that the accused is innocent until proved guilty. For other points the tribunal turned to the French and Soviet codes, particularly the rule compelling a defendant to take the stand. The men behind the bench served as both jury and judge, able to question defendants and witnesses at will.

Jurists in the future might argue — and many did — about the tribunal's validity and the principle involved. Trials of war criminals had been conducted in one shape or another for centuries. But this was the first time the leaders of a government were brought to a court accused of aggression, or starting a war. Such refinement was practically lost on those of us covering Nuremberg. I — and I suspect most — settled intently on the immediate proceedings, on every detail we could catch of the drama. The amber light on the judges' bench flashed on and off, and Justice Lawrence rapped with his gavel. The amber light was the signal from interpreters that the prosecutor was speaking too quickly and they couldn't follow.

"The German authorities deported from the Soviet Union to slavery about five million Soviet citizens. Such deportations were contrary to international conventions," said the chief Russian prosecutor, Rudenko, who then went into details of murder, torture, deliberate starvation, and plunder. Alfred Rosenberg, editor of the Nazi party newspaper *Voelkischer Beobachter* and Reich minister for eastern occupied territories, the most restless defendant, ran his fingers nervously through his thin hair, pulled the earphones on and off, rubbed his face, and bit his nails. Goering seemed to remain unimpressed. He scanned the windows in the gallery, through which cameramen took picture after picture.

Only Fritz Sauckel, a prime slave labor organizer, displayed any eagerness about the procedure. He sat forward in his chair, resembling a caricaturist's version of a German with shiny fat bald head, little moustache and narrow-collared blue suit. He nodded at the court's remarks, whispered every few minutes to von Schirach beside him, and looked as though he was taking in every word so some day he could tell his grandchildren how he, a one-time locksmith, had attended the Nuremberg trial.

"Of nine million, six hundred thousand Jews who lived in parts of Europe under Nazi domination," intoned a prosecutor, "it is conservatively estimated that five million, seven hundred thousand have disappeared, most of them deliberately put to death by Nazi conspirators." Julius Streitcher, arch Jew-baiter, glared at the judges, convinced — so a guard later told reporters — they, the judges, were all Jews. Shutting his pin-point eyes, perhaps he was thinking of the early 1920s when, in the same courtroom, he was convicted of criminal libel for an anti-Semitic story in his weekly paper, *Der Stuermer.*

There were stiff and dignified admirals, Karl Doenitz and Erich Raeder, attired not in navy uniforms but blue serge suits. They were members of the German High Command, which the indictment said was one of the Third Reich's six criminal organizations: "These persons had the major responsibility for the planning, preparation, initiation and waging of illegal wars." There were Franz von Papen, high-pressure diplomat, scion of an impoverished family of Westphalian nobility, now defended by his son; Baron Konstantin von Neurath, a German of the old school and more recently "protector of Bohemia and Moravia," at seventy-six the oldest in the group; Hjalmar Schacht, president of the Reichsbank, now, with his close-cropped grey hair and metal-framed glasses, more resembling a barber than banker; and the others.

Perhaps, as each late afternoon approached, they drifted back through the turbulent, bloody years, and imagined they were about to leave the Reich Chancellery after another conference with *der führer.* However, the voice that said the meeting was over for the time being was that of the presiding judge, an Englishman. The marching feet were those of the American guards who led them back to their cells and their memories.

The next day, the day after, and the days following, the proceedings continued. "In order to make their rule secure from attack," a prosecutor droned on, "the Nazi conspirators established and extended the system of terror against their opponents. Concentration camps were established early in 1933 under the direction of the defendant Goering."

Goering, leaning an elbow on an edge of the dock, held his cheek with two fingers of his right hand — in the characteristic pose I recalled from newsreel shots when he listened to Hitler. Next to him, Rudolf Hess, who attracted universal attention by making a wild flight to Scotland in 1941 on his own peace mission, stared ahead blankly. I wondered whether he was really unbalanced or just putting on a shrewd act. His eyebrows appeared even bushier than I had seen in photos, and his shirt collar was at least an inch too large. Occasionally his Adam's apple shifted slightly.

Sometimes I felt they were all unbelievably calm. Between the morning and afternoon sessions the prisoners had an hour and a half to themselves, to eat a lunch of cold bully beef in their seats. This was the occasion to envisage what they might be saying in private. I was in the room when Doenitz gathered a half dozen around him. Maybe he conceived an angle for their joint defence, because Goering and von Ribbentrop — the ex-champagne salesman who became Hitler's foreign minister — nodded soberly. Then they smiled with a look of confidence. You sensed they still clung to a hopeful outcome.

Only Hess was silent. He stood there, leaning on the dock, his hands clasped — looking as mad as a hatter. Maybe, I kept rebutting myself, he was not crazy after all. He spent his time in the second week's sessions reading a romance novel or doubling up in cramps so he could be escorted from the courtroom. One day, during a recess, Hess stood up, stretched his hands over his head, yawned, and shook himself — without altering his wooden expression. He might have been some carved, lifeless image. Who could have imagined he would outlive all his co-defendants and most of the other people in that room, dying in 1987 as the last occupant of Berlin's Spandau Prison, at the age of ninety-three?

But before that — eleven months after the trial opened, after two hundred and sixteen days of testimony — nine accused dropped on the gallows in Nuremberg, including Jodl, Keitel, von Ribbentrop, Streitcher, Sauckel and Rosenberg. Others received long prison sentences; only three were acquitted. Over the succeeding years, because of precedents at Nuremberg, thousands of Germans met justice determined by the allies or by other Germans. Long after the names of von Schirach or Sauckel had sunk into oblivion, the name of Nuremberg implanted in the minds of world leaders one fact: an individual who leads his people into a war of aggression faces a death penalty.

Nearly sixteen years were to elapse before I witnessed another legacy of Nuremberg — the inscribed principle that a person cannot absolve himself from crimes against humanity by arguing he simply followed a superior's orders. Adolf Eichmann, so argued — in vain — in Jerusalem.

5 "Two Gun" Cohen, et al

LIKE MANY MEN WHO SERVED OVERSEAS during World War II, I returned home restless and ill at ease. I imagine this condition was aggravated by the knowledge that no peacetime story could ever duplicate the drama of war. But human nature plays tricks to restore us to old patterns.

In the winter of 1944 the office had allowed me to come back for six weeks' leave. I recall an evening with friends at Moishe's, a Montreal steak house. Someone complained about slow service. Someone else that his steak was well done, when he had ordered it rare; in indignation, he summoned the waiter. All I could do was stare at the enormous slab of beef and think how it would feed a family of four in Paris. Instead of spending six weeks in Canada, I got back overseas in two weeks. I felt more comfortable there.

But now it was late 1946, and I was home for good, though I was determined that one way or another I would continue to explore the world and cover major events. The start was not propitious. I was appointed editor of *The Standard's* magazine section — a sedentary post. Not quite as bad a plight as that confronting ex-foreign correspondents of *The Chicago Tribune*. They were automatically put on the re-write desk to churn out obituaries — a savage method of bringing reporters down to size. Since people are people, I found myself, within weeks, complaining at Moishe's that my steak was too well done, and slow in arriving.

One pleasant happening during my wartime absence was the marriage of my sister Judith to a legendary personality, General Morris Abraham "Two Gun" Cohen. Morris spent his childhood in the Whitechapel district of London, where he learned to outfight other kids. He also learned to follow women down Petticoat Lane and lift their purses. Morris' father decided that what he needed was a more constructive challenge. So, Morris Cohen, aged sixteen, was sent to Wapella, Saskatchewan, where a farm job awaited him.

That was in 1905 and Western Canada was in a boom period of attracting thousands of immigrants. Morris quickly established himself as a land salesman. He did well, either collecting commissions or playing poker. Morris possessed deceptive hands — massive but not clumsy. He could deal cards as he desired. Later in life he said he never cheated an honest man. But he alone decided who was honest.

One evening in Saskatoon a hold-up man, pistol ready, entered the Chinese restaurant that Morris frequented. Before the owner could obey the command to empty the till, Morris clouted the bandit on the jaw. That instant reflex changed his life. From then on Morris Abraham Cohen, East End London Cockney Jew, was regarded by Chinese as one of them. They called him Mah Kun, the closest they could get to Morris Cohen. He grew in stature as a man of courage, honor and loyalty — so much so that the Chinese inducted him into a Tong, a secret society, and entrusted to him the safety of a remarkable man, Sun Yat-sen.

Sun Yat-sen, a physician, became convinced after China's defeat by Japan in 1895 that the Manchu dynasty must be overthrown. Exiled, he worked toward this goal with support from secret societies and overseas Chinese. Travel in North America, raising funds for the Kuomintang Party, which he founded, meant exposure to possible assassins. The Chinese community in Edmonton hired Morris as Sun's bodyguard.

The connection with the Chinese continued in World War I when Cohen, a Canadian army sergeant, directed coolie labor battalions maintaining railroad lines in France. In 1922 he travelled to China, to pick up again as bodyguard to Sun Yat-sen, now firmly established as first president of the Chinese republic. Morris became his aide-de-camp with the rank of general. But the job remained the same — protecting Sun.

Once, when two intruders, carrying Mauser pistols, were spotted climbing under Sun's train, Morris pulled out his own revolver and fired. Chinese guards took up the fight, and the two surrendered; they turned out to be professional killers hired by a Sun rival, a warlord. Cohen acquired a second Smith & Wesson revolver (hence the nickname "Two Gun") when he was slightly wounded in his left hand in another incident; he figured he might someday need to aim with either hand.

His real strength, however, lay in his talent for salesmanship and manoeuvring. The Chinese accepted him because his thought process was much like theirs — allowing face-saving in the pursuit of a deal or agreement. He honored commitments. His dedication to Sun, a revered figure, was renowned and appreciated — and consistent with Chinese custom of prime allegiance to an individual rather than to a cause. After Sun's death in 1925 Morris served other Kuomintang officials and embarked on a career as a wheeler-dealer. But he displayed continued devotion to Sun's widow.

Cohen, captured in 1941 by the Japanese, survived the notorious prisoner of war camp Stanley in Hong Kong. He was among a group of Americans and Canadians, aboard the Swedish liner Gripsholm, in a prisoner exchange. The Gripsholm docked in New York, and a special train brought the Canadians to Montreal. Morris, a burly figure, had lost considerable weight in Stanley. But photographs taken before imprisonment and after repatriation show the same broad, pugnacious face dominated by the broken nose of Whitechapel.

This was 1944. A mutual friend introduced Morris to Judith, who owned a successful dress shop, having started it during the Depression with a loan of two hundred dollars. She was forty and a divorcée without children. Morris was fifty-five and a bachelor. He liked to say that Judith won him because he was in a weakened condition. It was only natural that Judith, a romantic, would be attracted to this adventuresome figure, so different from most men. But he was also, beneath color and bluff, solid in character. They were married a few months later.

Morris talked about resuming his old life in China; Judith could hardly wait to share it. There were many stories — some true, many exaggerated — about Morris' wealth and generosity. He had, indeed, once chartered a train to transport guests hundreds of miles from Shanghai to Hong Kong for a friend's wedding. It was equally a fact that now he was penniless. He had made and lost — or given away — fortunes. He could claim a modest pension as Sun Yat-sen's bodyguard; but this he had steadfastly refused to do, saying the Chinese people owed him nothing.

China was in upheaval, in the midst of civil war, with the Communists rapidly overwhelming Kuomintang, or Nationalist, troops. By 1949 the last of the Kuomintang rulers fled to the island of Formosa. The country was closed to all travellers. But Hong Kong, a British colony, was open. Morris flew to Hong Kong to try to revive business contacts. I joined him for three months. I welcomed the opportunity to escape to a world that was not placid and predictable. My price for leave of absence from the office was a series of magazine articles.

We stayed at the Hong Kong Hotel, on Victoria Island, the heart of the colony. For a while we shared a room, until I could no longer tolerate Morris' snoring. "I don't know what you're complaining about," he said. "Wop May slept with me and he never complained."

Wilfrid "Wop" May achieved distinction in World War I as a novice fighter pilot. Manfred von Richthofen, the "Red Baron," was in hot pursuit of May, aiming for his eighty-first victim, when he himself was shot down by another allied flier. May went on to become one of Canada's leading bush pilots and later an executive in Canadian Pacific Airlines. It happened I had sat next to him on the long flight from Vancouver to Hong Kong. The only person I ever met who snored more thunderously than Morris Cohen was Wop May.

There were grander places than the Hong Kong Hotel, such as the Peninsula Hotel in Kowloon. But ours was creaky and seedy enough to make a visitor feel this was the real Orient of intrigue. There was no hint that Hong Kong would become the city of skyscrapers visible today. It remained, only a few years after the Japanese conflict, a sleepy colonial town of low-rise buildings barely scrubbed of the grime of wartime neglect. In the 1920s it could not have looked much different. At any moment Somerset Maugham, or one of his characters, might appear — in white suit.

Hong Kong was the best location from which to try for a visa to China. But none of Morris' contacts could help. Veteran newsmen, having made an exodus from Shanghai only a year earlier, sat around the bar of the Foreign Correspondents Club and sardonically wished me luck. I decided to try formal Canadian channels. After long delay, I managed to reach by telephone Chester Ronning, the Canadian chargé d'affaires in Chungking. I asked if he might be able employ diplomatic influence on my behalf.

"I doubt if you'll get a visa," he said, "but I'll see what I can do. What's your number in Hong Kong?" The phone in my room, from where I was calling, lacked any information on the dial. "Just a minute," I said, "I've got to look up the number in the phone book." Before I could make another move, a female voice cut in, and said, "The number is 28-631." Hong Kong was saturated with spies of all stripes. I still do not know whether the eavesdropper was an over eager Communist agent or a Nationalist agent. Or merely a snoopy switchboard operator? I like the spy version better.

The Communists were no more anxious than the Nationalists to sever the pipeline that fed valuable information through Hong Kong. With such information in hand, the next move became one of bluff or higher bidding. I picked up a story, for instance, about the Communists requiring an important cargo of aircraft parts that was stored in Hong Kong. They assigned a Panamanian shipping company to run the load through the Nationalist blockade of the China Seas. Late one night, two sister ships, the S.S. Rex and the S.S. Regina, four-thousand-ton freighters, anchored in Victoria Harbor, a couple of hundred yards off the colony's busy waterfront. Lighters brought out heavy wooden crates, their original markings hidden by streaks of black paint. Winches aboard the Rex creaked for hours as the cargo was loaded.

Meanwhile, a junk deliberately circled the Rex. When the freighter slipped away at dawn, the junk followed, and then vanished in the mist. Aboard the freighter, the crew reasoned that the junk had already reported to Formosa the activity it had detected. A full description of the vessel would now be flashed to every Nationalist warship in the China Seas. A couple of nights later, near the mouth of the Yangtze River, the Rex was challenged. Through the murkiness came the flicker of a signals lamp aboard a gunboat. "Turn south," said the gunboat.

The captain of the freighter, a Scotsman who had outwitted German U-boats in the Atlantic, signalled back, "Cannot turn. Steering disabled."

By first light of morning a Nationalist destroyer had joined the gunboat and now both warships closed in on the tiny freighter. The destroyer signalled, "We know you have airplane parts. Come to Formosa. We will pay twice Communist pay."

"Sugar aboard, no aircraft parts," replied the Rex. A skeptical Nationalist officer, followed by a dozen armed sailors, boarded the Rex. After an hour's search they discovered that, after all, the Rex carried only sugar. What they did not learn was the other part of a deceptive play. While attention focussed on the Rex, her sister ship Regina penetrated the blockade and was now safely en route to the north port of Tientsin — with the aircraft cargo.

After writing this account, I pondered about my own situation. I profoundly desired to get into China; normal procedures

Gerald Clark in an RCAF Canso Cataina flying boat, on an anti-submarine patrol off the coast of Nova Scotia in 1941.

General H.D.G. Crerar, commander of the First Canadian Army, briefs war correspondents, winter 1944. Gerald Clark, front row, third from left.

War correspondent Clark, Western Europe 1944, writes a despatch for *The Standard,* Montreal.

Canadians, participating in the liberation of Paris (August 1944), gather outside the Canadian legation where the Canadian flag flies for the first time in four years. Clark, fourth from left.

In a peacetime story in Kimberley, B.C., Clark becomes a hard rock miner.

In Hollywood, 1950, Clark plays a fierce pirate--as an extra.

In a Hollywood trailer for *The Great Lover,* Clark plays himself, a newspaperman, interviewing Bob Hope.

In conversation with Ava Gardner, on a Hollywood set.

Gerald Clark, on his first trip to Moscow, 1953, poses opposite the Kremlin.

In 1955, Canada's external affairs minister Lester B. Pearson enjoys banter with five Soviet vice premiers in Moscow. Clark stands behind Pearson.

Clark, on the Great Wall of China, 1958.

Clark, in Emmy-winning CBS television documentary, *The Face of Red China,* with Walter Cronkite.

Israeli prime minister Yitzhak Rabin, 1974, answers questions from Gerald Clark. Twenty years later, Rabin, again prime minister, took part in peace talks he had predicted.

In 1994, fifty years after touching down there, Gerald Clark revisits Courseulles-sur-mer in Normandy.

seemed useless, so why not something unorthodox: a run through the blockade on a freighter? It was neither expensive nor difficult to arrange passage on a Danish vessel. For a week I enjoyed a pleasant, totally uneventful trip, the only hazard a nightly bout of drinking Cherry Heering with a slightly mad Danish skipper.

We docked at Tientsin. I had thought I would at least be able to descend to the pier, and maybe persuade officials there to phone higher-ups in Peking, and maybe these would reward Canadian enterprise with a permit for temporary entry. But I never got past the two Chinese sentries at the top of the gangplank. I returned to Hong Kong on the same ship, rested but humbled.

The Hong Kong Hotel has long since vanished, but in those 1949 days General Morris A. Cohen still held court, just as he had done in the 1930s in Shanghai or Canton or wherever he happened to be. He sat in the same corner of the lobby, always in the same high-back, upholstered chair, while government officials or business people — British, Chinese, European — sought him out or responded to his messages. Sipping gimlets, they would exchange ideas, in convoluted language understood only by old China hands.

Mostly the ideas dealt with trade, how to jockey in an environment dominated, not by the Kuomintang, by the Communists. Old techniques no longer applied. The pre-1949 world was gone. No longer could individuals expect to collect five per cent or ten per cent for arranging a purchase of machine guns or railroad ties. Morris' problem was that he refused to recognize the change. He kept saying that communism was an aberration, that the Chinese would never accept it, that the Kuomintang would regain power.

The mainland might be discordant, but Hong Kong still retained memorable examples of Chinese entrepreneurial initiative. The colonial administration was proud of a newly opened comfort station equipped to handle ten men at a time. It was free. Pedicab runners could stop by, rush in, answer Nature, and rush out. The government even hired a caretaker to ensure the cleanliness of the comfort station. But soon newspapers began to carry stories of complaint. Pedicab runners and others in need found they had to wait in line — until they slipped the caretaker some change. Then, miraculously, a seat was vacated. What the enterprising caretaker had done, of course, was simply to hire ten men to squat all day, leaving their posts only on signal from him.

Ingenuity showed itself, too, on higher levels. Every Wednesday night during the opera season Radio Hong Kong broadcast the entire works from the Chinese opera house in Kowloon — five hours of it, from seven p.m. until midnight. But Radio Hong Kong also had an obligation to beam the BBC news in Cantonese at eleven every night. What to do? Could the managers of Radio Hong Kong interrupt the opera for the news, and offend opera listeners? Could they drop the news without alienating people who wanted the news? They compromised. They put on the news as usual, with the opera playing in the background.

It was in Hong Kong that I also discovered Chinese subtlety, exemplified by the *cheongsam* — the Chinese dress that covers the whole body. When a woman walks, the slit at her calf appears fleetingly and alluringly. The less said, the higher the drama. Morris told me the reason for the ancient and now forbidden practice of binding a girl's feet on birth: as she grew into womanhood she hobbled, developing muscles inside her thighs to heighten a man's sexual pleasures.

Such barbarity could hardly be condoned. But to this day I've deliberately avoided checking Morris' accuracy, lest the truth spoil a zesty story.

The Standard was still a good outlet for journalism — with few restraints on subject matter or individual style. Back in Montreal, I learned to relax and enjoy it, no longer as an editor but in my preferred pursuit, writing. The old paper had risen from a circulation of seventy thousand, most of it in Montreal, to three hundred and fifty thousand nationally. It continued to cover serious stories — enough to impel me to come up with what seemed an outlandish suggestion: a series on the Soviet Union.

It was outlandish because the Russians, under Stalin, granted visas to few foreign newspapermen, and only on a strict exchange basis: for every British correspondent resident in Moscow the Russians could claim a matching number in London; the same restriction applied to the Americans, French, and others. More pertinent was the fact that no Canadian journalist had received a visa in seven years, a hangover of a Soviet spy episode in Canada in late 1945. But this was now 1953 and Stalin had been dead a few months. I persuaded Glenn Gilbert, my editor, that timing might be right: the new regime might be more flexible.

I made several trips to Ottawa in an effort to sell the idea to officials at the Soviet embassy. Weeks passed, without any response. Then came a miraculous phone call from Ottawa — the visa was granted! I rushed into Gilbert's office, to be met not by congratulations but a stony silence, then a blunt, "You can't go."

Gilbert, it turned out, had bought a syndicated series by Perle Mesta, the socialite who had won the dubious title in Washington as "the hostess with the mostest," and also an appointment as U.S. ambassador to Luxemburg. Mesta had engaged her diplomatic passport to gain admission to the Soviet Union, where she wandered around with a can of California peaches defying the Russians to match its quality. She also described how the handles fell off the doors of shoddily built Russian taxis. It was hardly journalism in depth. Nor was there any awareness that Soviet priorities might lie in other directions. (A few years later the Russians sent Sputnik I aloft, beating the Americans in the first space flight).

I prepared to quit the paper, knowing my visa would give me entry not only to Russia but to *Maclean's* magazine and other major periodicals. Gilbert, meanwhile, realized he could never justify ignoring this opportunity for a first Canadian look at the

Soviet Union in the post-Stalin era. Grudgingly he approved my assignment with a biting comment, "It had better be good." But a day later a warm message from him awaited my arrival in Moscow. He was even more effusive when my series won a national newspaper award.

The stories I wrote covered earnest topics. The Russians, I related, were living and eating better than at any time in the past — and this is what made many believe in their system. Freedom of expression? That was something else. But in relative terms, had the average Russian known more freedom in the time of the czars? Despite wishful thinking in the West, there was no indication of mass discontent. Some of the pervasive propaganda about the decadence of capitalism seeped through. The latest volume of the Great Soviet Encyclopedia, published while I was there, featured a sixteen-page section on Canada with a description of how Canadian citizens are "grossly broken by police repression." The Russians, in many instances, accepted it.

As usual I found that sometimes the most whimsical anecdote might illustrate the most complex subject. There was, as a prime example, the matter of Soviet bureaucracy — monstrous and debilitating. But the Russians still retained an old practical streak, as demonstrated by the experience of an American diplomat. He had received an assignment to return to Washington. But first he needed to arrange to take his Great Dane with him by air. He appealed to Burobin, the official agency that handled the problems of foreign envoys, and was told that the dog would require a Soviet passport and would have to be crated.

Surprisingly, getting a passport for the Great Dane did not prove difficult. Then the American, an amateur carpenter, spent several evenings building an elaborate crate to the exact specifications laid down by the Russians. Tenderly he toted the Great Dane to the airport in the crate. He watched while porters carried it to the plane, and then, horrified, saw it would not fit through the doorway. The porters tried the crate sideways; they turned it upside down, with the dog's tail wagging toward the sky. It still would not go through. So, what did the Russians do? They smashed open the crate and led the dog in by a leash. The simple Russian credo: protect yourself with all the required routine; if this doesn't work, use your head.

Conversion of *The Standard* into *Weekend* made it more successful financially but far less interesting editorially. *Weekend*, a magazine supplement inserted in a score of newspapers across Canada, with millions in circulation, had to please a score of constituencies. An article I wrote on Las Vegas, tame by most measures, evoked concern at *The London Free Press*. Editors there thought it undignified for a family newspaper, and seriously considered not inserting that issue of *Weekend*. By contrast, *The Telegram* of Toronto, a lusty, tabloid-style publication, judged the piece too subdued — not enough cleavage in the illustrations. Inevitably, blandness beset *Weekend*.

Occasionally, an interesting subject came up. There was, for instance, an assignment to write a piece on Georges Simenon, the Belgian author whose stories about Inspector Maigret sold in phenomenal numbers. Simenon was married to a Canadian named Denise Ouimet. I spent a few days at his Connecticut estate. A prolific writer, Simenon turned out a book in ten days — no more, no less. He isolated himself in a wing of his home, and Denise mounted guard to ensure there were no interruptions. The slightest disturbance of this intense concentration meant loss of trend and abandonment of anything written so far.

At fifty, Simenon was obviously as intriguing a personality as any of the characters he created. He was candidly blunt about his excessive sexual need, satisfied largely with prostitutes. He estimated that he had bedded at least ten thousand women. Frequent visits to New York helped. He insisted that Denise appear absolutely virginal; he forbade her to wear even lipstick. One day, as we swam in his lake, I asked him, "What would you do if your wife slept with another man?" Simenon, halted in mid-stroke and glared. "I am like a Turk," he said. "I would kill her."

But few subjects like Simenon existed. Increasingly I found work frustrating. The clincher came one day in 1954 when Hugh Shaw, *Weekend* managing editor, called me into his office to discuss a manuscript of mine. He pointed to a word, *façade,* I had used in referring to a building's surface. He was going to change it. "Our readers won't understand it," he said.

"Let them look up a dictionary and learn a new word," I said.

No, the word had to go. On the spot I decided, so did I. It was time to make a change — my first in thirteen years. Probably Shaw was right; he was an editor and he was obliged to think of his kind of readership. But I needed a more challenging outlet that would encourage stories of some significance. So I saw John McConnell.

McConnell was now publisher of *The Montreal Star* as well as *Weekend.* He spoke to Ken Edey, managing editor of *The Star.* It was agreed I could move next door on St. James Street to *The Star.* It was not, of course, façade alone that did it; the incident reflected many irritations. But by such a simple, symbolic route — a difference over one word — are complex decisions sometimes arrived at.

Edey wanted a column from New York. I jumped at the opportunity, the freedom to roam through all types of subjects. The United Nations was my beat. So was Broadway. So was the art world. So was everything and anything, from interviews with Eleanor Roosevelt and Salvador Dali to a visit to the Little Church Around the Corner.

I saw Eleanor Roosevelt, widow of Franklin D. Roosevelt, in her office at the American Association for the United Nations. This exceptional woman still maintained, at age seventy, a work and social schedule that saw her up at seven a.m. and kept her going until midnight. Summers she spent in a small cottage at Hyde

Park, part of the president's estate; winters in a Manhattan apartment on East 62nd Street, shared by a maid and secretary. Most of the time she was on the road, filling five speaking engagements a week.

I asked her what she thought was the chief strength of her favorite subject, the United Nations. "Beyond anything else," she said, "the mere fact that so many nations get to know one another, and talk to one another, is in itself a great achievement." Her newspaper column, which she dictated in twenty minutes, touched whatever topic struck her at the moment. One day she commented on the H-bomb, saying she didn't believe it would ever be used as a weapon of war because it violated peoples' conscience; the next day she advised elderly women to keep busy by joining in community work.

Between the more rigid parts of her routine, Mrs. Roosevelt dictated replies to the hundred and fifty letters she received each day. Had she, I asked, a simple philosophy that guided her all her life? She smiled and said, "What came my way to do, I did."

Salvador Dali, master showman, was somewhat more ethereal. The Spanish artist, who graduated from surrealism to what he called "nuclear mysticism," landed in New York for the opening of his latest exhibition. His prize painting — limp watches hanging from dismembered bodies — was called "The Soft Watch." The inspiration for it came from, or via, his moustache — a widely photographed appendage that formed an arc, at least eight inches wide, twisting upward almost to his eyes.

Dali translated his thoughts from Spanish to French before emerging in English: "Eet tastes so good to be here in thees city of New York. Sometheeng cosmic, wheech I feel through my moostache, stimulates the eemagination. The moostache works not so well in Paree, France, or in Europe. But here? Eet gives me magnificent ideas."

In broad terms what Dali meant was this: Even he didn't take his moustache seriously until he read an ancient book that insisted that face hair served as a kind of antenna, catching ideas from the air and transmitting them to the brain. He wasn't certain why New York's cosmic atmosphere was better than Europe's. But there it was — a scientific Dali fact. Take it or leave it.

I took it. Only a few evenings earlier I had attended a rally in Madison Square Garden where twelve thousand men and women gathered to worship at the feet of Senator Joseph McCarthy. One of the speakers, Major Al Williams, an aviation pioneer of some note, stood on the stage and said in an awed voice: "When I look into your faces and see the burning expressions, the intense patriotism radiating from you, I am filled with a fever, with a spirit that has never before befallen me."

The audience chanted, "God bless McCarthy, thank God for McCarthy." Thus was reached the climax of a self-styled holy crusade to thwart "the hidden force" of Communists determined to enslave the people of the United States. The immediate protest was over the U.S. Senate's censure proceedings against McCarthy. Banners that circled the Garden proposed: "Censure Paul Revere for disturbing the peace."

McCarthyism reflected an ugly period. Salvador Dali made for a fun column. There were many other charming subjects. Irving Berlin, for one, was in a nostalgic mood when we sat at lunch at Dinty Moore's. Only two months earlier the Congress bestowed a gold medal on Berlin, principally for *God Bless America,* a long dormant song that became, almost overnight, when Kate Smith sang it, the unofficial national anthem.

It impelled Berlin to take stock of his background. The son of an immigrant cantor from Russia, he was brought up on the sidewalks of New York's Lower East Side. After only two years of schooling, he started warbling songs in saloons at seven dollars a week. He was not, he told me, inspired to become a song writer. He set out merely to write parodies of existing melodies. The first effort, *Marie from Sunny Italy,* paid him a total of thirty-six cents in royalties. But even before World War I he emerged as an international celebrity. Now he was a multimillionaire and the world's foremost composer of popular songs.

Everyone, regardless of age, recognized *Alexander's Ragtime Band* or *White Christmas*. But Berlin was distressed. "In the old days, before radio, records and television," he said, "people played songs instead of listening to them. Today they have so much music played to them that they don't get a chance to become part of it themselves." Berlin's sense of positive thinking helped him conquer insomnia. "I used to go to bed and worry about sleeping," he confessed, "until I found I was doing it the wrong way around." The cure? "Instead of sheep," he said, "count your blessings."

I picked up lessons from other celebrities. George Jessel, comedian and undisputed toastmaster-general of the United States, let me relay this priceless advice for aspiring after-dinner speakers: "Do not be afraid of the audience. They do not know what you are going to say, and you do, so you have the advantage over them. Speak slowly — and use the pause. Pause, look around the room, take a breath and then start speaking again. Silence can be as eloquent as words."

Much of my work was plain joy. One October night I went backstage of the Morosco Theatre for an interview with Tallulah Bankhead, perhaps the most irreverent, and one of the lustiest, of all actresses. "Oh Gawd, but I'm exhausted," she cried in her throaty voice, with a flourish of both arms. "Simply beat. Tired. Haven't got a spark of energy and all these people calling for tickets and I tell them the show's the hottest ticket in town and I haven't got any tickets. Did you see the world series? You didn't! I just cawn't understand anyone not seeing the series and I don't care what the critics say about the show, I think *Dear Charles* is dahling and all the cast is so wonderful. What did you say your name is, dahling?"

I told her for the sixth time, and she introduced me to Patsy Kelly, a comedienne who was visiting her, and said of me, "He represents an important paper in Toronto, Canada," and then went on: "I'm speaking seriously and I mean this with all my heart dahling I've never been in such a divine comedy Patsy is there any coffee left? And now I'm the honorary chairman of the Willie Mays day in Alabama where I come from. The series was divine, simply divine, did you see it? No! I cawn't understand anyone not seeing the series, what did you say your name is dahling?"

A couple more people had dropped into her dressing room, and she introduced me as belonging to "an important paper in Ottawa, Canada." "This is Reg," she said, waving dramatically toward a young man. "Reg is the son of Fay Bainter, you know that dahling lady of the stage and screen, how did you say your mother is keeping, Reg? That's wonderful and Willie Mays was here to see me the other day what a wonderful man and oh Gawd isn't it wonderful that my Giants my dear sainted Giants won this year? Did I tell you I'm on the Willie Mays committee? And *Dear Charles* is so delightful, it was a hit in London and Rome and Holland and not all plays are Pulitzer prize winners so who cares what the critics say if the audience laughs. What did you say your name is dahling?"

My favorite story was on the Little Church Around the Corner. I'm not sure why it lingers in my memory — perhaps because it murmured tranquility and old values in the midst of a city's tumult and uncertainty. Its reputation as "the marryingest church in the world" may have contributed. By the time I wrote a column, Dr. Randolph Ray had managed to officiate at more than twenty-five thousand weddings in his thirty-two years as rector. Dr. Ray, an Episcopalian, helped establish the myth that a middle-aisle trip in the Little Church was gilt-edged insurance against marital troubles. Among the long list of blunt answers he demanded of couples were these: "Are your backgrounds and interests similar? Do you really know enough about each other? Are you honestly in love?"

Ironically, the Little Church was launched on its way as a wedding centre by a funeral. For the first twenty years of its existence, the Church of the Transfiguration — the official appellation — was a quiet, unpublicized house of worship just off

Fifth Avenue on East 29th Street. Then, in 1870, an English actor named George Holland died in his Manhattan home. Holland's best friend, the popular American actor Joe Jefferson, rushed to the fashionable Church of the Atonement on Madison Avenue to make funeral arrangements. The minister shook his head and said firmly, "We cannot bury an actor."

Jefferson restrained his anger long enough to ask the minister if he could recommend a church that would consider burying a lowly actor. "Well," the clergyman replied, "there is a little church around the corner that does that sort of thing." After George Holland's funeral, word spread backstage of Manhattan theatres that the Church of the Transfiguration actually welcomed actors. Soon, the renamed Little Church Around the Corner became the spiritual headquarters for people of the theatre. Parish members over the years included John Drew, Maurice Barrymore, Dame May Whitty, George Arliss, Edwin Booth, Cornelia Otis Skinner, Raymond Massey, Katharine Cornell and Walter Hampden. Irene Castle and Ann Harding were among the performers married at the Little Church.

At the Little Church, too, memorial services were held in 1952 for Gertrude Lawrence. Dr. Ray summed it up for me: "I have buried more actors, baptized more actors' children, and married more actors than any other clergyman." Not only theatrical people were drawn to the retreat in thunderous Manhattan. A host of more obscure men and women were intrigued by the legends associated with it. As a result, Dr. Ray was prepared for any eventuality. At one wedding the bride yawned so widely that she dislocated her jaw. After rushing her to a hospital, the groom came back and called off the ceremony. He wasn't going to marry any woman, he announced, who was bored by her own wedding.

A New York column was a reporter's dream — limitless stimulation, endless variety. I rode on the final run of the train on stilts — the Third Avenue "El." I interviewed Helen Hayes, who called television plays "theatre in a bread box." I wandered Orchard

Street, the teeming, open air bazaar in Manhattan's Lower East Side, where a pushcart placard promised: "These shirts don't smell of herring."

I toiled hard, and I also got married — to Rosalie Arbess, a Montreal psychologist who worked in occupational therapy at a rehabilitation centre and taught at Sir George Williams (now Concordia) University. As a preamble to my proposal, I warned that life might become a bit nomadic — at least I hoped so. Rosalie said she wouldn't mind if we had to live in Zanzibar or Timbuktu. Exotic! I said, "How about Lachine?" Since Lachine had not yet claimed recognition as the childhood home of Saul Bellow, all one could say was that it was a quiet bedroom community adjacent to Montreal. I think my question won her.

We lived in Greenwich Village. We attended elegant receptions at the United Nations. We met interesting people. What more in life could anyone desire? Apart from a daily column, five times a week, I turned out a Saturday piece on the theatre. This meant attending all the openings, in season three or four a week. Most plays and musicals were duds, and I could easily have walked out after the first act. But Rosalie loved theatre, good or bad. She argued — convincingly — that any playwright who made it to Broadway deserved at least two and a half hours of my patience.

Looking back, I don't know how I did it all. Yet I thrived on the hectic and heavy schedule. Ken Edey was a great editor — bright, considerate, supportive. A graduate of a rugged school, *The Toronto Star*, he was also tough. My office in New York at first was in the Daily News building on 42nd Street near Third Avenue — private, handy to the United Nations, modern, air-conditioned. *The Star,* however, subscribed to the *Herald Tribune's* news service, and Edey decided I should move to the Herald Tribune building.

There was a glamorous history to the *Herald Tribune,* a paper more lively than its rival *New York Times*. But the building was across town, on 41st Street just west of Seventh Avenue —

ancient, not air-conditioned. Instead of a private office, I would occupy a corner in the crowded newsroom, next to an open window through which blew a steady stream of soot. Somehow, I managed, week after week, to find an excuse for avoiding the move. Then one day I received a Telex from Edey: "After this week to what address do you want your salary cheque sent."

The next day I took possession of a battered, cigarette-scarred desk that must have been familiar to reporters back in the 1850s of Horace Greeley, founder of the *Tribune*. There were compensations — including contact with a colorful and talented group of newspaper men and women, and access downstairs to Bleeck's, a fabled bar and restaurant. There were, too, excursions away from the oppressive heat of Manhattan. In our first summer, we made a swing through the straw hat theatre circuit of New England.

The next summer, Edey assigned me to do a series on southern states. We pulled into a gas station in rural South Carolina. Over the churning of a gas pump I heard the radio blaring inside the station. A local announcer appealed for anyone seeing a Nash convertible with New York licence plates — the number was given — to please contact the chief of police. It was my car. What was going on? Who could have known where I was? What emergency at home caused this histrionic entreaty?

I phoned the police chief. "I think it's good news," he said. "Your editor, Mr. Edey, wants you to call him."

Only Ken Edey, with his *Toronto Star* background, would have taken the high-tension steps of tracking down my car's make and licence number, estimating its whereabouts, and contacting various police departments. Only through sheer luck would I have heard this shot in the dark. It was indeed good news. The leaders of the Big Four — Eisenhower of the United States, Bulganin and Khrushchev of the Soviet Union, Eden of Britain, Faure of France — were to meet in Geneva at a summit conference. Edey wanted me to get ready to go to Geneva — with Rosalie — to cover it.

In July 1955 Geneva glowed. Our room at Hôtel de la Paix overlooked Lake Geneva, with its water spout shooting a gusher hundreds of feet skyward. The conference was held in the Palais des Nations, the cream colored building that once served the League of Nations and now the United Nations. Around the corner were cafés where Lenin, in pre-1917 exile, supposedly wrote revolutionary tracts. It was a sophisticated setting for the most important meeting between East and West since World War II. It could have marked the start in reduction of cold war stresses, but instead turned out to be merely the first in a long succession of fruitless meetings.

I learned, perhaps tardily, a disturbing fact about modern journalism: instant communications can be hazardous. About fifteen hundred media representatives, from nearly every country in the world, were gathered in the Maison de la Presse, near the Palais, some so heavily competitive that split seconds counted. At one point in a British press briefing it sounded as though London had broken with Washington over a disarmament issue. London siding with Moscow? That was big, extraordinary news, and a half dozen agency reporters rushed from the room to file bulletins — before the briefing was over. In the question period that followed, a misunderstanding was quickly cleared up. There had been no cleavage between the old allies. The joint Western plan was still intact.

News agency people did what they had to do; they sent immediate corrections. But by then many newspapers around the world, and many more radio stations, had flashed bulletins about discord in Anglo-American relations.

I formed an opinion then that I still cling to — the world might benefit enormously if political and diplomatic events were subject to a moratorium. In the early days of Queen Victoria, before cables, news travelled no more swiftly than a packet boat. If the emperor of China impugned the honor or worth of the British ambassador, and therefore England, it took weeks for the grave tidings to reach London. By then it was merely a forgotten incident.

Today, thanks to instant electronics, anger and insult can escalate to calamity and bloodshed. A freeze on news, of, say, twenty-four hours, could help calm tempers. Certainly, it would give reporters enough time to double-check the accuracy of what they're writing. Having said all this, I know it is unrealistic. Moreover, I'm not sure I would want, even after several decades' experience, to give up the thrill of immediacy.

The Geneva conference led to an assignment to accompany Lester Pearson, Canada's external affairs minister, on a mission to Moscow, New Delhi and Singapore. Soon after, in December 1955, I was appointed chief European correspondent of *The Star*. A few days before Christmas, we moved to London with our ten-week-old daughter Bette. I thought of Ogden Nash, America's foremost writer of whimsical verse, whom I met in New York a year earlier. It was Nash who wrote for all children, and his daughter Linell in particular, these immortal lines:

> *When she is snuffly*
> *She is perfectly luffly.*

This was my second tour of duty in London, a decade after the war. It was still to me the greatest city in the world, still a prime news centre and a convenient jump off point for anywhere in Europe. But perhaps most attractive was the distinctive character of the British. Some traits, such as nonchalance, could prove infuriating. We decided, for instance, that our "nappy" (diaper) service was incompetent. I looked up the phone book and found listed beneath it the name of another company. I called ours and said unless there was immediate improvement I would change to the other nappy service. "Oooh," said a very English female voice, "is there another nappy service in London?"

Most of the time, however, the individualism was charming — by Canadian measures, a trifle offbeat. I became friendly with Commander Charles Drage, an old friend of General Morris Cohen. Drage, retired from the Royal Navy, had operated in the Far East as an intelligence officer during much of Morris' heyday. Now he wrote biographies. A grandfather had served as physician to Queen Victoria. The family obviously possessed long and distinguished credentials. But any earlier wealth may have melted. The Drages still lived in a gracious old home in Sheffield Terrace, in central London, but shabbiness was ignored. If there were full time servants they were not visible.

Nonetheless, an expected way of life had to be maintained. One evening Rosalie and I arrived for dinner, to be greeted by Charles in dinner jacket. Since we were only a foursome, it had never occurred to me to dress; for Charles Drage it was routine. The dining room, in the basement, was dominated by a long refectory table, laden with fine old silverware. Charles sat at one end, his wife Enid at the other. Rosalie and I were in the centre. Mrs. Drage reached for the silver bell in front of her, tinkled it, and Commander Drage rose to serve dinner from the sideboard behind him. When the conversation touched on human relations, Enid proclaimed, "I don't care with whom Charles has an affair — so long as it's not with someone beneath my station in life."

The play *Auntie Mame* opened in London. We had seen it in New York, with Rosalind Russell in the lead. It had been an enormous success, rewarded with a long run. In London, Beatrice Lillie played to perfection Auntie Mame, a marvelously wacky character. The show was a dismal flop, closing after a brief run. British audiences couldn't see anything quaint or eccentric about Auntie Mame. Everyone had an Auntie Mame in the family.

My office was in the Daily Telegraph building, on Fleet Street. It was here that I breathed the air of history. Steele's *Tatler* and Addison's *Spectator* and other pamphlets had made their impact on the growth of journalism in Fleet Street. It was here, too, that

I was forced to relearn a process (called "objectivity") that I had learned, and forgotten, and undoubtedly would forget again.

One can talk ceaselessly about "objectivity" in reporting — the need to isolate one's personal feelings or emotions from a rendition of the facts of a story. So-called commentators do not pretend to strive for balance; they are editorialists, expressing opinion. Cautious journalists make an effort to reach that elusive, and probably non-existent, plateau of objectivity. The level is dependent on one's skill and experience and dedication, but a degree of prejudice must slip in. What is worse is the way in which one can proceed for a long stay on that plateau. Then, suddenly and inexplicably, it is flooded by emotion.

I remember a glaring example — coverage of the Suez crisis in 1956. I wrote angrily about Britain's collusion with France and Israel in an attack on Egypt to seize control of the Suez Canal, which Egypt's President Gamel Abdel Nasser had nationalized. Anthony Eden, the British prime minister, was a weak man trying to act like a strong man, a Churchill. Instinctively in my reporting, I took the same approach as *The Observer,* a liberal, progressive newspaper. It seemed to me that everyone I spoke to took the same approach: this was an outrageous act, a last gasp of a fading empire, an attempt to return to colonialism.

I thought the whole country felt the same way. But soon it was apparent the whole country did not feel that way. The majority — and opinion polls made this clear — were in support of Eden. "Hit the wogs," was the cry of the working man. I could have heard it much earlier if I had simply strolled into the pub next to *The Daily Telegraph.* White collar as well as blue collar men and women congregated there, but not the types who went to El Vino, the "intellectual" hangout a hundred yards along the street. It was a reminder to me how fragile and inconsistent is the measure called "objectivity," that one's own feelings or sense of logic or justice or values do not necessarily reflect the views of the majority.

Not every story was as complex or controversial as Suez. I can also think of John Bodkin Adams, whose story was merely sensational. Many years after the Pétain and Nuremberg trials, with their mass, universal precedents, it was relief to cover a "normal" trial — that is, of someone accused only of homicide. Moreover, no lawyer offered me a penny for mentioning his name, in contrast to practitioners in Montreal courts barely fifteen years before.

John Bodkin Adams, a physician, was charged with hastening by drug injection the deaths of wealthy elderly patients, to benefit from their wills. All Britain and much of the rest of the world hung on to every word of the proceedings. For me, sitting in the famous Court No. 1 of the Old Bailey, coverage invoked images of Agatha Christie and every odd character, including Scotland Yard detectives, ever seen in fiction. There were nervous nurses, and men in bowler hats who followed them on trains, sitting next to them, registering their conversations while pretending to read *The Times*. Best of all, there was "The Count," the Yard's Superintendent Herbert Hannam, in charge of the investigation.

Hannam came by the sobriquet because of his immaculate dress and appearance. In court one day he wore a single-breasted banker's grey suit, pearl grey tie, and white handkerchief jutting from breast pocket in precisely the proper angle. He looked and sounded dignified — forty-eight, steely grey hair parted in the centre, a rich voice. When "The Count" spoke, in firm, educated tones, he commanded attention. John Bodkin Adams, a chubby, rumpled man, ten years older, appeared absorbed in what Hannam said.

What he said was that he had confronted Dr. Adams with a list of prescriptions for drugs ordered by the doctor. In a later meeting he said to Adams, "On November 13th 1950 a patient of yours, Mrs. Edith Alice Morrell, died and you certified the cause of death to be cerebral thrombosis. I am now going to arrest you and take you to the local police station where you will be charged with the murder of Mrs. Morrell."

Adams, according to the superintendent, said, "Murder? Can you prove it was murder? I did not think you could prove murder. She was dying in any event."

Hannam then related that when they were passing through the hall of Adams' office-home, the doctor said to his receptionist, "I will see you in heaven." All this happened in Eastbourne, a coastal resort town, one morning in December, six years after Mrs. Morrell's death. Now, in the Old Bailey, Adams' defence lawyer, Geoffrey Lawrence, occupied centre stage. Lawrence, slight in figure but vigorous, had already made a reputation for demolishing the testimony of prosecution witnesses. Now the scene was of unparalleled drama.

Lawrence referred to what Hannam had described as his first "chance" meeting with Adams. "The first interview with Dr. Adams took place on October 1?" said Lawrence.

"Yes, sir," said Hannam from the witness box.

"Outside his house?"

"At the back of his house."

"The meeting was not by any design on your part?"

"That is so."

"What time did you say it happened?"

"Nine p.m."

"Was it dark?"

"Yes."

Lawrence, choosing his words methodically, said, "There were a number of coincidences that fell together if that was wholly a chance meeting, weren't there?" Hannam asked what Mr. Lawrence meant by "coincidences."

"You don't mean you don't understand my question, do you, superintendent?"

"It is impossible to understand what the coincidences were, sir, unless you help me to help you." The civility was overwhelming.

"It so happened," continued Lawrence, "that at the very moment when the doctor was outside his garage putting his car away you happened to be in his road?"

"I was passing by."

"Eastbourne is not a very small village, is it?"

"I don't think village is the right term at all, sir. It is a town."

"A very large town?"

Hannam would not agree.

Lawrence: "It so happened, quite by chance, at nine p.m. on October 1, in the dark, that you and Dr. Adams converged together outside the garage of his house? A remarkable coincidence."

"I don't think so."

"The truth of the matter," snapped Lawrence, "is that you were waylaying him there, isn't it?"

"Indeed, I was not," retorted Hannam. The gloves were still on, but the knuckles were beginning to show.

"There was a discussion about, some reference to, the chest of silver from Mrs. Morrell and you asked him about it?" (This alluded to silverware that the prosecution had alleged was willed to Dr. Adams, the "motive" for "murder.") Lawrence went on: "Did you know that at the time she died Dr. Adams had been cut out of the will altogether and not validly reinstated?"

"Yes, I think so."

"Did you know then, as you do now, that the only reason Dr. Adams got the chest of silver was by favor of Mr. Claud Morrell, the son?"

"It is my impression I did."

"You drew Dr. Adams' attention to the fact that on the cremation certificate he said he was not a beneficiary or not aware he was?"

"Yes."

"You knew," repeated Lawrence, "when she died he was not a beneficiary under her will?"

"Yes, I did."

"Did you refer to this fact when you spoke to Dr. Adams at this," and here Lawrence paused to underscore the next words, "at this utterly chance meeting?"

"No."

"You were drawing his attention to that certificate as if he had told a lie about it?"

"Yes."

"And all the time you knew he was not a beneficiary under the will?"

"He had...."

Lawrence interrupted sharply, "Is that right?" Now Hannam's irritation, too, was plainly visible. He began to answer, "No sir, he told me...." "Please answer my question," Lawrence shot back. Hannam finally answered it with a "yes." By now the gloves, for two strong men, were off.

Across the road from the Old Bailey stood a grand old pub, the Magpie and Stump. It was known as Court No. 7. The "regulars" — barristers, crime reporters and detectives — hustled in at lunch time for steak and kidney pie and a glass of brown ale. There they held their own unofficial forum on the trial. How persuasive was a leading British authority on morphine and heroin, Dr. Arthur Henry Douthwaite, when he concluded, about Mrs. Morrell, that Adams intended to "terminate her life?" On the other hand, what about Dr. Michael George Corbett Ashby, who declared that the possibility of death by natural causes "cannot be ruled out?"

Much of the talk for seventeen days, one of the longest murder trials in the history of the Old Bailey, was on the drama behind the drama, and of the brilliance of Lawrence. He stirred the "regulars" when he introduced the written records — school notebooks covered in bright red, royal blue, green and orange — kept by four nurses looking after the semi-paralyzed Mrs. Morrell.

This was a masterful, and possibly clinching, stroke — because it virtually shattered the testimony of two of the nurses who had relied on memory to describe what the prosecution alleged were "massive doses" of drugs used by Adams to "murder" his patient. The crown prosecutor, Sir Reginald Manningham-Buller, had built much of his case around the testimony of the nurses. Why had the police failed to find or produce the school notebooks, these vital records? Where had they been stored, or hidden? Not even at the Magpie and Stump could the pundits think of answers. Detectives looked away in embarrassed silence.

All this was before the era of laptop computers and modems. Correspondents still relied on telephones and cables. I arranged for a man from the cable company to stand by at the Magpie and Stump. The instant of the verdict, barely in time for my first edition, I rushed across the road. The cable man had a phone in hand, connected to his office. I scribbled, and he dictated. It was the day's lead story in *The Star* under an eight-column sweep: "Jury Acquits Dr. John Adams of Murder."

Somewhere along the line I had routinely applied for, and received after the requisite waiting period, a visa to Poland. I intended to use it when there was time to do a series on Communist East Europe. The time made itself. Unexpectedly, in the city of Poznan, Polish workers rioted in a demand for better living conditions — and implicitly more freedom. It took tanks, and hundreds of UB, secret police, to put authority in command again. *Tribyuna Luda,* the Communist party newspaper, blamed "hyenas from the West who feed on corpses." In fact the revolt was spontaneous. Many lives were lost, but quietly the regime did make concessions.

I had reached Poznan in a hurry. After reporting on the immediate situation, I looked around for feature material. Talking to Poles was not difficult. By nature demonstrative and outspoken, they sought out foreigners and served as voluntary guides and informants. If anything, the difficulty was in restraining them so they would not be exposed to police reprisal. "Go and tell your people," urged one man, "that it was we, the Poles, who brought about the riots. Talk of 'foreign provocateurs' is nonsense, and an insult to our courage."

I wandered through the streets taking pictures of buildings that had been pockmarked by rifle and machine gun fire. Outside one building, on Kochanowski Street, several men in uniform and plainclothes lurked on the stairway. As I focussed the camera, one of the men rushed toward me, his hand raised. The shutter clicked — and I found myself escorted inside the building. This, it turned out, was UB headquarters.

"This is a military building. Photographs are not permitted," said an officer. I said I had no way of knowing. "You are bluffing," said another. "What other photographs have you taken here?" I said I had shot only six today, mainly street scenes. "Well," he said, "we shall soon see. Your camera, please." I protested; he could have the film if necessary, but there was no need to take the camera. "Oh no," he said with a wry smile, as though to imply I might cloud the film in removing it. I gave up the camera.

The two men disappeared with it. A third, grinning, said, "You'd be better off sticking to photographs in the park." But one officer gave me a clue to the indoctrination that seeped down to some levels. He said Poland was a free country; it was not like America, where workers were oppressed, where McCarthy ruled, and liberty was unknown. I started to correct him, but he interrupted. "Capitalist propaganda," he said, stalking away.

It took twenty minutes and my camera was returned, with politeness and an apology that the negative would be brought to my hotel in an hour, when it had dried. Exactly on schedule a UB man knocked on my door. He held the film aloft, and ceremoniously snipped off the last shot — of the UB building. Then he had a drink with me.

I did not tell him, but probably he guessed the truth. I had been deliberately searching for the UB building, rationalizing that it was an important part of the story to learn what the secret police were thinking. In fact it was foolish and smart-alecky — the sort of action in later years I deplored in reporters I considered irresponsible. I could have wound up in a prison cell, of no use to myself or my newspaper. Luckily, the UB men turned out to be decent or concerned about image.

I have long appreciated the fraternity of newspaper work. I doubt if there is another profession quite like it. You can drop into almost any newspaper office in the world, identify yourself as representing a foreign publication, and someone will always be ready to help, providing background to a story or offering "morgue" — that is, library — facilities. All these courtesies, even the names and phone numbers of useful contacts, are yours— though it is highly unlikely you will ever be in a position to reciprocate. The donor knows that he or she one day might be in a similar plight, a stranger in a strange land, and someone else will return the favor.

Self-interest? Maybe, but I think it is more — the under-standing of a kindred soul. I have experienced this generosity in many places, even in some Communist countries, perhaps none more dramatically than in Budapest, July 1956. I was having coffee in Café Hungaria, exchanging small talk in a mixture of English and French with a Hungarian at the next table. "You say you are a journalist," he said. "You should go upstairs. It is the office of the party newspaper."

I had arrived late the night before, intending to soak in the atmosphere for a day or so before starting to work. But this was a tempting suggestion. So I walked up two flights and found myself asking a receptionist at *Népszabadság* for an editor who spoke English. There was no one around. But an editor who spoke French did emerge. He immediately whispered in my ear, "Rakosi has been thrown out." I barely recognized the name. This time, however, I knew it was not merely a general briefing by a congenial colleague but divulgence of dramatic news. Matyas Rakosi, feared and loathed, had been Hungary's unbending dictator since 1947. His Soviet masters, desiring more flexibility and popularity, had fired him.

Because of censorship and transmission complexities in the Communist bloc, I had made advance arrangements to phone *The Daily Telegraph* in London. It was well set up with highly skilled operators who knew how to record and transcribe messages from difficult areas; *Telegraph* staff correspondents sent news this way. We were not so well endowed at *The Star*. The deal was that if I ran into any worthwhile story I would dictate it to a *Telegraph* operator, who would refile it by cable to Montreal. *The Telegraph*, in exchange, could make use of the report.

Western news agencies relied on state radio broadcasts from Budapest for the announcement of Rakosi's dismissal. I was, by chance, the only foreign reporter in Hungary. My Rakosi account, fleshed out by analysis and interpretation I picked up at the British embassy, was the lead in *The Daily Telegraph*. But, as I discovered on my return to London, there was puzzlement among sub-editors about what I meant by a phrase I used in the next day's follow up. In describing the fears of Hungarians that any changes would be superficial, I said they were analyzing the "fine print." It was not a familiar expression to the English.

I can't remember how the sub-editors reworded it but I've no doubt it was elegant. The conservative *Daily Telegraph* possessed style. It demonstrated this during the John Bodkin Adams trial when it buried detailed reports inside the paper, so commuters could indulge their lusty taste for crime news without anyone else knowing what page they were reading.

Elegance on all levels was a distinctive mark of the better Fleet Street newspapers. Soon after my transfer to London, *The Times* introduced new ink on its presses. My publisher, John McConnell, asked me to get some details. Was the move made to improve quality? To cut costs? I made an appointment with the general manager and saw him in his office in Printing House Square. "From what point of view," I asked, "did *The Times* make this change?" He held back for no longer than a second and said, "From *The Times'* point of view, sir. From *The Times'* point of view."

The Café Hungaria was known, before the Communist takeover, as the New York Café, a flourishing haunt of Budapest's intelligentsia and literati. Closed for many years, it again attracted writers, composers, and painters. For me it was a marvelous treat to sip coffee in this vast, ornate room, beside the mirrored square pillars and under beaded chandeliers and high ceilings decorated with water nymphs. I could almost see Ferenc Molnár's ghost floating up there. But the conversation was defeatist, representative of the attitude of many of the ordinary Hungarians I met.

I couldn't help thinking of a difference. In Poland there was spirit, moving dynamically from the people themselves, speeding the process of liberalization. In Hungary there was docility, with men and women muffled in any demands for an independent role within the Soviet orbit. On that trip, which took me to Czechoslovakia as well as to Poland and Hungary, I wrote: "You can expect the Poles might rebel, and possibly the Czechs, but never the Hungarians." Three months later came the Hungarian uprising, the first major crack in the Soviet structure of East Europe. So much for prognostication.

6 A Call About China

IN THE SUMMER OF 1958 THE UNITED STATES verged on war with China over two obscure islands, Quemoy and Matsu in the Formosa Strait. The dispute — whether the islands belonged to the Communist mainland or the U.S. protégé, Nationalist Formosa (Taiwan) — amplified cold-war tensions. It also gave me one of my journalistic breaks.

My publisher at *The Montreal Star*, John McConnell, was also owner of North American Newspaper Alliance, a syndicate based in New York. NANA had a long history associated with some distinguished names. Ernest Hemingway, back in the 1930s and 1940s, had written for it. But competition now was tough, and NANA struggled to survive.

The Quemoy-Matsu crisis provided a rare opportunity. American journalists were barred by State Department regulations from travel to China. The Chinese were granting practically no visas to British or European reporters. So, a first-hand Western account of Peking's intentions in the Formosa Strait was unattainable. Perhaps a Canadian could get in?

That was the thought of someone in New York, and I was elected to try, from my base in London. I didn't take the effort too seriously. In 1949, when I was in Hong Kong with General Morris Cohen, I was frustrated in my attempts.

Morris, now divorced from my sister Judith, lived in London. We got along well, meeting periodically for lunch. I called him and asked if he had any ideas on how I should apply for a visa to China. "Cable Chou En-lai and say you're my brother-in-law," he roared.

This was the old Morris in top style, booming and confident. I had my doubts about how much influence he now carried. But I knew that a routine application at the Chinese embassy would yield nothing. So I sent a cable, addressed to Premier Chou En-Lai, Peking, People's Republic of China. I said: "The world receives its news about the Quemoy and Matsu situation from correspondents based in Taiwan. It is time you told your part of the story through a Canadian journalist, preferably me." I tacked on the inaccurate reference to my relationship to Mah Kun, the name familiar to Chinese who remembered Morris' bodyguard days with Sun Yat-sen.

Five days later I received a phone call from the Chinese embassy. I was astonished to get any acknowledgement. I was stunned at the message: My visa was ready. Could I drop around for it immediately? Within twenty minutes I presented myself to two young functionaries who awaited me at the door. I handed over my passport, and sank back in an over-stuffed easy chair while the functionaries vanished into another room. I drank the tea that had been proffered, and scanned magazines in English about China's revolution. I was still bewildered over my good fortune.

The two young functionaries finally — it seemed an hour, but it was much less — reappeared. Their expression was stern. One said, "We cannot give you a visa."

"No visa?" I echoed. "But it was approved by Premier Chou!"

"We cannot give you a visa when you carry this." He pointed to my passport — to a slip of paper stapled to the last page. It was a mimeographed notice issued by the Department of External Affairs, advising Canadian visitors to certain countries to report on arrival to a Canadian consulate or embassy. This was not mandatory; it was for their own security. Where no Canadian representation existed, the advice was to check in with the nearest British mission.

The list included such dictatorship states as Paraguay, where foreigners sometimes disappeared mysteriously, and several Communist countries, including "Mainland China."

That, of course, was what the Quemoy-Matsu crisis was all about — the claim of Peking that there was no "Mainland" China; there was only One China, including small and big islands such as Quemoy and Matsu — even Formosa. The faraway conflict had swept over me in London, threatening my chances for a trip to a country that had been closed to Westerners for nearly a decade. "Is it this that bothers you?" I asked, fingering the notice in my passport.

"Yes."

I pulled it from its staple and tore it up. The two Chinese officials stared at me, their mouths agape. I could imagine what they wanted to say: "Is this what you can do to a passport in Canada? In our country such treatment of a state document would be severely punished." The fact was, of course, that I hadn't mutilated or violated my passport; I had simply removed an extraneous attachment. In the process I may have struck a blow for freedom and democracy. I also got my visa.

The next day I was on my way, armed principally with a couple of books by C.P. Fitzgerald, one of the world's most eminent Sinologists. Fitzgerald, a British professor who had spent many years in China, now taught in Australia. I began to devour his words — his knowledge and understanding of China were monumental — the moment I stepped on a British Airways flight to Moscow. There I transferred to Aeroflot for the lengthy haul ahead on a TU-104.

Fifteen hours later, at nightfall, I was in Peking. My hotel, the Hsinchiao, was bleak but central. My room was clean and sparsely furnished, with a fixture I was to discover everywhere I later moved: a Thermos of hot tea. On my first day, I stopped at the hotel bar — an enormously long bar in a cavernous room. Only one other patron was there — a man who sat a dozen stools away. We exchanged a few words, in English. He was a slightly-built man in his late fifties — a ring of grey hair framing his bald head — who spoke with a soft British accent. He turned out to be C.P. Fitzgerald.

This was the first miracle in a voyage that was to prove endlessly captivating. It was the period of Mao Tse-tung's "Great Leap Forward," of the spread of communes, of the erection of home-made "blast furnaces" in every city and hamlet, of regimentation not without vitality from Shanghai to the hinterland.

Fitzgerald had left China a year after the Communist takeover in 1949. Every year since then he tried, unsuccessfully, to return. Peking refused a visa. Fitzgerald, though liberal and open-minded, was not the kind of person a new regime wanted floating around. He spoke fluent Mandarin, knew China and its ways, and possessed many contacts, especially among academics in a position to make substantial judgments. Unexpectedly, Fitzgerald had now received a visa, and had arrived only a few hours before me.

Of all the experts I could have hoped to hit upon, in all the world, none stood out more than C.P. Fitzgerald. And here he was, sitting beside me. For much of the rest of my stay I clung to him. I travelled with Fitzgerald whenever possible, benefitting from his ability to communicate and make comparisons. In one village, for instance, peasants said that communism was good to them. They now ate meat twice a month. I remarked to Fitzgerald that this didn't sound so impressive. He recalled that in this part of China they used to eat meat twice a year.

Private or personal contact with individuals in the New China was problematic. On his arrival, Fitzgerald had requested meetings with some of his old Chinese colleagues. He submitted a list to the ministry of cultural affairs, hoping for permission to see at least a few. Instead, he saw all of them — en masse. The ministry arranged a reception for the last night of Fitzgerald's stay, to which his old friends were invited. They came, accompanied by officials. Inevitably, conversations consisted not of topics of current value but of small talk. There was no time to meet them again. Nor could Fitzgerald return to Australia saying the Communist regime had denied him freedom of contact. He had seen the people he wanted to see, hadn't he?

That obliqueness was not necessarily Communist. It was also pure Chinese. I encountered another example at Peking University. The administration had sought to get rid of the dean of arts; he was old and feeble and not functioning properly. But he was a venerated figure. How could he be removed without loss to his dignity? The answer was simple. The administration doubled the dean's salary. Promptly he resigned, claiming he was not worthy of such reward. He had understood the message.

Everything I saw in China, everything I heard, was new — at least to me and most of the outside world. I possessed a virtual newspaper monopoly. As far as I could make out, the only other non-Communist journalists in the country were a reporter and photographer for *Der Stern,* the West German news magazine. Such exclusivity produced unparalleled efficiency. My contact from the start was a young Mr. Ho at the foreign ministry. He awaited my phone calls. He must have slept at the ministry; day or night he was on hand. It worked two ways. Mr. Ho, or others like him, always knew my exact whereabouts. Once, a cable arrived when I was talking to Fitzgerald in his room — that's where it was delivered.

Mr. Ho, who spoke good English, arranged all meetings with officials. Regardless of the ministry, the scene was much the same — plush chairs, a round table, and a cup of green tea constantly refilled by a woman who moved silently in and out of the room. In addition to the person I interviewed, there were invariably three or four other Chinese present — an interpreter and two men who sat in the background taking notes.

I never felt pressed for time. In some interviews I collected all I needed in an hour; others went on two or three hours. But it was always I who terminated the session. All along, I assumed, reports were going back to Mr. Ho — on the kind of questions I asked, on my attitude (was I attempting to do a serious job of reporting?). Mr. Ho as much as admitted this one day when he said, "We consider you to be a serious correspondent."

Did Mr. Ho mean by this a "sympathetic" correspondent?

"Not at all," he said. "We don't expect to convert you. We'll have no complaints if you report on China as you see it. We object when correspondents leave here and say that everything is bad."

I had asked for a meeting with Chen Yi, vice-premier and foreign minister. Early one morning I received a phone call from Mr. Ho. "Would you please stay in your room this afternoon," he said. "We may come and fetch you." I said I would be happy to stay. I knew the signal — an important interview was coming up.

The afternoon passed gloomily. At seven in the evening I rang Mr. Ho. "Should I keep on waiting?" I asked. "Or should I have dinner?"

"We suggest," said Mr. Ho, "that you have dinner."

"Would you like me to stand by tomorrow?" I said. "I'm supposed to go to the country to visit a commune, as you know. But I don't mind cancelling it."

"We suggest," said Mr. Ho, "that you visit the commune."

At four a.m., disconsolate, I rose to catch an early train. My usual interpreter was waiting in the lobby, and so was a Miss Chang of the foreign ministry. Miss Chang said she had never visited this particular commune and was now taking the opportunity of doing so. My spirits went up again, for Miss Chang's notebook jutted from the pocket of her blue boiler suit. There was hope that she was another examiner of my suitability to interview a leader.

Two days later, while I was having breakfast, I was summoned to the phone in the dining room. It was Mr. Ho. "Vice-premier Chen Yi," he said a bit breathlessly, "will receive you in an hour."

I don't know why there had been a previous false alarm, or why a final character investigation was required. In any event the session with Chen Yi lasted four hours — half that time spent by interpreters — and covered topics ranging from the Quemoy-Matsu crisis to Peking's expectation of replacing the Nationalists who occupied China's seat at the United Nations.

"We are patient, we know how to wait," said Chen Yi. "We do not lose anything by the present situation. On the contrary, we are receiving more and more sympathy and support from the people of the world. We are convinced we will ultimately enter the United Nations, just as the United States will ultimately withdraw from Taiwan. Time is in our favor."

The interview made the front page of *The New York Times* and many other papers. A series I wrote later from Hong Kong for NANA also gained wide publication. Walter O'Hearn, who had replaced Ken Edey as managing editor of *The Star,* cabled congratulations and asked me to return to London via New York. When I arrived in New York, I was greeted at the airport by O'Hearn, John McConnell, and several other executives of *The Star*. They had flown in from Montreal. A suite awaited me at the Algonquin Hotel. I never knew such lionizing — before or since.

The office had arranged television and radio interviews in New York. When I met Alice Weel, an associate producer at CBS television, I told her of *Der Stern* photographer Rolf Gilhausen. Apart from photos for his magazine, he had shot some film in China, using a small movie camera. I said I had no idea of its quality or what was on the film . Weel said she would relay the information.

A few days after I got back to London a letter arrived from New York. It was from Willis Kingsley Wing, a prominent literary agent. Had I, he asked, considered writing a book about China? I had not. With the exhilaration of getting out an exclusive series of articles, a book never occurred to me. I had spent barely six weeks in the country — acceptable for news coverage. But a book? What would my friend, the scholarly C.P. Fitzgerald, say about such audacity?

There was a phone discussion with Wing, who argued that I would not be attempting to emulate such authorities as Fitzgerald.

I would simply describe my limited observations and experiences in the style of a reporter. I said I'd think about it, because meanwhile an urgent message had arrived from CBS. Could I fly to New York right away? They had tracked down Rolf Gilhausen and obtained his movie footage. The film was extraordinary. CBS planned an hour's television documentary, and I was wanted to help with the script and narration. The show was scheduled to run on December 28 — eight days hence. I took off for New York on the next flight.

Though many years have elapsed, several points remain highlighted in my mind. First there was my introduction to the ways of major league networks. CBS asked me to come economy class; that's all the budget could afford. I didn't insist that I always flew first class for my newspaper. The story was too important for quibbling. I was anxious to get as wide an audience as possible for my message: Whether we liked it or not, many Chinese supported the Communists; for the first time a regime was taking effective steps to protect them against floods, famines, epidemics and other disasters that had always afflicted China. The Chinese were going through the greatest industrial transformation in history. If there was a threat to the West it was economic, not military. Not long ago the Chinese couldn't produce even an aspirin. Now they made all the penicillin their hospitals needed. The same kind of astonishing forward leaps in a variety of fields — automotive, electronics, chemical, railways — struck me wherever I travelled. Do not be misled by lurid tales of a society of "blue ants." Certainly there is some regimentation, but understand that the giant no longer sleeps.

A room had been reserved for me at the Roosevelt Hotel, across 45th Street from the old office building used by CBS News. An auditor informed me that my daily living allowance would be twenty-five dollars. When I pointed out that the room cost seventeen dollars, leaving me hardly enough for meals, he replied: "That's all Jack Benny gets." I said, "He can afford it." It was my first brave punch at CBS. But I lost the round. Twenty-five dollars a day was all I received.

I was listed as co-writer of the script, but Alice Weel, a gifted hand at television, put most of it together with the aid of my newspaper clippings. It was a phenomenal challenge to produce a full-length documentary in barely a week. December 28 was a Sunday, with the broadcast of *The Face of Red China* slated from 4:30 to 5:30 p.m. — hardly prime time. It was daring of the network, nonetheless, because of the serious subject matter during a Christmas holiday period.

Walter Cronkite appeared as the host. Early in the afternoon we recorded our voices over the film portions. The rest of the broadcast was to be live, Cronkite and I alternating in the narration. Suddenly, a half hour before air time, a meeting was called by a network vice-president. In attendance were the show's producer, Les Midgley, Cronkite, and several assistants.

The vice-president — I was so startled, I never did catch his name — said CBS was concerned about the tone of the presentation. In effect, he said it did not portray Communist China in a negative enough light. Therefore the network demanded a preface. An announcer would say that since American correspondents were not allowed to travel to China, CBS was unable to guarantee the objectivity of this account, filmed by a German cameraman and related by a Canadian correspondent.

There was utter silence. Midgley shrugged and looked unhappy. Cronkite, too, was plainly embarrassed. I said, as quietly as I knew how, "Apart from the fact that this is bad psychology — shooting down a report before the audience can decide for itself whether it is reliable — you cast doubt on my professionalism. If you go ahead with the precede, I walk off — on camera."

It was not a particularly audacious threat; I knew CBS could not afford such a revolt in public view. The vice-president motioned Midgley and the others into a quick, private conference. The derogatory preamble was dropped. We went on the air and completed the broadcast as originally planned.

I had only a little time before catching a flight back to London. Cronkite invited me for a drink. We sat in a bar on Third Avenue, still in makeup. The great reporter in Cronkite expressed itself in regrets over network behavior, and then in a barrage of questions about what it was like digging out material in China.

The Face of Red China, which gave the American people their first detailed view of the momentous social and economic developments in the most populous country in the world, won all of us an Emmy as the best documentary of the year. CBS also copped a Bell & Howell contract, the biggest of its kind, for a series of documentaries.

My visit to China taught me something not only about the Chinese but about myself — my ability to outface mandarins at an embassy or to stand up to moguls at a television network. It gave me as well an enormous lift. I wrote the book Willis Wing suggested. *Impatient Giant: Red China Today* became a success, financially and critically. *The New York Times* commended me for "superb reporting" which it called "balanced, thoughtful, perceptive." That was my supreme reward.

On March 21, 1960, in a place called Sharpeville, South Africa, white police opened fire on a couple of thousand black demonstrators, killing sixty-nine. Hours later, I received a phone call in London from Walter O'Hearn in Montreal. Could I get out there right away? It was quickly apparent that Sharpeville was more than just another incident of bloody repression; it contained ingredients of possibly historic significance. I booked myself on the first flight to Johannesburg, and had just stepped on the plane when I heard a Canadian-accented voice call my name.

It was Norman Phillips of *The Toronto Star.* He had arrived minutes earlier from Toronto, and barely made this connection. We spent the next ten days together on the story. We pooled our information. It was, we soon discovered, the kind of story in which reporters, up against rigidly entrenched and secretive authorities, must work together. Phillips and I were not in competition in the same city; even if we had been rivals, the principle of cooperation would have applied. The bigger obligation to journalism, and the public it serves, takes over. When reporters operate under this principle, bureaucracy, anywhere, stands less chance of suppressing information.

South Africa was still a member of the Commonwealth (it would withdraw a year later) and, as Canadians, our passports got us in. American and other foreign journalists were compelled to wait anxiously abroad for visas. Minutes after we cleared immigration and customs in Johannesburg airport, we set out in our rented car for Vereeniging, thirty-five miles to the south.

It was almost impossible to relate the lovely and tranquil countryside, rich in foliage and dotted with attractive ranch-style houses, occupied by whites, to the setting of tension and poverty and carnage that lay ahead. The streets of Vereeniging, a modern, well laid out town, were filled with armored cars roaring toward Sharpeville, two miles away. Sharpeville, known as a "location," was a fenced-in reservation of earthen streets and one-room shanties. There the black Africans, who worked in the light industries or the steel mill at Vereeniging, lived and slept and died.

Our introduction to white South Africa came from a ramrod-straight Afrikaner, a police colonel named Pine Piennar, in charge of the armed checkpoint that prevented us penetrating inside the location. "You have just arrived here," he said. "You do not understand these savages." What was the colonel's explanation for the slayings? Piennar, weary after sleepless days and nights, said, "The natives have had some grievances, but these have existed for many years. It is only now that they are led and incited by small groups."

"What kind of groups?"

He lowered his voice and said, "You know, the Communists." Then he added more vehemently, "When the Communists get twenty thousand people together — let alone savages — something is bound to happen." For me there was a gloomy flashback to another time and place — Poznan, four years ago, when the Poles demonstrated because they wanted more bread and more rights. In Poznan, while the bodies of slain men and women were still being identified, just as they were now still being identified in Sharpeville, a police colonel snapped, "They were incited by capitalist agents." Police states appeared to be universal in their mentalities and techniques. Only the labels were changed.

South African police were not menaced by twenty thousand "savages." The real number of demonstrators, as eye-witnesses later testified, was closer to two thousand. These men and women descended on the police station in Sharpeville deliberately to be arrested. Some burned their "pass books," identity documents which, by compulsion, they carried everywhere, and produced on demand by any police officer. Failure to do so meant jail.

Sharpeville started as a passive demonstration against the white man's inhuman laws that reduced black movements and freedom almost to the point of slavery. But the figures — twenty thousand or two thousand — were unimportant. The significant fact was that the blacks did not retreat, despite the deaths and injuries. Instead, for the first time they sensed the sudden panic of the white men who had opened machine-gun fire on them. In subsequent days they continued their march forward. In Durban and Cape Town and other cities, thousands gathered at memorial services, despite a government prohibition.

The government mobilized army regiments and air force squadrons, in addition to all police units. This did not prevent a "day of mourning" called by black leaders. It brought industry in Johannesburg and other centres to a halt. Never had the country seen such an impressive — and for the whites, terrifying — display of native solidarity. There was little doubt, blacks told me, that if sufficient numbers had been organized and armed, rising at several points simultaneously, the whites would have been overwhelmed.

As it was, the military, rushing forces from place to place in response to urgent calls, could barely keep unarmed people subdued.

Over the years, in subsequent visits to South Africa, I met more and more whites who faced the reality that their world of complete and unquestioned domination was nearing an end. Even back in 1960 it was astonishing to note that many whites sensed that the demands of the modern world were catching up. A white taxi driver unwittingly summarized the attitude and apprehension. "The natives," he said, "are getting too confident. Only this morning our maid had the nerve to use the toaster for her own bread."

There were two principal black leaders, Chief Albert Luthuli, head of the African National Congress, and Robert Mangaliso Sobukwe, head of the more aggressive Pan-Africanist Congress. Norm Phillips set out to interview Luthuli while my mission was to locate Sobukwe. I never did find him — at least not then. He was already in jail, charged with incitement to riot. Fifteen years elapsed before I met Sobukwe, in a semi-clandestine way. Phillips' timing was better than mine. He spoke to Luthuli in Pretoria hours before Luthuli's arrest.

"If only five hundred thousand burn their passes," said Luthuli, "the police might be able to put that number in jail. But they cannot do it if all of us burn our passes." There were fourteen million blacks in South Africa at the time, compared with three million whites, the majority Afrikaners. Luthuli was sensitive to white fears. With great prescience he said: "The only solution is to ensure that Africans become saturated with democracy. The question of tyranny of numbers would be moderated if we made sure that people had come to accept democracy as their way of life."

But he accused white South Africans — especially members of the Nationalist Party of Prime Minister Henrik F. Verwoerd, a vociferous exponent of apartheid, or apartness — of doing nothing to provide proper training in democracy. "The Afrikaners," Luthuli said, "have no contact with Africans except on a master-servant basis." Later, Luthuli was awarded the Nobel Peace Prize.

A state of emergency proclamation gave the Verwoerd government dictatorial powers. The police possessed the authority to arrest anyone without warrant. Newspapers, constantly threatened with closure, were powerless even to publish the names of those arrested. The smothering was effective. I arrived in Cape Town, to meet members of parliament opposed to government policy, and was questioned for several desperate minutes about individuals in Johannesburg. Did I know of their fate? Did anyone know whether detainees were still held in the central police station, or had they been sent to concentration camps?

Foreign journalists were still able to cable their reports, but there was a fear that censorship might be imposed at any moment. I ran into trouble when the Columbia Broadcasting System, unable to obtain a visa for any of its own correspondents, asked me to broadcast to New York. A circuit was set up through the South African Broadcasting Corporation. I reached the Johannesburg studios, only to be informed by a senior official that I was barred from the air. He cited the emergency proclamation. I shouted, "This is a great way to gain world understanding." He shouted back, "We don't give a damn what the outside world thinks." He was not alone. Afrikaner pride and stubbornness, which had sheltered a people and culture for more than a century, had reached a fevered level.

My fate was hardly comparable with that of Phillips. He was arrested and jailed in Durban for three days for reporting a police attack on Nyanga, one of two big African locations outside Cape Town. This may have impelled Tom Hopkinson, a great British journalist, to write some kind words about us in his memoirs, *In the Fiery Continent,* two years later.

Hopkinson, who had edited London's *Picture Post* in its heyday and then moved to South Africa to take over the magazine *Drum,* described how it was difficult to get any work done during the Sharpeville crisis. The press of half the world, he wrote, poured into *Drum* offices in Johannesburg, asking questions and favors. Then came the pat on the back: "Of all our visitors, two of those who applied themselves most seriously to trying to find out what the trouble was about were two Canadians, Norman Phillips of *The Toronto Star*, and Gerald Clark of *The Montreal Star*."

Soon after landing in London from Johannesburg I packed again — this time for a return to Montreal. We had spent nearly five glorious years in London, but Rosalie now suffered from cancer. The office did not hesitate when I said we wanted to move back home. Walter O'Hearn was managing editor, but his boss, as well as mine, was George V. Ferguson, the editor-in-chief. I was appointed an associate editor, a glorified title for editorial writer — but I accepted it with the understanding that foreign assignments would still take priority.

More than ever, after my exposure to London as a repository of history and gateway to international stories, I was convinced that my chief interest lay in foreign affairs. *The Star* was an ideal place for employment. Montreal was still the largest city in Canada, the financial and business centre with much of its orientation toward Europe. *The Star,* apart from bureaus in Ottawa and Washington, had long devoted space and money to correspondents in Europe and coverage of news from abroad. It was a solid and sophisticated newspaper of high repute.

I had never worked for *The Star* in Montreal. In 1953, when I switched from *Weekend* it was to go straight to New York. The Star's building then, on St. James Street, exuded a kind of decayed charm, dating to 1900 (the paper was founded in 1869). John McConnell knew that proper expansion was long overdue. A fine new structure, back to back with the old, and facing Craig Street (now St. Antoine Street), started to go up in the mid-1950s.

Thanks to the shrewd connivance of Ken Edey, I could claim indirect credit for a touch of creature comfort on Craig Street. McConnell had not believed it necessary to spend extra millions in air-conditioning the new building. Edey knew it was essential. He had me contact experts on air-conditioning in New York, and I wrote a terse series of articles. The thrust was simple: air-conditioning, rather than costing money, saved money in improved productivity. McConnell yielded. Now, established in a small but comfortable private office, I was a beneficiary, along with thirteen hundred other Star employes.

The Star, as I confirmed close up, was a great newspaper — the best, I thought, in the country. Certainly no other paper could claim a more distinguished or sagacious editor than George Ferguson. Ferguson was a product of *The Winnipeg Free Press,* the spawning ground for some of Canada's best and most liberal newspapermen. J.W. McConnell, *The Star's* owner, had considered him far too radical for a paper like *The Star,* but McConnell's son, John G., preparing to take over as publisher, surreptitiously established Ferguson in an office across the street. There Ferguson wrote refreshing editorials, which John quietly slipped into the paper. When John officially took over its direction Ferguson emerged in the open.

There were other changes in Montreal and the province, the kind that people on the spot often fail to recognize because these creep in gradually and without seeming important. A word that struck me on my return in 1960 was "separatism." It kept popping up in everyday conversation and I was never quite clear what it meant until I asked for explanations. Only then did I learn that an old Quebec phenomenon — the striving of some French Canadians for independence — was recurring. I suggested a closer look, and Max McMahon, an editorial writer, wrote what turned out to be a startling analysis of how the country stood on the edge of crisis. Canada was becoming something of an international story, but, engaging as it was, I was still drawn to other parts of the world where conflict was resolved not by debate but by violent upheaval. Simply put, I felt that people at home needed constant reminders that our problems were trivial compared with ferocious events in much of the world.

One excursion led me to the Belgian Congo, where the Belgian colonial power was being overthrown by the Congolese in fierce combat. I reported it not entirely in sympathy with the whites. A letter awaited me when I got back to Montreal. It said it was too bad I had never sent my wife to the Congo where she could have been raped by the blacks. It ended with a false signature, "A. Paperman.' Since Rosalie had died not long ago, and Paperman was the name of a Jewish undertaker in Montreal, I felt sickened — so much so that I carried the letter into George Ferguson's office and wordlessly placed it on the desk before him. I don't know what kind of commiseration I needed or expected. All I remember is that he shook his head in revulsion and said that personal gloom as well as satisfaction was a price of journalism. He might have added that some demented readers followed one's career.

On a March afternoon in 1961 McConnell called me into his office to ask how I would feel about covering the Eichmann trial. Walter O'Hearn, managing editor, had already raised the same question. He wondered if, as a Jew, I might suffer emotionally in hearing testimony about the man accused of organizing the transport of millions of Jews destined for extermination. I told McConnell what I had told O'Hearn: I was a Jew, I was a Canadian, and I was a newspaperman.

It was a measure of both men's sensitivity that the question even arose. It was a measure of my uncertainty that I was not sure — I am still not sure — what priority I give to journalism. I like to think that as a professional I can detach my feelings from any specific situation. It is not always possible, of course. I reaffirmed this during the Eichmann trial, when, two or three times, hearing a hideous account of atrocities, I made my way out of the courtroom to gulp fresh air or throw up. But other reporters — non-Jews — did the same.

Back of my mind, perhaps, was the sense that many relatives of mine, never known to me, died because their ancestors did not, or could not, migrate to the New World. If my father had not quit the Austrian empire, would I have lived to watch these proceedings? Would there be grandchildren of mine to read these words? I still like to believe, though, that I functioned with hardly a thought other than getting the story, getting it right, and getting it back to the office.

It was a profound experience. It turned out to be the first of forty trips I was to make to Israel, a troubled and fascinating land. I learned on that visit in 1961, and again in 1991, and on every visit between, that no other country can match it for news interest. Israel's biggest export is not polished diamonds or electronic instruments or citrus fruit. It is news. Some scholars argue that this was predestined, that the Bible itself was the original media story, with the Jews placing themselves at its centre. This may be an intriguing concept, even fanciful, but the fact is that since its start in 1948 modern Israel has hardly left the front pages or network broadcasts for more than brief periods.

Apart from wars, several events are noteworthy, including a historic visit by an Egyptian leader, Anwar Sadat, that led to Israel's peace with its strongest adversary; a Palestinian uprising that persists; and violent disputes between Jews because they were either Ashkenazic or Sephardic, or religious or non-religious, or because they just happened to think differently from one another. One feels a constant turbulence, a striving to reach almost unattainable values and standards.

The setting of my introduction in 1961 could not have been more fitting: a modest hotel called the Holy Land, in the Judean hills, about seven miles from the centre of Jerusalem. A minibus transported guests to and from town. In religious terms, I am neither knowledgeable nor observant. But there was no escaping the special quality of the backdrop. The low hills were virtually denuded of greenery, worn to a brown surface over the millennia. One could visualize the prophets trudging through ancient pathways.

I remarked on this one day to a passenger sitting next to me, a woman from the Bronx. "Ech," she said. "These mountains are all right. But we have the Catskills."

The setting for the Eichmann trial was quite different, the courtroom a converted auditorium in Jerusalem's new cultural centre, Beit Ha'am. Pressed into service to accommodate five hundred reporters from around the world, plus hundreds of witnesses and observers, it was austerely lined with buff brick, an unappealing sample of modern functionalism and security. There, behind a bullet-proof glass cage, sat Adolf Eichmann, accused of crimes against humanity and the Jewish people, the highest ranking Nazi caught since the Nuremberg trial.

I formed some of my most lasting impressions not inside but outside the courtroom. On the evening before the trial's opening I stood in the square facing Beit Ha'am. Hundreds of Israelis were there, many survivors of the death camps. They stood and stared, in silence, as though their vision could penetrate the limestone walls and focus on Eichmann himself. Or were they pondering the meaning of justice? Harsh searchlights came into play, to silhouette on the roof of Beit Ha'am and nearby buildings the figures of Israeli soldiers, their submachine guns visible and challenging. Eichmann, it was made clear, would not be the successful target of any rescuer — or of any assassin.

In the morning, clusters of people lingered in the square, still shrouded in absolute silence. The eerie hush clung on and on, until the voice of a tiny girl, perhaps five or six, cried out, "Is he the man who killed my granny?" Her mother, without answering, led the child away by the hand.

On another memorable occasion I fell into conversation with an Israeli youth of twelve. In weeks he would celebrate his bar-mitzvah, just as Israel itself would turn thirteen. He was terribly puzzled. His school history books described the prowess of Israeli soldiers in the two wars they had fought up to then — the War of Independence in 1948-49 and the Suez campaign of 1956. He simply could not understand how Jews were slaughtered in Europe. "Why didn't they send in the Israeli army to save them?" he asked.

Of course no Israeli army existed until 1948. Many Israeli parents, particularly those who had escaped Europe or outlived refugee terror, deliberately sought to shield their children from what they regarded as the unbearable past. That attitude changed over the years, as young Israelis learned, thanks partly to the Eichmann trial, how six million Jews were not led en masse to their graves. Instead they were victims, in small numbers, of the most sinister and efficient timetable of genocide ever devised.

Today Israeli children receive frank schooling and visit Yad Vashem, the memorial to the Holocaust in Jerusalem, and Beth Hatefutsoth, the museum of the Jewish diaspora in Tel Aviv. They acquire a deep understanding of the tragic period — and some glory such as the Warsaw ghetto uprising — known to their parents and grandparents. But in those days, starting in April 1961, many older people refused to tune in the radio carrying live the proceedings from Beit Ha'am. They could not endure a ceaseless reminder of the doom of loved ones or their own escape from death. That, too, changed after a short while — days in some cases, weeks in others. Gradually, all Israel tuned in on the Eichmann trial.

A year had passed since Eichmann's abduction in Buenos Aires, where he worked in an auto assembly plant and lived with his family on Garibaldi Street, in a lower-middle-class neighborhood. He called himself Ricardo Klement, but agents of Mossad, the Israeli intelligence service that tracked him down, referred to him by the code name Attila. They seized him moments after he alighted from a bus near his home, and pushed him into a car. Drugged and disguised as a drunken El Al steward to avoid Argentinian or neo-Nazi scrutiny, he was flown to Israel.

Former SS Obersturmführer Adolf Eichmann, familiar from his youthful picture in SS uniform with high-crowned hat, now appeared unfamiliar in his mid-fifties. Earphones rigidly in place, he sat in the dock dressed in a dark blue suit, white shirt, and tie of horizontal stripes, issued by the Israelis. He wore this combination like a uniform, day after day. Baldness reached over his forehead. Now he wore eyeglasses, where before there were none. But witnesses recognized him all too well. Moritz Fleischmann spoke haltingly, and obviously in pain, when he recalled what Eichmann told him and a half dozen other leaders of Vienna's Jewish community. Austria, Eichmann said, would finally be cleared of all Jews "in the shortest possible way."

"Who said that?" asked the Israeli prosecutor.

"He, Eichmann," replied Fleischmann.

"Do you remember his face?"

"Yes, though he was younger then and wore no spectacles."

"Younger than when?"

"Younger than today."

"Do you see him today?"

Fleischmann paused, as though catching his breath, and peered at the dock. There was total stillness in the room. Then Fleischmann said, "Yes, he is here opposite me. I do identify him."

Moshe Beisky told of the horrors at his concentration camp, where the children were led away to the sound of lullabies over loud speakers, never again to see their tormented mothers. "We were put to work for the SS disinfection unit in the ghetto of Riga," said Leona Neumann. "The clothing of people already killed was sent to us for cleaning, disinfection and repair. It was later sent to German clothing stores. One day one of the men screamed. He recognized the bloodstained coat of his little daughter who had been shot."

Other witnesses recounted the method of gassing, and how bodies were heaped in carts and hauled to the ovens. Still others described the pulverizing of bones in grinding machines, and the dispersal of ashes. The verbal testimony of scores of men and women was augmented by written evidence drawn from millions of documents — originals and microfilms kept by methodical Germans and now in storage at Yad Vashem.

Throughout his trial Eichmann maintained two arguments: one, that he was simply a soldier obeying orders; two, he was merely a transport officer, responsible for getting prisoners to concentration camps but not what happened to them there. The prosecution argued that, as head of the Gestapo's Jewish section, he supervised the Nazi policies of deportation, slave labor, torture, medical experimentation, and mass murder in the concentration camps.

For the witnesses it was obviously a gruelling experience reliving their nightmares. For Israelis generally there was reaffirmation, if any was needed, of the crucial importance of preserving a homeland where any Jew, from anywhere, could find sanctuary. The messages, the notes of irony, were almost endless. In his cell Eichmann ate the kosher food of Israel. West German legal observers, who stayed at the Holy Land Hotel, learned about matzo during the Passover period. They kept an awkward distance from other guests at the hotel. The time had not yet arrived when Germans were welcomed by Jews.

What about the prisoner, the person, Eichmann himself? What was my reaction to him? When I first saw him I thought the remarkable feature about Eichmann was that he looked so unremarkable — he might pass on the street for a book salesman or a bank accountant. Nor did I believe he was sadistic, that he derived sick pleasure from his task. Such an explanation would have been too simple, too neat. It was more frightening than that, and it took time to realize the real simplicity: He was a dedicated civil servant, in the old German style — methodical, conscientious — but found, I am sure, in some measure, in every country of the world.

A revealing clue to the make-up of this kind of person, of the rigidity of character and position, materialized during the Israeli police interrogation of Eichmann. At one point his chief examiner, Captain Avner Less, confronted Eichmann with Gestapo documents marked "top secret," intended for lieutenant-colonels and over. Now, fifteen years later, years in which he had masked himself as a civilian, *Colonel* Eichmann could not forget his rank. "*Captain* Less," he said, "you can't possibly expect me to discuss these with you?"

7 From Canaan to Fink's

IT WAS ALSO IN 1961 THAT I WAS INTRODUCED to Fink's bar and restaurant, a tiny establishment filled with color and lore. Fink's was situated in the heart of West Jerusalem, as distinct from the nearby walled Old City, still in the hands of the Jordanians. Its founder, Moshe Fink, a Hungarian émigré, stepped ashore in Palestine in 1933 laden with a large container of jam and a love for Zionism. Wrapped in paper and concealed in the jam was an automatic pistol, complete with magazine and bullets. A British security officer at dock side, looking for just such weapons, dug his finger into the jam, pronounced it delectable and missed the rest of the contents.

The pistol was Fink's first contribution to the Haganah, the undercover Jewish defence organization. It was not his last, for the restaurant that he opened in 1935 quickly became a *sleak*, the Hebrew word for a hidden arsenal. In this instance the implications were broad. Fink's *sleak* was a secret central post office, with Haganah agents relaying messages to one another from various parts of the country. Zionist leaders and intellectuals, such as philosopher Martin Buber, congregated there, but so did lesser, anonymous figures in the Haganah.

It was an age of colorful, enterprising individuals. David Rothschild had arrived in Palestine from his native Bavaria soon after Hitler took power in 1933. A construction worker, he helped to build, among other things, a golf course for the British. He also carried crates in a soda-bottling plant, and then he took a job as a waiter, saving enough money so that by 1946 he could enter Fink's as a partner. Rothschild ran the bar while Fink taught him the restaurant business. Within months Rothschild was on the way to becoming sole owner.

The next two years, 1947 and 1948, were among the most dramatic in the story of Fink's, for the very beginning and the early survival of a Jewish state, and all within it, were at stake. The British announced that, after troublesome decades of trying to run Palestine under old mandate commitments, they were pulling out. On November 29, 1947 the United Nations voted to divide Palestine between the Arabs and Jews. Rothschild, in ecstasy when the news came over the radio, joined the customers who ran out to King George V Avenue, shouting, "We have a state!"

The celebration was premature. The Jews accepted the partition plan, but the Arabs rejected it. Even before the British withdrawal the Arabs began their attacks, besieging Jerusalem. The Haganah over the years had accumulated rudimentary caches of rifles and other small weapons — some smuggled in from abroad, others home-made. Now they accelerated their efforts. Particularly crucial was the obtaining of heavy equipment — and the logical course was through British soldiers in covert, illegal deals.

The British liked Fink's — it was central and the only real bar in Jerusalem in those days. For Rothschild there was no dilemma. While he was reluctant to admit unescorted women he did not know, he was also a long-standing member of the Haganah. He asked no questions. At least some of the women who came in with British officers and sergeants, or met them at the bar, were Haganah agents. Trades were arranged in cash or kind.

During the last months of the mandate, the Haganah managed to build its arsenal. Enterprising British soldiers brought half-tracks or lorries and parked them in the courtyard of a former German school, around the corner from Fink's. Haganah drivers took them away. Some contained rifles and light machine guns, others uniforms. When the Haganah was able to emerge openly as the first Jewish army in two thousand years, it wore British battle dress.

The greatest coup came with the acquisition of two armored cars equipped with two-inch guns. These proved invaluable. Jerusalem was cut off by Jordanian troops. On April 20, 1948, a convoy, attempting to break through from Tel Aviv, came under severe attack. The Palmach, Haganah's striking force, rushed out reinforcements from Jerusalem including one of the armored cars. It saved the convoy.

I find it easy to imagine the clandestine whispers and old happenings in a dim interior, the lighting and atmosphere of Fink's unchanged over the years. The combined bar and restaurant is diminutive — nine metres in length, five in width — and contains only six tables with a maximum seating capacity of twenty-five. The bar was, and still is, flanked by a dozen tall, tightly packed stools. This legendary character remains intact.

Media representatives of scores of countries, after listening to harrowing details about Eichmann during the day, unwound at night at Fink's. One of the devotees, Bill Corrigan, of New York Irish heritage, sat at the bar wearing a black *yarmulke*, skull cap, with the white letters PRESS — a gift from his NBC colleagues. Fink's provided more than good drinks and food. We enjoyed Rothschild's recounting how British and Haganah intelligence officers sat on these very bar stools, pumping one another and sometimes even swapping information. The nights were enlivened when Haganah veterans joined us and provided details that not many years back were secret.

Inevitably there was the story of how, seconds after British police vacated their headquarters in the old Russian compound, Haganah agents entered it, preventing Arabs from seizing this strategic position. The pre-arrangement, including an exchange of money, was conducted at Fink's. Rothschild, in shrugging off Fink's role, appended the usual disclaimer, "It was not my business." He expressed his philosophy: "The difference between a restaurateur and a journalist is that you can write what you know. I must shut up with what I know."

Fink's was to prove my mecca on almost every subsequent visit. My appearance sometimes was only ritualistic — to see David

Rothschild and whether he had made any changes in his martinis or establishment. In the thirty years I have known it, there have been no changes. But I suppose nothing will ever duplicate 1961, when Fink's provided a gathering place of inestimable camaraderie and recreational value.

The kidnapping of Eichmann, and his hearing, had a double purpose: to educate a young generation about the fate of Jews during the Nazi era; to remind the world that the hunt for surviving perpetrators was not over. By inference there was a third message: no longer could Jews be persecuted without an organized state demanding justice. Not since 70 A.D., when the Romans destroyed Jerusalem, had any Jew been in a position to judge crimes against his people. A Dutch journalist who sat next to me in Beit Ha'am remarked: "I cannot get over the absence of emotion, the respect this court has for the law."

The Eichmann trial lasted more than four months, followed by nearly four months of deliberations by the tribunal. On December 10, 1961 the three judges delivered their verdict of guilt on all counts of crimes against humanity and the Jewish people. Eichmann was hanged and cremated on May 31,1962, his ashes scattered at sea to discourage any attempt by fanatics to transform a burial site into a shrine. He was the only person ever executed in the state of Israel.

Many years later, in 1991, I read a book, *Eichmann In My Hands*, by one of Eichmann's Mossad captors, Peter Z. Malkin. Technically, Malkin was the first Israeli to get his hands on Eichmann. He leapt at him, knocking him to the ground near his home in Buenos Aires. Malkin's concluding words: "Evil does not exist in isolation. It is the product of amorality by consensus. Could it happen again? Who can say? I only know it is a question which we must never stop asking." The Israeli response — "never again" — is at the bedrock of caution in dealing with the Palestine

Liberation Organization or any state whose trustworthiness is in doubt.

Looking back at the Eichmann trial, I would like to have seen more emphasis on the broader indictment: crimes against humanity, against people generally. Revenge by Jews was only part of the drama. The message that needed — and still needs — to be underscored is that no longer can a handful of men decide indiscriminately, without facing consequences, whether masses of innocent people should live or die. In 1993 the world tumbled to this question, and at least sought solutions, in the horror of "ethnic cleansing" that permeated the civil war in the former Yugoslavia.

My next contact with Israel, June 1967, came in hasty departure for what turned out to be the Six-Day War, though, of course, no one expected it to end so quickly. Getting to the front — or rather, fronts, involving the Sinai, the Golan Heights, Jordan — was relatively easy. The government press office provided buses for foreign journalists who didn't mind group travel. Or you could rent a car — or hail a taxi! There was no problem in Tel Aviv finding any number of cab drivers — veterans of the 1948 War of Independence or the Suez campaign of 1956 — too old now for active service but eager to see what was going on. They were willing to drive you, provided you had the necessary fare (negotiable in advance) and your Israeli press pass to get you through military check points. This seemingly crazy way to cover a war was not unprecedented. At one point in World War II you could take a tramway in Antwerp to within strolling distance of the front.

I shared a cab from Tel Aviv to Jerusalem with novelist Saul Bellow, there for *Newsday*. I'd introduced myself to him in the airport at Athens while we — with scores of others — waited for El Al flights to resume service after a brief security hiatus. We had talked cursorily about Montreal and a suburb, Lachine, where Bellow was born and spent his boyhood.

Now the objective was to enter Jerusalem's walled Old City — for nearly twenty years, since 1948, in Jordanian possession, with barbed wire and machine guns denying entry to Jews. Almost as though calculated by a West Jerusalem welcoming committee, there, on King George V Avenue, with a parcel under his arm, stood David Rothschild. We waved to one another.

Israeli soldiers were clearing away the last Jordanian soldiers from East Jerusalem. The whole of the city fell into Israeli hands. It was a short walk through narrow alleys into biblical history, to the remnant of the wall that once surrounded Herod's temple, with some of the stones supposedly dating back to Solomon's temple. Jews for two thousand years mourned at this wall the destruction of their temple. It became known as the Wailing Wall or the Western Wall. Standing there now were unshaven Jewish soldiers, some just staring, some worshipping, a few thrusting hastily scribbled notes of prayer in the stone cracks before going again into combat. They were smelly from the sweat and tension of battle, the apotheosis of "dirty Jews."

I felt emotional, and I knew what my father, dead sixteen years, would have felt. In his memory I said the only words in Hebrew I could recall, "Baruch atah adonoy...." They were the wrong words — "Blessed are you, our God..." — used in common prayer. I should have recited some of the *kaddish,* the prayer for the dead, but I didn't remember it.

Many years later I recounted to an Israeli how I touched the stone wall and it was so sententious it felt hot. "The month was June," said he. "What did you expect? A cold wall?" It was a characteristic, dour reaction. Israelis abide no nonsense. That was borne out only days after the capture of the Old City, when realism arrived in the form of security.

To me, there was something symbolic, not only about the Western Wall but the approaches to it — the constricted lanes, the proximity of old buildings. The wall was separated from facing houses by an alley no wider than fifteen feet, almost the embodiment of Jewish confinement or oppression over the centuries. But the narrowness also denoted difficulty of protection against Arab sniping or ambushing or even Jewish crushing. Thousands of Israelis, on a pilgrimage or simply sightseeing, streamed in to visit the Western Wall. The government decreed the demolition of adjacent buildings and the creation of a huge open square. It offered space and defence, but it took away some of my sensation of awe.

I don't know what Bellow felt. Ten years later, reading his memoir, *To Jerusalem and Back*, I still didn't know. But he referred to something in another region that had escaped my attention: so many canvas or burlap sacks, which must have fallen from speeding trucks, lying scattered in the Sinai desert. It was only after a while that he realized they contained the bodies of Egyptian soldiers. This was his first glimpse of a battlefield, and it shook him. Maybe I was too acclimated after European war scenes to absorb the sight. But I did record an oddity: thousands of pairs of empty boots — abandoned by terrified Egyptian soldiers, most of peasant stock and poverty, who could run faster barefoot in the sand.

From the start it was apparent that Israelis were on the way to a stunning victory. In the first three hours of warfare they gained mastery of the skies, and in the next three days control of the Sinai and west bank of the Jordan river. By the time of the cease-fire they occupied the Golan Heights, from where Syrian artillery since 1948 had fired at will on Israeli kibbutz settlements and fishermen in the Sea of Galilee below. But I had no idea of the scope of the triumph when I leapt at an invitation from the press department. It was to join three other foreign newsmen — a Briton, an American, a Frenchman — to make the first complete swing through the Sinai Peninsula, starting with the Gaza strip and ending at the bottom tip, Sharm el-Sheikh.

We took off from Tel Aviv in an Israeli air force C-47, the fuselage painted in green and brown camouflage, with the Star of David on wing tips. The last time I had flown in one of these old workhorses was to watch the German surrender at Reims. Now two graphic highlights imbedded themselves in my mind. The first was the view, as we swung low — about two hundred feet — over the Mitla pass, a major route through barren hills about forty kilometres east of the Suez Canal.

Of all the hellish scenes I had seen in World War II, nothing matched that of the Mitla Pass. Here Egyptian tanks funnelled together from several directions, and here they ended in a mass graveyard. Israeli fighter-bombers had hit the leading tanks and blocked passage to the tanks behind. These in turn were picked off by Israeli armor. Egyptian tanks sprawled over the road and tumbled into ravines in huge clusters, like dead black beetles rolled over on their backs. There were hundreds upon hundreds of them.

By 1973 the Egyptians were going to show skill in modern warfare. But in 1967, still of *fellaheen*, or peasant, simplicity, they could not cope with the sophisticated Soviet equipment in their hands. I remember the words of an Israeli gunnery major who, sitting next to me in the plane, peered down in silence at the devastation and then said: "It's like giving a gold fountain pen to someone who can't read or write. What will he do with it?" Left unsaid was another point. The Egyptians lacked Israeli motivation: survival.

The second lingering image is of Sharm el-Sheikh, the promontory at the south end of Sinai Peninsula. Control of it meant control of the Straits of Tiran and any ships heading for Israel from the Red Sea. It was the closing of the straits by Egypt's President Nasser, and the fear that Egypt and Syria were about to attack, that led Israel to strike first on Monday morning, June 5. Now it was Sunday, June 11, and the fighting was finished.

Sharm el-Sheikh turned out to be enigmatic. The approaches, as we came across the Gulf of Suez, looked about as hospitable as the face of the moon — sandy cliffs bereft of living matter. The C-47 propellers churned up a cloud of dust, obscuring the horizon. But once we alighted, we could see the clear blue waters of the Straits of Tiran and the Red Sea. Israeli soldiers, with little else to do except fight the heat now, swam in the Red Sea. There were no local inhabitants. There never had been, except a few wandering Bedouins. Egyptian garrison troops had fled with their artillery, leaving behind mounds of shells, rations of dates, and Soviet trucks. "For the Egyptians this was just a piece of sand," said the gunnery major. "For us it was life or death."

I spent several days on follow-up stories: the last of the Arab snipers cleared from the Gaza strip; the return of young soldiers, and couples strolling hand in hand down Dizengoff Street in Tel Aviv; the Israeli fears of a sell-out by the United Nations; the gratitude toward the United States for its moral, material and financial support. But I wanted something that might round it all up, put the war and its aftermath into sensitive and knowledgeable perspective. How should I go about it?

One afternoon, relaxing beside the pool at the Tel Aviv Hilton, the answer struck me: an interview with David Ben-Gurion. He was the one person — the revered father of modern Israel, the prime minister who led his country through its first two wars — whose words would carry great substance. Now eighty, in retirement, Ben-Gurion spent most of his time on a small kibbutz, Sde Boker, in the Negev. He also retained his old home in Tel Aviv. Where was he now? More important, who did I know who could help me get an appointment? Ben-Gurion granted few interviews.

Pondering these questions, between laps, I suddenly thought of an article I had read years ago. The theme was about the virtue of the direct approach. The article cited an example of the editor of the *New York Herald Tribune* who wanted to meet with Bernard Baruch, financier and adviser to every U.S. president from Woodrow Wilson to Dwight Eisenhower. The editor called the chief of his bureau in Washington to see if he knew anyone who knew Baruch; he got his managing editor to check other possible sources. Meanwhile, a cub reporter, observing the commotion, looked up the Manhattan phone book under "B," found a listing, and dialed a number. A man answered, the reporter asked,

"May I speak with Mr. Bernard Baruch?" The man said, "Baruch speaking."

I climbed from the pool, took the elevator to the sixth floor (I occupied Room 621), sat on the edge of the bed in my wet swim suit, and picked up the phone. The hotel operator came on. "Could you please get me David Ben-Gurion," I said. "One moment, sir," she said. I heard the quick ringing. At least it was not long distance. Then another woman's voice, in Hebrew, "Kem." Yes. I said: "May I speak with Mr. Ben-Gurion, please?" The voice answered in English, "Who wants him?"

I gave my name and the name of my newspaper.

"So, what do you want?"

I said, "May I ask who I'm speaking to?"

"Who?" she echoed in exasperation. "This is Paula, who else?"

It then registered: the legendary Paula Ben-Gurion, David Ben-Gurion's wife of a half century who zealously protected him from all intruders. I explained that I had covered the war, and would be very grateful for an interview with the former prime minister.

"Impossible," said Paula. "A thousand journalists have asked."

I was not going to argue that only six hundred foreigners had been accredited. I pleaded on the grounds that Canadians had always felt fondly about David Ben-Gurion. I got nowhere. I tried other approaches. Nothing worked. Finally, before quitting, I said, "*Nu*, Mrs. Ben-Gurion, I hope your grandsons came through the war all right." A catch-all Yiddish word, "nu" is literally untranslatable ("so? well?") but as international as chopped liver.

There was stillness on the other end. Then Paula spoke again, "You said your name is Clark. You used 'nu.' You're a Jewish boy?"

Before I could answer, she added hastily, "Not that it matters!"

Forty minutes later I was sitting in David Ben-Gurion's study in his modest home in central Tel Aviv. I asked the obvious question: Will a peace agreement now become possible? Ben-Gurion said that peace in the Middle East depended first on Nasser, and if Nasser remained stubborn it depended next on relations between the Soviet Union and the United States, and these in turn depended on the unity of Europe. Thus, in a concise sentence, one of the most celebrated and profound men of the age summarized for me the complexity of an Arab-Israeli settlement.

We sat for an hour in a study that contained thousands of books spilling into two adjacent rooms. On one subject he spoke in harmony with the huge majority of Israelis: the future of the reunified Jerusalem was not open to negotiations. He pointed out that if the Arabs had accepted the United Nations partition plan of 1947 Jerusalem would be an international zone today. But now that it was in Israeli hands, after long denial of admission of Jews to the Old City, it was too late to go back even to international status. I was to hear in the 1990s the same argument from even the most liberal and flexible of Israelis.

But back then, in 1967, Ben-Gurion was more farsighted and moderate than many of his old colleagues. He would, for instance, return the Sinai Peninsula, including Sharm el-Sheikh, once Egypt agreed to sign a peace treaty. More astonishing still, he would also return to Syria the Golan Heights.

Ben-Gurion's proposals depended on one essential: inducing Arab leaders to sit at the same conference table with Israelis. "How do you get them to do it?" I said. Ben-Gurion looked like a tiny, innocent pixy with his bushy white hair and open-neck shirt, but really he was a hardheaded individual who had dealt closely with Arabs most of his adult life. He just shrugged. Plainly he did not know. "But one thing is clear," he said. "No other Arab state will make peace until Nasser decides to." And if Nasser remains immovable, will Israel continue to sit in the Sinai indefinitely? "In history," said Ben-Gurion with emphasis, "there is no such word as indefinitely."

The extent of Ben-Gurion's prescience took on more meaning with the passage of time. In 1979 Nasser's successor, Anwar Sadat, did sign a peace treaty, and the Sinai reverted to Egypt. Israelis and Syrians still debated the future of the Golan Heights. But the improved climate of Middle East diplomacy in mid-1994 raised hopes for a settlement. Arabs and Jews were getting to sit at the same conference table, thanks largely to a new relationship between Washington and Moscow. In a striking example, Israel and Jordan reached an agreement ending their state of war that had lasted forty-six years. By December 1994 Jordanian and Israeli tourists crossed the frontier in both directions.

My interview with Ben-Gurion was a lovely experience, and a two-letter word had brought it about. I celebrated by driving to Jerusalem and Fink's. Jerusalem was shelled during the Six-Day War, but David Rothschild greeted me with the exclamation, "We never closed." Not even the Windmill Theatre of wartime London made this claim more proudly.

In Montreal visitors to Expo 67 overwhelmed a boutique featuring Israeli goods. Such was the sentiment for Israel that they bought every copy the owners could import of the hit recording *Jerusalem of Gold*. In New York, and on television, comedians wrote and rewrote jokes about Superman. In this instance Superman was an Israeli, taking on single-handedly hordes of Arab marauders. The image of the Jew as a fighting man had never stood taller. Jews of the Diaspora luxuriated in the glory.

Israelis? Almost from the start they decried the euphoria. The Six-Day War was a traumatic experience. For them the reality was how to survive amid unyielding massive hostility. Even with victory there remained the collective fear that the Arabs needed to win only one battle — and that would be the end of Israel and probably of its inhabitants.

Some Israelis derived comfort from the feeling that a buffer now existed. Within days demonstrators paraded outside the Knesset, Israel's parliament, with banners: "Do not return occupied areas." But there was little doubt that most were prepared to accept a peace settlement on almost any terms, including a withdrawal from land they had not coveted in the first place.

In two years I was back in Israel, and by now a depressing letdown had set in — a realization that another generation remained trapped in the perennial state of emergency that began in 1948. The country had a new prime minister, Mrs. Golda Meir, and the same old problems. "We are told over and over again," she said when I interviewed her, "that we cannot press Nasser to make peace with Israel because he is frustrated, and modern psychology teaches that when a person is frustrated you must deal carefully with him."

She paused only momentarily and went on: "What is he frustrated about? That he wanted to destroy us — every man, woman and child of us — and he just didn't succeed, so he is frustrated? What are we asking of him? That we want to occupy Egypt? We are asking him, 'All right, you tried and couldn't make it. Now we want peace with you.' I don't know where there has ever been a situation where people luckily won the war, and then turned around to the loser and said, 'Would you please come and sit with us so we can have peace?'" Golda Meir was a shrewd and tough woman.

My work in Montreal took a fresh turn in 1968. Frank B. Walker, a protégé of George Ferguson on *The Winnipeg Free Press,* replaced Ferguson when he retired as editor-in-chief of *The Star.* I became the editor, with responsibility mainly for the editorial and opposite editorial pages. Walker, who served as a naval officer in World War II and later a war correspondent, was an old colleague. Our temperaments complemented one another's. He lived for the paper, day and night — but inside the walls of *The Star's* new building. Rarely did he leave Montreal, spurning even vacations. By contrast I still sought big events in the outside world.

Walker, sensitive to the changes in Quebec, hired several French-Canadian reporters. But the international scene continued to rate prime importance. Our bureaus expanded from London and Paris to Bonn and Moscow. Walker encouraged my travels, believing individual reportage built the paper's personality. One of the minor challenges in his life was to see if he could locate me by phone when I was on a trip abroad. Sometimes it wasn't difficult. He knew I frequented Fink's in Jerusalem. On two occasions he reached me there. He just wanted to know if the martinis were properly chilled.

Mrs. Golda Meir was still prime minister when the Egyptians struck on Yom Kippur day, October 6, in 1973. This time the Egyptian leader, Anwar Sadat, nearly succeeded. Faulty reading of intelligence reports left Israel unprepared. Dumbfounded reservists rushed from synagogues in prayer shawls to join their units. Front-line soldiers along the Suez Canal took a terrible beating. But the outside world knew little of any setback.

I got there a day later — with hundreds of other reporters — thinking this might be a repeat of 1967. I even retraced my routine of six years ago — a taxi from the airport directly to Beit Sokolov, the government press centre in Tel Aviv, without even a pause at a hotel. It was nearly midnight, and indeed like old times. There on duty as a military spokesman was a reservist with whom I became friendly in 1967 — Meron Medzini, in regular life a political science professor (his mother had migrated from Milwaukee to Palestine with Golda Meir in 1921).

On the street, outside Beit Sokolov, I even ran into another political scientist I knew from McGill University — Michael Brecher, who now taught at Hebrew University in Jerusalem. He and some colleagues were going to drive up to the Golan Heights out of curiosity — just like the restless taxi drivers did during the Six-Day War.

But this was not old times. It was not a Six-Day War. The Egyptians later called it, not without justification, the Six-Hour War, in reference to how long it took them to cross the Suez Canal, penetrating deep into Israeli positions. No longer did thousands of discarded boots litter the desert. Instead, Egyptian infantrymen rode on the side of tanks — in the style of Russians in World War II — and they attacked in wave after wave, heedless of casualties.

At first the public accepted Golda Meir's explanation that the Israeli decision not to strike first, as in 1967, was a political one to avoid world condemnation. But after a few days, everyone seemed to know that over-confidence was to blame. At two p.m. on Yom Kippur, on two separate fronts, the Egyptians and Syrians made their coordinated assault. Why were some Israeli soldiers on the Suez line taking afternoon naps? Why were some on the Golan Heights taking showers? These were the nagging questions.

The simple fact was that Israeli generals, who enjoyed a reputation for unorthodoxy, turned out to be much like generals anywhere at almost any stage in history. They allowed this war to start where the last one had left off. They thought that any Arab attack would conform to the old pattern, that it would be preceded by a long artillery barrage, giving Israelis time to bring up reserves. Instead, the Egyptians came across the Suez Canal in full daylight, in amphibious tanks and rubber dinghies, so swiftly and with such skill that one Israeli lieutenant told me that he was not sure whether the men approaching his outpost from the rear were Israeli reinforcements or Egyptian infiltrators.

I alternated fronts in my coverage — one day the long, long drive to the Suez sector, the next to the closer, but equally exhausting, Golan Heights. The Israelis never felt hatred for Egyptians; at worst they thought Egyptians misguided, and, at least until this war, innocents without any ability to fight. By contrast, there was a deep loathing of Syrians — who were, in the Israeli mind, unscrupulous and bloodthirsty, exemplified by the pre-1967 shelling of the Galilee region. The feeling was reciprocated. Syrians detested Israelis. The virulent language on both sides was identical. Listen to this: "Of course hatred can exist when our prisoners are tortured and killed." An Israeli talking? No, it was Syria's deputy foreign minister, Abdul Ghani al Rafai, speaking to me a year later in Damascus.

Now, on the Golan Heights, I stood on the main road, fourteen kilometres inside Syria and only forty from Damascus. It was the road taken by St. Paul and, in more modern times, enabled British General Edmund Allenby and his allied troops to complete the disintegration of the Ottoman empire in 1918. An Israeli tank rumbled by, white Hebrew letters painted crudely on its muddy side: "There is a God. Forward to Damascus." But the Israelis did not intend to reach the Syrian capital. Their preoccupation was with the other front and the much bigger force of Egyptians.

In two weeks there had been a turnabout — enough to get Israeli armor across the Suez Canal but not enough to alleviate the disconsolate Israeli mood. This was a nation of sadness, mourning not only its dead but its faith in peace and hope for the future. It began on the personal level, for the mother who had a premonition about her son. She sat by the window waiting for the government team that conveyed the news of a fatality, that tried to console and to comfort. When the team — a social worker, a psychiatrist, another mother with experience of grief — did arrive, she simply said, "Just tell me where it was and when. Then leave me alone. I prefer to cry in privacy." An Israeli friend of mine, who recounted the incident, added, "We are all crying in privacy."

Much of the sorrow was in the sense of futility, of bitterness that history had not delivered a measure of security. Were Israelis destined to fight a war every six years, as they had since the country's creation? The haunting question came into everyday conversation.

There were some heartening notes — the determined fashion, for instance, in which the United States came to Israel's side. "I had two immediate fears when the Arabs attacked," said a Jerusalemite. "The first was the casualties we would suffer, and that fear remains. The second was of strangulation, of being left without supplies, without replacement of equipment. I am not an emotional man. But yesterday, when I saw an American transport flying overhead, I wanted to weep with joy. I felt there is a lifeline after all."

That lifeline was crucial, and so was the cease-fire when it came after sixteen days. I spent the last night at the Suez Canal, huddled in a blanket against the chill desert air. In every war, it seems, no matter how mobile it becomes, there must be scenes reminiscent of films of World War I, with the night illuminated by flares sent up by both sides. I watched the flares and wondered. Had nothing changed? The Israelis had turned back the Egyptians and Syrians. It was victory because it was survival. But there could be no gloating, no joy.

What I could not know — what no one could know — was that a profound change was just beginning. Anwar Sadat was tired of seeing Egyptians, who had carried the main load in four wars with Israel, dying and bleeding themselves economically for other Arabs. He was also sufficiently confident, after restoring Egyptian pride and dignity in the first days of the Yom Kippur War, to start thinking of peace with Israel.

On November 19, 1977 — four years, one month, thirteen days after the outbreak of the Yom Kippur War — I stood with hundreds of Israelis outside the King David Hotel in Jerusalem awaiting the arrival of Sadat. I was to meet him for an interview in Cairo two years later, but I don't believe even that occasion matched the thrill of this moment under a star-filled sky in Jerusalem. Here was the president of Egypt, an old enemy of Israelis, plunging into their midst in an unprecedented gesture of faith and goodwill. It took enormous courage and statesmanship.

Walker Cronkite, the broadcaster, could take credit for acting as go-between. In separate television interviews, he threw the question of a meeting at Sadat and Menachem Begin, Israel's prime minister. Obviously feelers must have been underway through diplomats, but the Cronkite prodding enabled Sadat to accept the challenge. And now the jumble of impressions, most in disbelief, hopped one upon another. These mounted with the arrival of the Sadat plane, his standing in the open doorway on Israeli soil, blinking into the powerful array of television lights.

"Did you ever expect to see a sight like this in your lifetime?" I asked a twenty-three-year-old woman. She replied, "Not so soon, not so soon. Everyone said it would never be before I was sixty or seventy." How did she feel now? "Shivery," she said. "All shivery with excitement."

In hundreds of thousands of homes the television sets were on — indeed they stayed on all weekend — as families and groups of friends gathered to watch. Sadat started down the gangway, and some people broke into applause — in their homes, sixty kilometres from the airport. It was a spontaneous, instinctive gesture of friendship and welcome. If Sadat couldn't hear it, they could feel better for having expressed it. And when the Egyptian national anthem was played, followed by Hatikvah, the Israeli anthem, there were many twenty-three-year-olds, and fifty-three-year-olds, who felt all shivery inside.

I would like to know how many did not notice a lump in their throats. For Mrs. Rose Sheffer, fixed to the TV screen, it was an emotional ordeal. Her son David, a first-year law student, died in the Sinai in 1973, and now the man who ordered that war stood before her. Bitterness, hatred — did she feel these things? "No, no," she answered, then she sobbed and said, "Half my heart is with him, with Sadat, in my hope for peace. The other half is with my boy and all the other boys who lie in what I call the Hill of Youth. I thought, if only there could be a miracle. If only these boys could rise and rejoice with the nation."

But this aspect of tragedy is forgotten for the moment by others, if not by Mrs. Sheffer, for here comes the motorcade, the limousines with the dignitaries and security men, and now the car with Sadat approaching the King David Hotel. He steps out, and there is great applause — rather than wild cheering. Warm applause, but still with some inhibition — the self-restraint imposed by too many expectations in the past, too many disappointments. But maybe, maybe this time....

The next day in the Knesset, Sadat says, "We do not want to encircle each other with rockets or with missiles......I have come to establish peace." He also says that a Palestinian homeland is the "key to peace." This sends different shivers — negative ones — through Israelis, for the question of Palestinian rights has only arisen since Israel's conquests in 1967. Sadat and Begin make their final public remarks at a press conference held before eight hundred reporters. It is almost an anti-climax, productive of hand-shaking but no startling revelations for a peace formula.

It is all over in slightly more than forty-two hours, and Sadat is on his way home. Instantly the debate begins among Israelis. "Nothing good can come of the visit," says a taxi driver. "Wait, wait," agrees a switchboard operator. "It will be worse. All they want to do is push us into the sea." "You are wrong," says an academic. "This is a breakthrough, a historic event. No other Arab leader even concedes the reality of Israel's existence." Instant peace has not descended on Israel. Nor has instant war. In its place is something that has never been tried before: instant communication. When you communicate you can have hope. For the first time in thirty years, thanks to the massive requirements of the media, it is now possible to telephone from Israel to Cairo. Yes, says the dubious switchboard operator, but will the line be cut again?

In fact on March 26, 1979 a peace accord was signed by Sadat and Begin in Washington, under the patronage of President Jimmy Carter. There was little jubilation in Israel. For the average person the news was still difficult to comprehend. In the simplest terms Israel was returning the Sinai in exchange for peace with its biggest foe. But the nation's soul was divided, some recognizing the positive dimension, others fearing the elimination of the protective Sinai. A psychologist, Professor Hans Kreitler of Tel Aviv University, said this was not the kind of news that brings elation. In eleven years, since the 1967 war, people became accustomed to the security of buffer zones. "Peace is a promise," said Kreitler, "but the Sinai is real."

I marked the occasion with drinks and dinner at Fink's. David Rothschild remembered a journey my daughter Bette had taken with me from Cairo to Jerusalem, back in 1969. I remembered it, too, for Bette, thirteen, had picked up a stomach bug in Egypt, and Rothschild insisted on dispensing the cure: chicken soup. It worked. He also reminisced about another visitor, Henry Kissinger, one of the few illustrious figures who tried, and failed, to gain admission to the unparalleled institution that is Fink's.

Kissinger, the U.S. secretary of state, was conducting his shuttle diplomacy between Egypt and Israel in 1973 when an accompanying correspondent, Marvin Kalb of CBS, urged him to break away from the King David Hotel and dine at Fink's. A Kissinger lieutenant phoned Rothschild and said Kissinger would be coming along in an hour with a small group of aides — but for security reasons the restaurant must be emptied. Rothschild was not about to clear his tables and bar of faithful patrons — tourists as well as Jerusalemites — and said so.

Kissinger attempted on another occasion — "without prior conditions," as Rothschild, in the language of diplomacy, liked to put it. This time, however, it was for Friday night, and Fink's is closed on the sabbath eve. So Kissinger again failed, and Rothschild had to get along with the memories of Golda Meir, Moshe Dayan and other mere mortals who had favored his establishment. The publicity mileage, however, was considerable. Newspapers ran stories headed, "Kissinger Meets His Match."

8 Israel's Other Wars

ISRAEL DOESN'T NEED ARABS OR WARS to supply tension. It retains its own built-in stresses and strains. A simple illustration was provided for me one Friday evening when an old friend, Adin Talbar, drove me to his home for dinner. We had met in Montreal in 1960 when Talbar was Israeli consul for economic affairs. We kept in touch when he later took charge of foreign trade in Israel's ministry of trade, and now that he operated his own business running trade fairs.

Talbar was heading for his home on Bnai Brit Street in West Jerusalem. Bnai Brit adjoins Mea Shearim, the ultra-orthodox quarter. For twenty-four hours, under religious law, riding on the Sabbath is forbidden in Mea Shearim, and violators who by-pass police barricades risk stoning. Just as we were approaching Bnai Brit, three little girls, the oldest perhaps twelve, the youngest seven or eight, stepped into the roadway beyond the barricades and shouted, "Shabbat, Shabbat."

That was all. There was no heaving of stones, no abusive language — merely an innocuous reminder that this was the Sabbath. But it was enough for Talbar. He pulled up the car sharply and leaned from his window to call out at the girls. He had as many rights as they, he shouted, and they had to respect those rights, including the right to drive, just as he respected their rights to strict adherence to the Sabbath.

The girls, neat and shiny in their bright frocks, their hair tidily done up in braids, stood in silence while Talbar delivered his lecture. It was hard to judge if they were unnerved or embarrassed. Neither. They were just waiting for Talbar to pause, and then the twelve-year-old said, "But it is the Sabbath, and you know it is forbidden to ride on the Sabbath." "Yes," chimed in the youngest, "it is the Sabbath." Talbar tried his spiel once more, with the same unsatisfactory results. Then he drove off, muttering grimly, "The future generation — as rigid as their parents."

Not many months later, when I was back in Israel, the situation had turned mean and bloody. It was no longer just a question of riding on the Sabbath. It was a question of whether religious law was going to prevail. In some cities, notably Tel Aviv and Haifa, buses operate on the Sabbath and cinemas are open. In Jerusalem there is no public transport and cinemas are closed — or at least they were until a couple of owners found a loophole in municipal by-laws and decided to stay open. This, to the ultra-orthodox, known in Hebrew as *Haredim* ("those who are God-fearing"), meant warfare.

Jerusalem has a special meaning to the *Haredim*. They deliberately settled here, not because it is Israel's capital but because it is the Holy City. Indeed, for them Israel as a state does not exist; it will only deserve recognition after the Messiah arrives, and this will happen only when the purity of religious law has been fully established. In their eyes the opening of cinemas on the Sabbath, a day devoted to prayer and meditation, is desecration of the worst sort. To the secularists it is not unreasonable to go to the movies, especially since the cinemas do not encroach on *Haredi* territory.

Israeli Jews fall roughly into four categories: approximately forty-five per cent, either immigrants or Sabras (native-born), are non-observant; they rarely attend synagogue services. The next largest group, about thirty-five per cent, mostly Sephardim who are observant but not strictly so, call themselves "traditional Jews." "Orthodox" Jews, who are highly observant and regularly go to synagogues, comprise about fifteen per cent; they accept that secularism and Judaism can co-exist. The *Haredim* make up only about five per cent of the population, but their strength is political as well as religious.

Israel inherited Britain's parliamentary system, but not its penchant for two or three manageable parties. From the start, as many as a dozen fragmented parties have characterized Israeli politics. Ben-Gurion, even before the state existed, had to make peace with religious elements by agreeing that the Sabbath — from sundown Friday to sundown Saturday — would be the official day of rest. Problems of interpretation have followed ever since, and virtually every prime minister has had to accept religious demands in order to retain a majority in the Knesset.

Most recently *Haredi* politicians, who command only a few of the Knesset's one hundred and twenty seats (with more moderate religious parties occupying perhaps another eight seats), have held the balance of power between Labor and Likud. They are therefore courted. Yielding to the extremists can be costly in many ways. A veteran of El Al says wearily, "We are the only airline in the world that flies three hundred days a year." El Al is grounded on the Sabbath and High Holidays.

After witnessing a street clash between secular and *Haredi* demonstrators, I retreated to Fink's bar and said to David Rothschild, "It is sad to see Jew against Jew." "Why?" he retorted. "The *Haredim* do nothing for this country. They refuse to serve in the army. They stay in their yeshivas and pay no taxes. But if I want to drive on the Sabbath or go to a movie they won't let me. Is that freedom? I see nothing sad about hitting back — Jew or no Jew."

The next day I met with Dov Patkin, an Australian who portrayed himself as "a returnee to Judaism." Not far from his apartment in Mea Shearim a banner stretched across the street. In English, and intended for tourists, it warned, "Jewish daughter! The Torah obligates you to dress modestly!" This meant long sleeves, closed neckline, no slacks.

Patkin described his father as "a modern Jew" — a bomber pilot in the Royal Australian Air Force who was shot down and killed over Germany in 1944. Dov studied sociology and philosophy at the University of Melbourne. This led to an interest in religion:

"I wanted to rediscover my Jewish roots." So much so that in 1967 he gravitated to an ultra-orthodox Hassidic sect in Jerusalem. Now, at forty-seven, he divided his time between continued religious studies and teaching in a *yeshiva.*

Patkin paid no allegiance to contemporary Israel for a simple reason: "In 1948 a group of Jews decided to set up a state. They ignored the state of Israel that had been set up thousands of years ago and the Jews who have always been here enforcing the laws of Judaism. So the real question is, Who has to recognize whom?" He had an equally simple explanation for *Haredi* rejection of the army: "We cannot serve under generals who are not religious. My field marshal is God."

The *Haredim* count on increasing numbers from three sources: people like Patkin who are "returnees;" the migration of ultra-orthodox Jews from the United States and Canada; and a high birth rate. The average number of children in *Haredi* families is eight, in secular families 2.2 — a procreation pattern that is worrisome to the seculars. Patkin is the father of ten, ranging from nineteen years to four months; he is also a grandfather.

"Do you encourage your children to go out and demonstrate?" I asked him.

"On the contrary," he said. "I forbid them. It's not safe."

"Do you demonstrate?"

"Of course I do. I have no choice. When my rabbis tell me to go out to remind people of the joys of the Sabbath, I obey. It is written in the Torah."

It is precisely this kind of fundamentalism that agitates the seculars and other non-*Haredim.* "It's no different from Khomeneism," says Adin Talbar's son, Asa, a sophisticated young publicist who lives in Tel Aviv. Another group also upsets Asa: the Jews who settle the West Bank. "If I'm driving through the West Bank and see an Arab looking for a lift, and he doesn't appear threatening, I'll give it to him," he says. "But I won't to a Jew if I think he's from a settlement." The enmity applies particularly to members of

Gush Emunim ("Bloc of the Faithful"), a religious Zionist movement that originated in 1974, a year after the Yom Kippur war, when Israeli spirits were low. People met in private homes to discuss what might be done to minimize Israel's vulnerability.

One of them, as I recall it, said, "We decided that the Arabs had no intention of coming to the peace table voluntarily, but maybe we could make them come if they saw we were here to stay. Besides, Judea and Samaria were not ours to give back. God gave the area to us. How could we give it back?"

Judea and Samaria are the Biblical references to what the rest of the world knows as the West Bank, which covers nearly six thousand square kilometres. Thus, twin motivations — security and religion — pushed a movement into aggressive political action. The first Gush Emunim settlement, Kedumim, was established — without government approval — in 1975 near the militantly pro-Palestine town of Nablus. Yitzhak Rabin, who had replaced Golda Meir as prime minister, ordered the settlers to leave. They simply squatted and organized religious services.

To people like Professor Yeshayahu Leibowitz, a noted authority on Judaism as well as biochemistry, Gush Emunim represented "paganism, not Zionism." But the movement continued to expand and the number of settlements multiplied.

When I first saw Kedumim in 1977 it was little more than a collection of pre-fabricated huts and trailers alongside dirt roads. One of the residents, Mrs. Daniella Weiss, of American and Polish parentage, was a teacher of English literature. A decade later Mrs. Weiss was Gush Emunim's general-secretary. She still lived in Kedumim, but now she and her husband, an importer of precious metals and exporter of jewelry, and four children occupied a villa of five bedrooms and two bathrooms.

Kedumim had grown from ten families to three hundred — a community with gardens and pavements and shops but no changes in ideology. "Judea and Samaria is where our nation was molded," said Mrs. Weiss. "We are here to stay. If the Arabs get this message from us consistently, they will seek their national expression somewhere else."

The *Gush Emunim* movement received early encouragement from Menachem Begin and his Likud bloc. Following Likud's election victory in 1977 the settlement of occupied territories was not confined to religious zealots. As deliberate government policy to establish a stronger Jewish presence, secular Jews were encouraged to move to the West Bank. The inducement was largely economic — low-cost housing — though patriotism was also invoked.

In a place called Ariel the mayor, Ron Nachman, talks of how the neck of Israel was only fifteen kilometres wide before the 1967 war, leading to the constant fear that its severing would isolate Haifa and the north from the rest of the country. Now the West Bank provides a substantial buffer, with people like himself, halfway between the Jordanian border and the Mediterranean, arguing that they serve a vital function simply by being there. "There is a historic link," says Nachman, "but I'm talking about the security link. We, in Ariel, are the belly button of Israel."

Ariel did not exist until August 1978. Nachman, a thirty-five-year-old personnel director with Israel Military Industries, and fourth generation Israeli (his ancestors were among the first arrivals from Russia in 1882), led a group of forty families to put down roots in rocky and hilly countryside the Palestinians call "The Mountain of Death." Ten years later you approached Ariel through Arab olive groves, suddenly to encounter, not a primordial settlement but a modern town of eight thousand residents. With obvious pride they pointed to their shopping centre, day care centres, schools, public swimming pool and sports stadium.

Fifteen construction companies put up housing developments in the knowledge that land was cheap, and banks with government incentives were providing inexpensive mortgages. A two-bedroom apartment cost $42,000, a town house of four bedrooms and two bathrooms, $75,000 — thirty to sixty per cent less than comparable accommodation in Tel Aviv, forty kilometres away. Nachman liked to say "we're yuppies." Indeed, ninety per cent of the inhabitants were secular, most of them young professionals.

Dr. Mordechai Tamarkin, a thirty-five-year-old gynaecologist, had lived in Ariel eight years and thought nothing of the hour's drive to his hospital in Tel Aviv. "I treat it as a way of getting fresh air," he said. But there's much more: "I wanted to participate in what was going on in Israel, to continue the pioneering. For one who believes in holding the territory, as I do, it's important to stabilize it." But what about the Arabs whose lives have been disrupted? "They accept our existence in Samaria, because we are here and we have won the war."

The Arabs, of course, did not accept such existence. In 1987 a few Palestinians impulsively began what soon took on the markings of an uprising. To the astonishment of everyone — Palestinians as well as Israelis — it did not peter out. It continued as the *intifada*.

In 1979, on the eve of Sadat and Begin signing a treaty, I wrote a series of articles titled, "Can Israel survive peace?" The theme, about internal clashes, touched not only on *Haredim* but other broad categories of Jews. These were the Sephardim, of Middle East origin — so-called "Oriental" Jews — and Ashkenazim. The Ashkenazim looked to Europe for much of their culture and posture. All they shared with the Sephardim was religion.

Antagonism arrived with new immigrants. "Oriental" Jews claimed that Ashkenazic Jews dominated the country politically and economically, relegating the Orientals to menial jobs or sending them to settle remote areas close to dangerous Arab frontiers. There was some truth in the claim, but the Ashkenazim defended themselves on the grounds they possessed the experience of modern statehood, to say nothing of higher education, including a knowledge of technology. A graphic story of contrast, which I heard repeatedly, dealt with Operation Magic Carpet.

The name arose in the early days of Israel's formation, when a mixed fleet of old DC-3s and other planes belonging to the freshly organized airline, El Al, airlifted forty-five thousand Yemenites to the land of their ancestors. A simple, tough and honest people, the Yemenites had preserved their religion despite two thousand years of separation. But they could draw on little else to connect them to European Jews. Inhabitants of mountains and deserts of the Arabian peninsula, most had scant awareness of automobiles, let alone airplanes. Inevitably there was anxiety and nervousness as they waited to board the planes. But wise men among the Yemenites had said all would be well because it was happening as predicted in Leviticus: "And they shall be borne home on the wings of eagles."

The interior of the planes were primitive, equipped with neither stewardesses nor galleys. Therefore, when a young Yemenite entered the cockpit and offered an American radio operator, Joe Swery, a steaming cup of tea, he accepted it with gratitude. Then he jolted himself upright. Where had the tea come from? Swery dashed into the cabin. There, in the middle of the floor, squatted a group of men. They enjoyed a kettle of tea boiling over a Primus stove. Swery grabbed the kettle and doused the fire with the hot water. The story entered Israeli folklore as a hardy example of East and West coming together.

That coming together remained tenuous as late as the 1970s. The Orientals, most of whom lived in poor neighborhoods of Jerusalem, Tel Aviv and other cities, took to the streets in vehement demonstrations spearheaded by a militant group, the Black Panthers. The prime minister, the Labor party's Golda Meir, was quoted as saying, "What do they want? We have given them so much." The "we" and "they" attitude cost the Labor party dearly. It was a principal reason the Orientals, who numbered well over half the population, helped Menchem Begin's bloc come to office in the 1977 election.

Several years later, in 1988, I wrote about Israel's Fortieth anniversary — an anniversary regarded as significant because in Biblical terms it denotes the passage of a full generation. Which way were the Israelis heading? Toward a calmer future or continued agitation? One of the more grievous internal points of friction appeared close to resolution. A younger generation of Oriental and European Jews met in the army and began to understand and like one another. Many Sephardic and Ashkenazic Jews married.

Another important equalizer was economics. Orientals met success in the business world and professions. If you needed casual evidence, the Sonesta Hotel in Eilat, a Red Sea resort, offered it. Though Sephardim are usually of darker complexion than Ashkenazim, it was hard to distinguish affluent young couples in the Sonesta's lobby or bar. In a common denominator, the men wore Guccis, the women looked as though they stepped from smart shops in Milan.

A more intensive indication of advancement was found in the Knesset; one-quarter of the members were Sephardim, still not in proportion to population but a substantial gain nonetheless. The Sephardim were penetrating the power structure. Israel Kessar, a Yemenite, was elected secretary-general of the Histadrut, the forceful federation of trade unions. General Moshe Levy, an Iraqi, served as Israel's chief of staff.

The new, more hopeful mood of Sephardim was reflected by Dede Ben Shitrit. Of Moroccan parentage, Shitrit, thirty-six, first received national attention as a professional soccer player. Now he was a Labor party member of Jerusalem's municipal council. He cited some basic statistics to tell me why he was a supporter of Labor rather than Likud. In 1977, seventy per cent of prison inmates were Sephardic, eighty per cent of university students were Ashkenazic. A decade later, after Likud held long unbroken rule and then a half share in a coalition government, the figures remained unaltered.

"Only a Labor government will help improve conditions," said Shitrit. He based this calculation on a belief that Labor was much readier than Likud to make a settlement with Palestinians — and until that settlement is reached, and while heavy defence expenditures go on, money will not be available for social improvements. Shitrit became one of the leaders of Peace Now, the movement that sprang up in 1978 among reserve officers and academics and spread rapidly to the general public.

There is still friction between Sephardic and Ashkenazic Jews. "But it is not really serious," says Shitrit. "Nobody stops me doing what I want to do or becoming what I want to become. It is nothing like the conflict that exists between the religious and the secular." Oddly, it was while the Sephardic-Ashkenazic issue began to cool that the religious-secular controversy, never far from the surface, started to boil.

The Sephardic-Ashkenazic situation improves with time, the Haredim-secular debate fluctuates. But tension with Arabs remains immutable, changing only in form. Whether it is external or internal, the dominant characteristic of life in Israel and occupied territories is the use of physical force. The kind of spark that can flare with deadly swiftness showed itself in December 1987 when four Palestinians died in a collision with an Israeli army lorry in Gaza.

Rumors swept Arabs that the crash was deliberate, in retaliation for the stabbing of an Israeli. Palestinians rose spontaneously, heaving rocks at Israeli patrols. The soldiers responded with gunfire. Such was the strain that developed in the occupied territories in 1988 that even Ron Nachman, the ebullient mayor of Ariel, was caught in it. He had boasted to me, only months earlier, that he was so trusting of his Arab barber in a neighboring village that he enjoyed a shave under his straight Arab razor. When I phoned Nachman now, he confessed rediscovery of shaving himself.

No one thought it would last. Instead, the *intifada* radiated, affecting life not only for Arabs and Jews in the West Bank but for people in Israel Itself. The wife of Adin Talbar, Ziva, was a Sabra, born in Jerusalem, an ambulance driver for the British in World War II and an Israeli major in the 1948 War of Independence. Ziva Talbar remembers how she was able, not many years ago, to drive to Ramallah, in the West Bank, to visit an old Arab friend, Fatima Khalidi, whose late husband had gone to a British officer training school in Palestine with Adin in 1942. In 1948, the two men fought on opposing fronts; after the 1967 war they resumed their friendship.

One day on her way back from seeing Fatima, Ziva stopped at an Arab fruit stall in Ramallah to buy some grapes. An Israeli border guard confronted her and shouted, "What are you doing here? Don't you realize you are in danger?"

"What is the point of all this?" Ziva said to the frontier guard. "Where is it all going to end if people can't meet in a market place?" The guard shrugged and led her to her car.

Arab hostility, Ziva senses, has grown, and will not end until Palestinians feel at home in the West Bank. She hardly lacks courage, as her record certifies. But today she will not expose herself by driving to Ramallah. Occasionally Fatima comes to visit her in West Jerusalem.

In 1988, four months after the start of the *intifada,* I joined Israelis on a patrol in the Gaza Strip. It was in a personnel carrier, and noteworthy for a couple of reasons. The soldiers, old reservists as well as young recruits, were ready to use their Galil automatic rifles as they saw fit. They were also ready to talk freely about possible political solutions. Everyone had an opinion: end the occupation, annex the territories, give up the territories, make peace, you can't trust the Arabs, you can't trust our government. On and on — strong, outspoken.

In 1990 I went out again in Gaza, but it was quite different. The soldiers, all of them eighteen years old, and fresh from basic training, were under strict instructions to keep to plastic bullets, to fire "live" ammunition only on orders from a superior or when their lives were threatened. An infraction could result in a courtmartial. Indeed, sixty-two soldiers, were serving, or had served, prison sentences.

The patrol moved along cautiously. Periodically the men crouched, to scan corners and fields. Obviously they were aware that it was along this deserted stretch of Shech Ajlin that a month earlier an Israeli patrol was ambushed, with two young soldiers shot to death — one of the first instances of assailants resorting to "hot" weaponry. I witnessed no startling events on that day's patrol. But the next day Palestinians claimed that forty-two men, women and children were shot and wounded by Israeli troops in scattered Gaza Strip clashes.

The anguished question is this: How does a soldier define "threatened?" Especially in an army that proudly boasts of a concept called "purity of arms," the idea that blood-letting is justified only as a last resort? It was what the *intifada* was doing to Israeli morale, and the Israeli image abroad, that led the army to its stricter guidelines.

It also led to a reinforced dictum that the army must keep out of politics. Hence, when I spoke to the young foot soldiers after their patrol, I heard only generalities and shibboleths, giveaways that they had been carefully primed to say nothing controversial to media members. I heard not a single comment about Palestinian rights or non-rights, about trusting or not trusting Yasir Arafat and the Palestine Liberation Organization.

Instead, a young man named Maoz from Tel Aviv, said, "We're here to stop disorder." Kovi, from Haifa: "I heard stories before about what was going on in Gaza. Now I see for myself." Yigal, from Nazareth: "The army is the army. It must be obeyed." I knew what Maoz and Kovi and Yigal thought — or at least what other eighteen-year-olds think before they put on a uniform. But this political conformity was so alien to the free swinging style of the past.

So, too, was the army's technique of dealing with the *intifada*. Soldiers still carried truncheons, but rarely did they wade into mobs, wielding the sticks. Instead, according to the commander of the infantry unit I visited, "We now concentrate on the masked agitators. They're the ones who heat up the demonstrations." It was a tactic that started a year after the *intifada* itself, resulting largely in thirteen thousand Palestinians remaining in prison in 1990.

Over the next few days I would gather the story from the other point of view, meeting young "terrorists," as the Israelis called them, or "activists," as the Palestinians called themselves. Meanwhile what had started as a "shepherd's war" — the name given to skirmishes between Arabs and Jews in the mandate period of Palestine — dramatically highlighted the argument that delays in answering Palestinian insistence on a homeland were no longer feasible.

One of the great challenges of journalism comes under the heading of "objectivity." It is always easier to keep to one version of a story than attempt to balance it with another point of view. The problem with the latter approach is that it knocks out preconceptions and clichés. The day after I accompanied an Israeli patrol in Gaza I started on my own trail of young Palestinians. It was not difficult to pick up. Palestinian journalists in East Jerusalem eagerly help colleagues from the West. Propaganda? Public relations? Professional camaraderie? I try to evaluate each case of helpfulness — and I have met many Arabs over the years in Syria, Egypt, Jordan, Lebanon, the West Bank — on its own merits.

Certainly I detected nothing sinister in my introduction by a journalist in the West Bank to a seventeen-year-old Palestinian named Saed. The deal, almost always, is that surnames are not used, a safeguard for the individual against Israeli arrest. Israelis make the same request to protect their soldiers in case of capture. For Saed, our meeting was a refreshing breather. He had been on the run from Israeli pursuers for several days, hiding and usually sleeping in West Bank fields or in friends' houses. But now he was home near Ramallah, for two hours at least, for this pre-arranged session. His mother smiled proudly when Saed quietly described his continued battles against the Israelis.

Saed was only slightly younger than the patrolling Israeli youths who are conscripts for three years before becoming reservists for another thirty years. Saed had enlisted in his "army," a rag-tag mob, at the age of fifteen in December 1987 when the *intifada* erupted. No one expected it to last, but it became a stunning propaganda success, drawing world attention to Saed's cause. Now Saed is a veteran leader, one of the dwindling but extremely effective band of youthful activists whose main weapons remain rocks, and occasionally petrol bombs. Their objective is unambiguous: the replacement of Israeli-occupied territories with a Palestinian home-land.

When I met him, Saed had served six months in a detention centre for hurling stones at Israeli soldiers. "Holy stones," a young woman characterizes them, "because they come from our soil." The weapons directed against activists like Saed include computers. Soldiers and officers of Shin Bet, the Israeli internal security service, came to his home, but Saed was in hiding. A patrol picked him up when he dared emerge on a Ramallah street. A soldier radioed in Saed's ID card number, and someone punched it in a terminal. Saed went to jail.

Saed carries a green ID card, which means he has an arrest record (for those unblemished the color is orange) and subject to close questioning any time a patrol asks for identification. There is cunning and stealth in the way he now gets around. The guile is hardly one-sided. Not long ago Israelis on the hunt would arrive at a suspect's house in easily recognizable military vehicles. In places like densely crowded refugee camps the warning signal — a whistle formed by two fingers in the mouth — resounded from corner to corner. Now plainclothesmen approach in commandeered taxis bearing Arab licence plates.

That's what led to the arrest of one of Saher's brothers, picked up in Kadora, a United Nations camp in the West Bank. Saher is an eighteen-year-old who has lived all her life only in Kadora. Her family still regards as "home" the village of Lefta, and Saher is determined to return there. The trouble is that Lefta has been part of Israel since the state's creation in 1948. This situation arouses in many Israelis the fear that the demand for a Palestinian "homeland" is only the starter. What, they ask, will people like Saher claim next: Jaffa? Haifa? Jerusalem?

The brother who was arrested, twenty years old, is still in prison. Another, fourteen, is out after serving four months for erecting a street barricade. A third, sixteen, is on the run. The father is dead, and the family's financial providers are Saher's older sister, who works in a nursery, and another brother who earns four hundred shekels (two hundred and forty dollars) a month as a laborer. Thus the family must depend on UN handouts of rice, sugar and flour.

Israelis suffered economically from the *intifada* — with drastic slides in tourism and the construction industry — but few abroad are aware that simultaneously Arabs of the occupied territories suffered a fifty per cent drop in living standards. How much longer can they go on? Saher, who sometimes stays at the forefront of agitators to taunt Israelis, says, "Until we have a homeland." Saher's fifty-year-old mother, Amal, answers the question with a shrug. It is a wordless but expressive answer meaning, "Only Allah knows," or "As long as necessary."

What makes Amal's reaction of interest is the changed relationship between parents and children in the brief years since *intifada's* birth. Before, there was outright condemnation by the young that the older generation had been too passive, had done nothing to thwart the Israelis since their occupation in 1967. "No one led us in the struggle," explains Amal. Earlier, Saher might have frowned at this excuse, but now she ignores it because her mother adds: "I take part. Ever since I saw soldiers beat my sons, I go out with the young people."

Saed's mother, a well educated, affluent woman in her forties, is even more forthright. "We didn't imagine the occupation would last," she says. "We were stupid. Now I am following my son." So thrilled is she about her own activist role that she brings out a copy of *Palestine Revolution,* a PLO weekly magazine published in Cyprus. There, haranguing Israeli troops, she dominates a color photo. "Kill me if you want," she is shouting, "but we don't want you here."

Saed is as proud of his mother as she is of him. He is also cautious about the use of "hot" weapons by Arabs, fearing any such escalation would result in massive retaliation — not so much in the form of Israeli tanks, which are always available but never used. "We don't want them to justify the transfer of population, the destruction of Palestinian society," he says.

One of the things that strikes me about Saed, and others of his generation I have met, is the kind of advanced maturity that cloaks teenhood. Saed talks more like a seventy-year-old than a seventeen-year-old. Perhaps it is the consequence of a prison term. In any case, he has his own explanation for the narrowing of the gap between parents and children: "A few years ago activists were regarded by older people as abnormal. Now they represent normalcy."

There is little doubt that the *intifada* was a spontaneous uprising, primarily by youth, catching the PLO by surprise as much as it did the Israelis. The PLO has since tried to assert its leadership, but with limited success. Musa, a seventeen-year-old who returned recently to the UN refugee camp of Jalazone after ten months' detention, insists that the PLO represents Palestinians. But he betrays skepticism about adults generally:

"The PLO conducted an armed struggle for twenty years, but it didn't have the same effect as the *intifada.* We, as the generation of the *intifada,* look at other nations, especially Israel, and see what they have and we want the same — a state, independence, a future." Thus Musa, while supporting Arafat, feels more comfortable in the knowledge that he and Saed and their peers still form *intifada's* spearhead. He also believes that Palestinians must stand on their own; they cannot count on support from Arab regimes. "The suffering of Palestinians is not only from Israelis but from other Arabs," he says, referring to the pre-1967 days of Jordanian rule. But in view of Israel's military strength, "the military option for us is not realistic." So the solution must be a political one.

What assurances can Israel expect about its continued security? Musa's family comes from the village of Beit Nabala. It is now plowed under as part of Ben-Gurion Airport. Does Musa expect to reclaim the land burying Beit Nabala? He doesn't respond directly. "Israel is there now," says Musa. "When there is a Palestine, we will live peacefully. Until there's a political solution, the rocks will continue." The details of a political solution are left in abeyance.

I see one inexorable conclusion. Palestinian youth are not discomfited by debates that beset Israelis who argue in favor of annexation and transfer of entire populations, and others who say, conversely, that Israelis must vacate the occupied territories. Variation in approach is minor among Palestinian youth. Almost as a whole they separate themselves from politicians — to a far greater extent than do Israelis. Their single objective is attainment of nationhood.

One evening I sat in Fink's with an internationally acclaimed Israeli photographer, David Rubinger. A Viennese who migrated in 1939 to Palestine, Rubinger remembers the Jewish underground resistance fighters, of the Haganah. They struggled against the British for a homeland up to the eve of Israeli independence. Back from a recent assignment photographing young *intifada* fighters,

Rubinger said, "I couldn't help comparing them with the young Jews of 1947. They possess the same kind of ideological dedication and readiness to die."

Most Israelis do not like to hear such comment. It is simpler to think that a fight for survival holds one dimension only. Israelis keep constantly in mind the history of modern times — the mass extermination of six million Jews. It is equally true that Palestinians, as they keep repeating, were not responsible for the Holocaust.

Visionaries have always existed in Israel. David Ben-Gurion was an example. So was Abba Eban, whom I interviewed in 1987, twenty years after Ben-Gurion. In Israel's short history, none of its leaders played a more prominent role on the world stage than Eban, first as ambassador to the United Nations and later as foreign minister.

Eban, born in Cape Town, was educated at Cambridge University, where he sharpened his skills as a debater. I first admired those skills, and his Churchillian eloquence, when I covered the UN in the early 1950s. His resonant voice kept perfect harmony with his tall and distinguished appearance. Many Israelis resented Eban's liberal, outspoken frankness and obvious disdain for creatures of lesser intellect. Few could match his ability — funded by exceptional brilliance, knowledge and erudition — to look at present realities and project the future.

Eban was chairman of the Knesset's foreign affairs and security committee when I saw him at his home in Herzlia, overlooking the Mediterranean Sea. "Some Israelis," I said, "demand the annexation of the West Bank and the Gaza Strip despite the large Palestinian populations. How do you answer them?"

Eban said: "Any country that deliberately put itself in a position where more than a third of its population were members of a foreign nation which didn't want to belong to it, and had no allegiance whatever to it, would be acting suicidally. Democracy in Israel would not survive annexation of the West Bank and Gaza populations. By the end of the century we would become just another country in which Jews are a minority. Then let's not give the Palestinians the vote, say some of the annexationists. But this would be a horrifying anticlimax to the history and struggle of the Jewish people.

" The Jews had to fight hard for hundreds of years for the idea that they must have the same rights as anybody else in any country where they live. And now, if Israel were to impose one law for its own people and another for the Palestinians, we would lose the support of world Jewry and of the Western nations. We must, therefore, separate from the Palestinians. Only by agreeing that they should live in a Jordanian-Palestinian state, can we maintain both our predominance and our democratic vocation in Israel."

A few months later, I spoke with Eban at his office in the Knesset. Much had changed, even in that brief period. Very few now spoke of annexation. "The impression I have, from everyone I've talked to in Israel — right, left, centre — is that the status quo is finished," I said.

"That's very important," said Eban, "because a few months ago that wasn't the case. There was a mentality which said that something that lasted twenty years might last another ten years. Nobody is saying this today."

"So the uprising has achieved at least that much?"

"It has achieved its purpose, yes. It has achieved it because the status quo itself is inherently defective. If the status quo were inherently harmonious and normal, then the uprising wouldn't have affected it. The occupation and the rule over foreign people is in itself abnormal. Therefore, under the pressure of the uprising, it showed cracks."

"Can you see any real pressure on Israel, economic and so on, from the United States, for a settlement of the Palestinian issue?"

"The real pressure is the pressure of our own interests, and, of course, the pressure created by the fact that there is nobody in the world who believes we should hang on to the territories. Why should they believe it when we won our legitimacy on the basis of a contract in which we said we would share sovereignty and share territory in the area west of the Jordan? How can a nation turn its back on its own birth certificate?"

"As you know, there are people in Israel who say world opinion doesn't matter. What does it count for?"

"I don't know any country that can live in total isolation of world opinion. The United States can't, for example. Even the Soviet Union [adapted] its policies to its need for image. If there are great, huge empires which can't ignore world opinion it's ludicrous to think Israel can."

All these things Eban said three and four years before the move in 1991 toward an international peace conference dealing with the Middle East. The talks were a predictable outcome of the Gulf War and the new harmony between the United States and Russia. If the Israelis were more amenable, it was partly because the old concept of buffer zones providing security had altered. Iraq's Saddam Hussein changed that concept when he sent Scuds, launched from hundreds of kilometres away, over borders and crashing into Tel Aviv and Haifa.

Scuds with explosive warheads were bad enough. I remember how Londoners bravely met the Scud's ancestors, German V2 rockets, in 1944. What made it different this time was the hideous mystery — whether the missiles might contain something worse than explosives: mustard gas or nerve gas, anthrax microbes or equally deadly agents that would spread and destroy life, rather than buildings, over a wide area.

I thought of George Bernard Shaw. Back in 1946, when I was stationed in London, my newspaper planned a special supplement on the dawn of the nuclear age. Still fresh was the devastation of atomic bombs on Hiroshima and Nagasaki. I was asked to contact Shaw for his comments. Realizing I had scant chance of an interview with the distinguished playwright, I sent him a letter. I received in reply a penny postcard — written in his famous chicken scribble. Shaw visualized a new weapon to replace the atomic bomb — a weapon that would wipe out everyone but leave undamaged the material spoils to the victors. Some Jerusalemites, spared explosive Scuds because of Al-Aksa Mosque and Dome on the Rock, the third holiest site in Islam, felt that chemical or biological weapons could hit them before Tel Aviv.

There was a new deep fear in Israel. I had never before witnessed anything like it. In the Six-Day War, in the Yom Kippur War, in the *intifada,* the pattern was basically the same: soldiers on the ground in combat with an enemy on the ground. They were trained for their mission. This time, two ugly ingredients predominated: uncertainty and frustration. The soldiers were now spectators. In the past, civilians accepted their own role as spectators. They sent their soldiers into battle with prayers for their safety. Now when the men departed to fulfil their reservist duties it was they who trembled — for the wives and children they left behind.

Yet Israelis, always highly individualistic and quarrelsome, followed a disciplined routine without demur or hesitation. When the sirens wailed, they slapped on gas masks and rushed — not sauntered — to a "sealed room."

The Babich family — Rivka Babich, a forty-eight-year-old pediatric nurse, her husband Joseph, marketing manager for an ice cream company, and son Jacob, seventeen, lived in a modest apartment in Kirat Shalom, a Tel Aviv residential district. They had followed government-directed instructions, buying packing tape to cover gaps in window frames and prepare a sealed room as protection against gas or bacteriological attack. A towel, soaked in a solution of baking soda, would cut off any noxious entry under the door. Bottled water and canned food, stocked in the sealed room, would sustain the family for a week if necessary.

The age of nuclear isolation, dreaded by all humanity, might be finally at hand. The Babich routine quickly became deeply implanted. Even the Siamese cat, Moli, ran to the sealed room, to hide under the bed. She refused to emerge until the Babiches removed their masks.

That was the story when I visited the Babiches in their home during the early weeks of the Gulf War — a family representative not only of contemporary Israel but of any family, anywhere, that might face the perils and uncertainty of modern missile attack. When the sirens sounded, they went off not only in Tel Aviv. They were heard simultaneously through the length and breadth of Israel. The whole nation had entered into a collective experience. It was the first time that the veteran of sixty and the grandchild of six were involved in the same war of the unknown.

It was also the first time Israel, in its insistence on self-reliance, had ever accepted the presence of U.S. troops on its soil, a breakthrough of profound significance. A battery of Patriot anti-missile missiles, manned by Americans, was stationed less than a half kilometre from the Babich apartment. Rivka complained that she couldn't approach the soldiers to hand them some home-baked cookies: "There are so many Israelis trying to get near them, the police are stopping us."

The inter-dependence of governments and peoples could hardly have found a deeper demonstration than in the sealed rooms. Relatives and friends dropped by in the evening to visit the Babiches, wordlessly expressing gratitude for one another's company. They all shared space in the sealed room.

There was another side effect, the impact on men — and it was not merely a blow to the macho image — on the reservist sitting in a sealed room, watching children in gas masks, watching helplessly, unable to retaliate. He approved of the government's restraint, compliance with a policy not to hit back, because that was precisely the reaction Saddam sought to win favor in the Arab world. Nonetheless, it still left the Israeli feeling impotent. Jacob, a high school student, prepared to enter military service next year with other eighteen-year-olds. "In all our wars that I've read about," he said, "we were able to hit back, and when we did, Israel won every time." He had no more to say. It was all implied — helplessness.

"Helplessness," said Dr. Haim Dasberg, a Jerusalem psychiatrist, "is the most fearful sensation people can experience." I saw one aspect of this, a flashback into history, when I sat in a sealed room in my hotel with a fifteen-year-old high school student and his grandfather. I asked the boy if he had difficulty putting on his gas mask. "No," he said, "but my grandfather does. It reminds him of the Holocaust." When I looked at the elderly man, a survivor of Nazi Germany, I sensed what was going on in his mind. Gas connoted only one thing: death camps.

Dr. Dasberg spent his boyhood in hiding in occupied Amsterdam; his father perished in a gas chamber. He lectures widely on the Holocaust, with the reminder that a quarter of a million Israelis living today came out of occupied Europe. "The gas mask is immediately symbolic," he said, "but it goes beyond that. The goal of war is to defeat an army and force a peace, but not to kill. Genocide is to kill everyone and wipe out the memory of them. To hear Saddam Hussein express a wish to kill half Israel, and then for us to endure his missiles, means to many a threatened repeat of what happened in Europe."

Some attitudes change, some do not. Jerusalem remains non-negotiable, even among Israelis who are prepared to see a Palestine state established in the West Bank. A few are willing to allow Jerusalem to become internationalized in exchange for a comprehensive peace treaty with all Arabs — but only a few. Such is Jerusalem's value — historic, religious — that the overwhelming majority would fight to keep it. "A person can live without an arm, without a leg," said Mayor Teddy Kollek. "He can't live without a heart."

The view toward Germans has modified, tending to the positive. Adin Talbar, as an eleven-year-old in Berlin, saw his father dragged off by the Gestapo. In 1935, when his father, a prominent physician and author, was released from concentration camp, the family moved to Palestine. Adin admits that he took a long time to come to terms with his native land of Germany. "We Jews wanted to build a new country," he says, "but I saw, after the war, Germany also becoming a new country. The world goes on. You can't hate forever."

For the last several years Talbar has run his own business organizing trade fairs abroad — two-thirds in West Germany — for Israeli products. His contribution in establishing rapprochement included bringing over the first German sports teams to play in Israel. In recognition of this work, the West German government, at a ceremony in the German Embassy, presented him with a civilian medal, the Cross of Honor. Talbar could not help but think of the award his father had won for bravery in German trenches during World War I. A lingering touch of bitterness emerged when he told the gathering in the embassy, "I will put my medal in a drawer next to the Iron Cross of my father."

When I look back on more than thirty years of contact with Israel I recall being entertained by people in their homes, with cold tea and peanuts; that was what they could afford in 1961. Today, thanks to relative affluence, I am likely to be offered wine and canapés. But Israel remains a country in ferment, as though events that began with the establishment of the state in 1948 refuse to wind down. One feels an insatiable striving of Israelis to reach almost unattainable values and standards.

Many visitors are drawn to the country precisely because of its stimulation and excitement. Several times a year Zubin Mehta, former conductor of the Montreal Symphony Orchestra and later music director of the New York Philharmonic, conducts the Israel Philharmonic. I wondered why he spent so much of his time with Israeli musicians. "They are electric," he told me. The description applies to practically all Israelis in this land of chronic tension.

* * *

Still, one institution stays unchanged and predictable — Fink's. Inevitably in 1991, Scuds or no Scuds, I made my appearance there. David Rothschild, close to eighty, was still in residence, pouring delicately mixed martinis. Two plastic penguins on a shelf bobbed their beaks up and down in a glass of water, Rothschild adding a few drops of vinegar every night to revitalize them. The penguins — or their earlier mates — have performed there as long as I can remember.

Nothing, but nothing, is allowed to change. Even the two chefs have been fixtures in Fink's for a quarter century. The goulash soup, for which Fink's achieved international renown, is prepared exactly as it was generations ago. It requires years before a new dish makes an appearance. Rothschild brought back his last innovation, Tafelspitz, from Austria in 1985. Tafelspitz is a shoulder cut of boiled beef covered with a mild horseradish sauce. The event was newsworthy enough for *The Jerusalem Post* to report it.

"We change our shirts, but not our menu," said a whimsical Rothschild.

Fink's thick volumes of tributes and autographs keep multiplying. Rothschild remembers the favorite dishes of his "regulars" who make frequent trips to Israel. Zubin Mehta comes in for Wiener schnitzel. Violinist Isaac Stern takes goulash soup, brimming with meat, sausage and potatoes and well seasoned with paprika. Pablo Casals, the renowned cellist, was also an admirer of the goulash soup. But in his last years, too infirm after a concert to come in person, he sent a musical emissary, Alexander Schneider, to bring a container to his suite in the King David Hotel. This had something of the touch of an old Haganah operation. The King David, a kosher hotel, was forbidden by rabbinical law to allow non-kosher food inside its doors. Rothschild, asking no questions, pretended he did not know the goulash soup's destination.

His son-in-law, Shmuel Azriely, is training to take his place. Does Azriely ever tire of the Haganah nostalgia of old-timers who drop by? "On the contrary," he says, "they never bore me. They have the privilege of being first, of having started this country." An educator, Azriely, has fallen willingly and neatly into line, respecting and emulating Rothschild's practices and values. "I don't want to change anything here by so much as a millimetre," he says. It is a comforting thought.

Fink's bar holds echoes of arms dealing while the British were still there. The quintessential touch, however, was the smuggling in of Israel's first fighter planes — ironically, Messerschmitt 109s, German aircraft newly built in Czechoslovakia under licence. They arrived in parts — a wing, an engine tucked into the belly of a C-46 — and were put together surreptitiously by Jewish mechanics.

Aharon Remez, the chief of staff of the Haganah's "air arm" — a grandiose title since the "air arm" consisted initially of a Tiger Moth — had trained as a Royal Air Force fighter pilot in Canada and flown a Spitfire against ME-109s over Germany. By the time the Arabs invaded, Remez could count not only on the Tiger Moth but one Spitfire, assembled from cannibalized wrecks left behind by the British, four ME-109s, with another ten under preparation in Czechoslovakia, a couple of C-47s and two B-17s. This compared with one hundred and fifty Egyptian fighters and bombers plus Iraqi aircraft — a total of two hundred Arab planes.

Ben-Gurion, then Israel's prime minister, refused to allow his chief of air staff to risk himself in combat. "Anyway," as Remez told me, "we had more pilots than planes." These included Ezer Weizman, a veteran of the Royal Air Force in the world war that had ended only three years earlier. There were also one Jewish veteran of the Soviet air force and more than one hundred volunteers — Christian as well as Jewish — from the U.S., Britain, South Africa and Canada. A Canadian ace, George "Buzz" Beurling, with twenty-nine "kills" to his credit, died in an air crash en route to Israel.

On May 29, 1948 Weizman and three others, wearing Luftwaffe helmets and flying boots, went into action in the ME-109s. One plane was shot down, but the others helped ground units to save Tel Aviv by bombing and strafing an advancing Egyptian column. Days later there was another threat when two Egyptian bombers approached the city. An Israeli flier took off in an ME-109 and demolished both Egyptian planes. That was the turning point. From then on, many more aircraft arrived, including disassembled P-51s (Mustangs) smuggled out of the United States as agricultural equipment.

When I interviewed him in 1988, Weizman still owned and flew on occasion, not an ME-109, but a Spitfire. The walls of his office in Jerusalem — he was a cabinet minister — held framed photos of crew mates in the RAF and the Israeli air force, which he commanded in the 1960s. "For years we taught ourselves how not to die," he said. "Now we must teach ourselves how to live."

This process included finding peace with the Palestinians — a revolutionary thought for many Israelis when Weizman enunciated it. Weizman was intelligent, decent — and erratic politically. He had switched from Labor to Likud and back again to Labor. Dovish, his main foe in a left-right unity cabinet was the hawkish Ariel Sharon, a rigid, uncompromising advocate of Jewish settlements in the occupied territories.

Weizman took from his desk a copy of the Camp David agreement, the fabric for peace in the Middle East endorsed by President Jimmy Carter, President Anwar Sadat and Prime Minister Menachem Begin in 1978. He made me read the passage which states that Palestinians should participate in further negotiations. Then he accused Israel of "dilly-dallying."

"The West Bank and Gaza Strip are negotiable," he said. "The Israeli government is holding things up because the country is split in two. Therefore the delay is in our hands."

Those were strong and brave words, and one might have expected Weizman to be shoved into the background. But that is not the way political life necessarily spins in Israel. Weizman resigned amid controversy that he had held illegal talks with the Palestine Liberation Organization, an accusation neither confirmed nor denied. In May 1993 he returned to prominence — elected by the Knesset, with a Labor coalition in the barest majority, as Israel's seventh president. His uncle, Chaim Weizmann, a principal founder of the state, was Israel's first president. I recalled Ezer Weizman saying, "My father decided that one 'n' was good enough for us."

Israel's president enjoys no real political power; his duties are mostly ceremonial. But Weizman, who had played a key role in the accord with Egypt, made it clear that he intended to take part in further development of the Middle East peace process. Then he curbed the blunt talk for which he is famous. At a reception, he deflected awkward questions, telling reporters he was hungry and that hungry people often speak foolishly. "Let's eat," he said. Weizman's predecessor, Chaim Herzog, held the presidency for two five-year terms. Weizman's election signalled, at least among many Israelis, optimism for the future.

That optimism was borne out faster than anyone could have anticipated.

In 1974 I spent an hour in conversation with Yitzhak Rabin, the prime minister. Rabin spoke in deep and precise voice, in short, articulate sentences — the personification of a solid old soldier, which is exactly what he was. Rabin liked direct questions, to which he could give straight answers — no wasting of words. You did not think of approaching him with a philosophic question, but I tried one. "What," I asked him, "is your dream for Israel? Not a dream about borders or politics, but about people and even the role Palestinians might play in it? In a sense, perhaps, the way Ben-Gurion used to express a dream about the migration of all Jews to Israel?"

"Well," said Rabin, "I believe that the purpose of Israel, the essence of its existence, is to be a Jewish state. When I say a Jewish state it doesn't mean that all Jews have to live here. I'm realistic enough to know that such an assumption cannot be carried out. I would like to see many more Jews coming over to Israel, to have a population of five, six or seven million Jews who would live and work in a Jewish state. I also see non-Jews — Christians or Moslems — living here with no problem."

It was to come about — largely because of the influx of Russians — that the Jewish population would indeed rise to five million. Rabin was always known as a pragmatist and keen analyst. But it was the next statement that drew him also in the unexpected character of something of a visionary: "I believe that within former Palestine — that includes the east and west banks of the River Jordan — there will be two states. One a Jewish state, the kind I have defined for you. And eastward of it a Jordanian-Palestinian state where the Palestinians and the Jordanians would find freedom to express their own identity. It doesn't seem feasible tomorrow, but in the long run I believe that this is the best solution for the area."

As for the public postures of Arafat and other Arab leaders, Rabin returned to current realities: "If they are ready to negotiate, to reach practical arrangements, if they want to have peace, let them not just state it. Let them agree to negotiate directly with us. Or let them do it secretly through an intermediary."

Those thoughts were expressed two decades ago. Who could have anticipated that in September 1993, Rabin, again Israel's prime minister, and Chairman Arafat would announce the stunning news that Israel and the Palestine Liberation Organization recognized each another? Or that the breakthrough was made possible through an intermediary, Norway's foreign minister? Soon afterward began the slow but essential process of evolving a pattern of co-existence within the framework of a possible Jordanian-Palestinian federation. Among the initial tangible steps, in May 1994, Israeli soldiers withdrew from the Gaza Strip. Palestinian police moved in.

It was another historic step in the shaping of a new Middle East, sixteen years after the first historic step — Sadat's daring visit to Jerusalem.

9 Terror in the Andes

JOURNALISTIC FRATERNITY WAS NEVER better demonstrated than during my second trip to South Africa, in 1975, when I was determined to interview Robert Sobukwe, who was still in detention. A courageous South African newspaperman, Benjamin Pogrund, a contact from Sharpeville days, contrived a meeting for me. I never questioned Pogrund how he did it, but I knew he was exposing himself to reprisal; government agents frowned on such manoeuvring. I kept his name out of print, but any lingering danger eventually vanished. Pogrund, in his fifties and disconsolate about his country's future, moved to London several years later to take up a new career in journalism.

Sobukwe was unknown to the outside world in 1960, and hardly recognized even in South Africa. A teacher of Bantu language and leader of a fledgling black-consciousness movement, the Pan-Africanist Congress, he travelled around the countryside in a Volkswagen Beetle to enlist supporters. He preached non-violence in the campaign to eliminate apartheid. Then, as a gesture of desperation, he urged blacks at Sharpeville to heap their pass books in a bonfire — and both he and Sharpeville suddenly entered history.

The price Sobukwe paid for this civil disobedience was nine years in prison, mostly on the infamous Robben Island, where he was kept in solitary confinement in a small stockade encased in barbed wire. Another inmate on Robben Island was a former colleague and competitor named Nelson Mandela. But Mandela was not yet a legendary figure. Black lore centred on Sobukwe. He was revered and looked upon as a possible saviour.

Released from Robben Island, Sobukwe had now lived, for the last five years, under terms of "banning." The Russians, in the periods of both the Czars and the Communists, knew a similar device: Siberia. Banning in South Africa signified not only restriction to a specific town or place — in Sobukwe's case it was Kimberley, deliberately chosen by the government because he had no friends there — but adherence to strict rules. You could speak to only one person at a time; more than one, in the state's eyes, would constitute a crowd and therefore a political demonstration. You were not allowed to enter a building where anything was printed or published, or an institution, such as a school, where anything was taught.

Sobukwe, unable to return to teaching, took a job as a clerk in a black lawyer's office and decided to study law through correspondence with the University of South Africa. He started his own practice in 1975 in Kimberley's adjacent black location of Galeshewe, where he lived. A standing curfew allowed him to leave his house only from six a.m. to seven p.m. He was not allowed to travel beyond the limits of Galeshewe or Kimberley.

No South African newspaper was permitted to quote Sobukwe; thus, in theory, he was never heard. Nor, in theory, did he hear what was going on. But for all practical purposes, Sobukwe, a non-person, was strikingly well informed, and so was the black community about his thinking. The oral network was remarkable in 1960; it was even more sophisticated in 1975. "Sobukwe's behavior and his dignity are examples for all of us," a black journalist told me.

After an hour's flight from Johannesburg, I met Sobukwe for tea in the mixed tea room at the original Kimberley diamond mine. It was one of the few places in South Africa where such fraternization between whites and blacks was not prohibited. The mine, which closed down in 1914, was now a tourist attraction.

For three hours we talked, until it was time for Sobukwe to catch a black bus that would get him home before curfew. To protect Sobukwe, I took no notes.

Sobukwe, who was fifty-one, showed no bitterness over his long imprisonment and banishment. One is bitter, he said, when there is no hope; but for Africans there was hope. I was struck by how he could say this, though only a few minor concessions had appeared since Sharpeville. The indignity and injustice of pass books — and all they implied — remained in place. Apartheid was as rigid as ever. The Afrikaner, under Verwoerd's successor, Prime Minister B.J. Vorster, gave no sign of backing down.

Nevertheless, Sobukwe exuded immense serenity and understanding, along with almost a Gandhi-like quality of soft and gentle language. The Afrikaner had no other place to go, Sobukwe said, because he was not a European at heart; the English South African could turn to nearly the whole world. The issue, therefore, was between Afrikaner and African, and time was on the African's side. Did this mean that violent revolution was inevitable? It was not inevitable, but what was inevitable was the end to Afrikaner exclusivity. No one at Sharpeville had expected violence — neither black organizers nor white authorities. Now the whites were prepared physically, and so were young blacks, at least psychologically. The flashpoints were impossible to detect.

How much time was left? Sobukwe did not respond directly. Instead, he told of his brother, an Anglican bishop,who was once asked how he felt about Robert's activism. "The trouble with Robert," replied the bishop, "is that he is trying to play God by advancing the clock one hour past midnight. The trouble with Vorster is that he, too, is trying to play God by setting the clock back one hour to eleven p.m. When God is ready, the clock will strike at twelve and then we will have equanimity."

It was a delicate and beautiful thought, said Sobukwe. But obviously he was far from persuaded that the clock would strike properly. Time, he repeated, was on the African's side and that was why he held no bitterness — only hope. Sobukwe, denied permission to emigrate to the United States where he was offered teaching posts, died of cancer in 1978. His old rival, Nelson Mandela, took on new prominence despite continued isolation on Robben Island.

As in Israel, the news always flows in South Africa. Fresh players take centre stage, but the basic, intense story remains the same — how to make significant changes, or preserve the status quo, or achieve reassuring compromise. The Luthulis and Sobukwes were names in text books when I returned several years later for *Reader's Digest*. Now the Tutus and the Buthelezis stood in the forefront. The world still watched while white South Africans considered how much alteration was necessary to satisfy the blacks.

On the surface many superficial abrasions had been removed. I was impressed and encouraged to see that the tokenism of a mixed tourist tea room in Kimberley was now widespread. In many restaurants, in many cities, blacks now sat at tables alongside whites. The petty apartheid, of separate park benches for whites and non-whites, had been erased almost everywhere. And some blacks were now able to ascend to decent economic and professional levels. But was it nearly enough? Earlier, black ambitions had focussed on destruction of the hated pass books and their symbolism. What now?

On my previous visits, I found the leading industry in Soweto, the sprawling black township or "location" outside Johannesburg, consisted of undertaking. This time the biggest entrepreneur in Soweto, Richard Maponya, operated not only a funeral parlor. His name also appeared on a fleet of buses, a filling station, a General Motors car dealership, and a stable of fifty-five racehorses. Maponya's big jewel was his three-year-old combination store — supermarket and soft goods — with twenty-one check-out counters.

If business opportunities had improved for men like Maponya, what about his political life? Maponya held no ambition to enter politics himself, but in common with all blacks he believed that whites must begin to relinquish control. As a start, it was necessary to talk to such recognized black leaders as Mandela. Maponya was not to know, of course, that Mandela would remain in prison until 1990. "I see nations that don't agree with one another ideologically, talking to one another," Maponya said. "So I want to see our government talking to the Mandelas of this world. Only by talking, can we resolve our differences."

Maponya, aged fifty-five and a moderate, was not representative of a younger generation. I did not need to look further than to Shireen Ngwanya, a thirty-year-old black reporter who volunteered to drive me around Soweto. I had been warned by whites in Johannesburg that I would be stoned by children in Soweto. Youngsters — ten, eleven years old — stood in clusters around squalid street corners where mud roads converged. But they were hardly menacing.

Instead of rocks, they held out battered tin cans, and they smiled appreciatively when I dropped in a few coins. The money was to help them buy grass seeds and a few ornaments so they could replace the garbage at street corners with semblances of green space and parks. It was a touching idea. Shireen decided our first stop should be the home of her mother. It was a simple single storey four-room house, more lavish than most in Soweto because it boasted running water. Mrs. Ngwanya, fifty, commented on the difference between generations. "Kids today are not cooperative at all," she said. "I suppose it's because they have nothing to do." This was about the boycott that had been going on for five months, pupils refusing to attend schools. It was not an uncommon protest. I remarked that at least some were keeping busy by fabricating tiny parks. "Yes," sighed Mrs. Ngwanya. "It's better than throwing stones."

"It's better to throw stones," said Shireen.

And that, I thought, summed up much of the story of South Africa: an older generation, wanting an improved life, but within the limits of the established authority, the government; a younger generation in effect saying the older generation had failed and no longer counted, that the whites would respond only to militancy, to force. Never far from anyone's mind was the knowledge that blacks outnumbered whites nearly five to one.

What did South Africa's most celebrated clergyman, Anglican Bishop Desmond Tutu, the black Nobel Peace Prize winner, see ahead? "South Africa is going to be free," he said. "We will have a true democracy, and there will almost certainly be a black as head of affairs. That is going to happen. The question is how it is going to happen. There is very real concern, especially in the black community, that it happen with a minimum of violence. But the way things are going, with the intransigence of the government...." Here he broke off, leaving the rest untold but implied: the pattern of violence was likely to continue and even accelerate.

Such blunt and public comments, accompanied by his threats to lead blacks in civil disobedience, hardly endeared Bishop Tutu to the more fanatical whites. A Johannesburg taxi driver, realizing, as he took me to St. Alban's church, that I was to meet Bishop Tutu, murmured, "I don't know why someone hasn't put a bullet in his head." When I related this to Bishop Tutu, he appeared shaken and said, "Well, they put a bullet through Martin Luther King's head. They did the same with Gandhi."

On that trip in 1986 I flew to the province of Natal to speak to a prominent white and a prominent black. Forty years earlier, author Alan Paton wrote the classic *Cry, the Beloved Country.* In it a black clergyman, Msimangu, says of the whites: "I have one great fear in my heart, that one day when they turn to loving they will find we are turned to hating." I asked Paton, at his home in Pietermaritzburg, to comment. "Yes," he said, "that thought, to a greater extent than I feared, has come true. It is one of the most quoted passages from the book."

In 1960, in the aftermath of the Sharpeville massacre, police jailed several whites along with hundreds of blacks who condemned the government. Hearing the news, Paton, at the time national president of the Liberal Party, said, "I am feeling a bit ashamed of myself for not being arrested. I must have slipped up somewhere in my activities."

Over the years Paton continued to write and rail, both at home and abroad, about South African injustices. Had Paton, eighty-two, ever considered throwing up his hands in despair and leaving South Africa for good? "Once, in 1976, when rioting broke out in Soweto," he confessed. "But after a very short time — twenty-four hours — I realized that if others could stay, then I should stay."

A couple of hundred kilometres northwest of Pieter-maritzburg lay the town of Ulundi, in a gently hilly area of KwaZulu, once known as Zululand. Ulundi was my destination. There I was to meet Chief Mangosuthu Buthelezi, chief minister of KwaZulu, a "homeland."

The "homeland" system had its origin in the 1960s when the South African government set aside ten regions to be populated by ethnic sub-groups among the blacks. The concept supposedly gave the blacks autonomy, a status they neither sought nor were asked about. In fact what it did was to reserve thirteen per cent of the nation's territory for three-quarters of the population. The remaining eighty-seven per cent, "white" territory, covered the best agricultural land, the gold and diamond mines, and all the principal cities. The "homelands" not only lay scattered about the outer reaches of the country, far from urban centres, but fragmented — Lebowa, for instance, into thirteen pieces.

The Afrikaner government strategy was a familiar one: to divide and rule. By confinement to specified areas, the Zulus, Xhosas and other tribal groups, would in theory be unable to build black unity. Blacks would be allowed to venture into dormitory townships like Soweto by permit only — when required to provide cheap labor in mines or city factories. Millions of blacks, though born in townships, were shunted around the country into unproductive regions with which they had no affinity and where there was little prospect of employment. Many drifted back into the townships illegally. Thus the scheme was faulty as well as unjust. The government, nonetheless, clung to the argument that homelands provided an answer to race problems.

The existence of homelands was one of the main causes of tension. Among blacks it created disillusionment and a feeling that forcible uprooting of people from familiar surroundings, such as Soweto, could be answered only by force. President P.W. Botha was sufficiently sensitive to the black mood of the 1980s to speak vaguely of some kind of confederation or federation and even "citizenship" that would give blacks limited access to white areas. But blacks asked themselves a basic question: What good is "citizenship" unless it is accompanied by political rights?

In turn, many whites feared that even the vaguest notion of "citizenship" would lead inevitably to one-man-one-vote — and therefore a black majority government. "Remember one thing," an Afrikaner political leader, C.P. "Connie" Mulder, told me. "The whites are not going to sit still and let their country disappear from below their feet. They would take up arms — let's be quite frank about it."

Since the blacks heavily outnumbered the whites, wouldn't the results be inevitable? Mulder, with a smile of confidence, replied, "It depends on who has the best weapons." Was this a flashback to the ancestral stand of Afrikaners, or Boers, against hordes of Zulus? "We will try to prevent that, but...." The rest of Mulder's sentence was left dangling. But the inference was clear: the whites hadn't even begun to use their heavy arsenal.

It was in 1834 that the Boers, pushed out of the coastal area of southern Africa by the British, started on their celebrated Great Trek. In ox-drawn wagons, and in search of fresh territory, they set off for the interior. A new enemy, a Zulu army, confronted them. But superior technology and weaponry — firearms, including cannon, versus spears — gave the whites the advantage. In a decisive battle, four hundred and sixty-four Boers defeated twelve thousand Zulus.

Chief Buthelezi is a descendant of Zulu kings and generals who fought the Boers and later the British. It was in Ulundi that the Zulus suffered their last decisive defeat, by the British. Buthelezi, while he hopes his people will "rise from the ashes," does not cling to the site for maudlin reasons. Rather, he considers it ideal because of a nearby rail line and other infrastructure features. He refused to accept "independence" for KwaZulu on the grounds it would become a complete satellite of Pretoria, entitled to "crumbs of charity." As it is, KwaZulu depends on Pretoria's largesse for eighty per cent of its budget.

Buthelezi was able to retain his liberty of spirit and talk and action because he was a leading champion of non-violent transition in South Africa. Many whites acclaimed him, while many blacks, including young Zulus, condemned him for working within the system. His formula called for the franchise for everyone, blacks as well as whites, but with an initial built-in veto for minorities, providing whites with confidence. That was the theory — that whites would feel reassured about their safety and freedom.

A few days before my meeting with Buthelezi a group of Zulus and Pondos, a main tribal group, clashed, leaving sixty dead. When I mentioned this as just the sort of tribal conflict whites used as an excuse to resist majority rule, Buthelezi shot back, "The Afrikaners and the British fought a full-scale war, and there isn't much love lost between them." This was a commentary on the Anglo-Boer war (1899-1902), and continued enmity between the two white tribes who formed an uneasy alliance to establish a South Africa that still functioned.

But what had it to do with an ability of blacks to govern? Buthelezi was an aristocratic man — haughty, overbearing and unattractive, I thought. He declined to answer directly. Instead he explained that the Zulus and Pondos had never been at war, and the recent collision was caused not by tribalism but by economic desperation — over claims for water, land and jobs. Buthelezi said with some bitterness, "The whites use our adversity to try to justify their prejudices."

Buthelezi was a kind of linchpin, helping to maintain some dialogue between blacks and whites. He was undoubtedly the most important black political leader at liberty in South Africa — until Mandela's release. It was not difficult to anticipate the coming contest between these two powerful personalities. Buthelezi's Inkatha Freedom Party, a political organization of Zulus, and Mandela's African National Congress had been bitter opponents for years, engaging in frequent skirmishes costly in lives. I quoted to Buthelezi figures from public opinion polls showing his popularity far below that of Mandela. He shrugged this off with an irritated refusal to be compared with a man "who has been put in jail as a criminal."

The lifting of the ban against the African National Congress by the relatively benign government of President F.W. de Klerk, who replaced P.W. Botha, was yet to come. So were intensified battles between the Inkatha and the ANC, adding to old Afrikaner claims that "kafirs" were still savages, and under black majority rule whites would be decimated. By the 1990s the population had grown even more disproportionate: thirty million blacks, five million whites.

Soon after my talk with Buthelezi I had a lunch interview in Pretoria with Louis Nel, the deputy minister of information and chief government spokesman. I kept a minicassette recorder on the table in full view, and as my final question, after an hour and half of hearing banalities, asked Nel if he could live under a black president. He was visibly startled, but finally said in a low voice, "Yes." This was political dynamite. I doubt if many senior government people had ever faced such a question, or answered it affirmatively.

A week later, when I was back in Montreal, I listened to radio reports of a new crisis in South Africa's government. Some members were accused of taking too soft a position on apartheid. Their careers were in peril. Minutes later I received a phone call from Pretoria, from Nel. Would I, he asked me, consider not using the reference he had made to accepting black rule? I agreed to kill it. "I owe you one," he said gratefully. It was not, from my point of view, a bad promise for the future.

I wasn't being too magnanimous. I couldn't have used the quote anyway. *Reader's Digest* was insistent on verifying information, and my tape, unknown both to Nel and me, had run out at the last moment; it missed his crucial "yes." I only made this discovery when I replayed the tape. Anyway, Nel, soon afterward, left the government over a policy dispute, so I'm not sure how valuable was his IOU.

Nel could not know then, nor could anyone else, that in 1994 life under a black president would become a reality. After the country's first democratic election, Nelson Mandela replaced de Klerk as president of South Africa — a momentous development generated thirty-four years earlier at an obscure place called Sharpeville.

Hotels can provide much more than shelter. They also trigger memories of people, places, times, customs, noteworthy events. I like to recall the following:

• Prominent in my recollections is Sofia, with the cupolas of its Orthodox churches and love of the Bulgarians for the Russians who liberated them in 1878 after centuries of Turkish rule. I left a pair of black suede shoes outside the door of my hotel room — for brushing. In the morning I found them polished — well, not exactly polished. No amount of diligent labor could create a sheen. I still wonder what the attendant must have thought as he toiled away, with mounting frustration. I know what I thought when I discarded the shoes.

• Before embarking for Lagos, I saw the Nigerian high commissioner, or ambassador — an imposingly massive black — in Ottawa. He was helpful and cordial, giving me his card with an inscription, "Please offer any assistance required by the bearer." On arrival I found the usual blatant attempts of African petty officials to extract a little blackmail. Soldiers bearing submachine guns glowered while customs inspectors made it clear I would have difficulty passing without a handout of dollars. I bridled, thought of the high commissioner's card, and whipped it from my wallet. A customs man stared at it, then beamed and exclaimed, "Ah, you are the Nigerian high commissioner to Canada." I found myself escorted without delay through all formalities. My baggage piled into the trunk of a government limousine, and with police motorcycle sirens clearing traffic, I was grandly escorted to my hotel.

• Some hotels remain permanently etched in memory: Raffles in Singapore, because of the tale told every new guest — that the Singapore sling was invented when a British planter urgently required a tranquilizer after discovering a tiger beneath the billiards table. In Nairobi, there was the Norfolk, to which other planters rode every evening for their "sundowners," a lovely, descriptive word.

• In Phnom Penh, Cambodia, I left Le Royal early one morning to catch the only daily flight to Bangkok. At the airport I was informed that, though I was an hour early, I had missed it. There was no choice but to return to Le Royal. I changed into a swim suit, applied suntan lotion and deposited myself at poolside for quiet reflection that one must adapt to the mysterious ways of the Far East or perish. Within five minutes a breathless hotel employee shouted in my ear that my plane was only now arriving. They would hold it for me if I got to the airport within a half hour. Suntan lotion and all, I made it, wondering again about the mysterious ways of the Orient.

• When the people of Guinea, the old French African colony, refused to join the new French Community, departing colonial officers took revenge. They demolished power stations and poured concrete into the sewage system of Conakry. As a result, Conakry was one of the most dismal capitals I have ever seen. Forewarned, I carried bottled water in my baggage. I did not anticipate that the only edible food would be bananas that children hawked on the mud streets. Ahmed Sékou Touré, the dictator-president, gave me a tour. He drove his own car, with no visible bodyguards, to prove he enjoyed popularity and no one faced danger. But I couldn't wait to escape to my next stop, Abidjan, in the Ivory Coast. There the luxurious Hôtel Ivoire, in a magnificent setting with swimming pool, beckoned. I dug into my bag, unsuccessfully, for trunks. Then I remembered the quick, shady shuffling of two floor boys who were supposedly cleaning my room in Conakry when I walked in without warning. To this day I suspect someone might be wandering the jungles of Guinea in an old pair of Canadian swim shorts.

• The St. Georges in Beirut encapsulated the old style media favorite. It provided the best in accommodation, food, and service. For foreign correspondents covering the Middle East, the bar was not only a beacon for reunions but a mail drop. Letters and messages from all over the world awaited reporters. The St. Georges for me, however, is most vividly remembered for the doubting stare of a room clerk who registered my daughter Bette, aged thirteen, in my room. Vladimir Nabokov's novel *Lolita,* about the sexual exploits of a teen-ager, was still a best-seller. Did I look like "a dirty old man?" The stare made me feel like one, but the point, in decadent Beirut, was that no one considered it suitable to issue a challenge.

There is a marvelous, simplistic quality to wandering the world these days. The operative word is "economics." Ignore for a moment the poor who sleep on the sidewalks outside your hotel, as they do in Calcutta. Instead, look at the people in the hotel coffee shop, whether it is Camellia Corner, at the Okura in Tokyo, or the Ibis at the Nile Hilton in Cairo. They share affluence. They dress the same, they are chic, and any children with them sit quietly in reverence, as though aware that fate has bestowed on them a special status.

The greatest hotel in the world? I can't decide. Of the hotels I've stayed at — including Venus' luxurious Cipriani, Rome's Hassler, Paris' Plaza Athénée, Cape Town's Mount Nelson, where war correspondent Winston Churchill stayed after escaping from the Boers — there are a couple that stand out for different reasons. Jerusalem's American Colony exudes a distinctive history and flavor, with shadows of Lawrence of Arabia flitting under the lemon trees in the courtyard. The Okura stations young hostesses, in classical kimonos, to bow as you enter an elevator. Japan, a male dominated society? It is the only country I have ever visited where the chambermaids, in cleaning Okura bathrooms, deliberately leave the toilet seat up. (I have no idea of the procedure when a female guest occupies a room).

I do know my favorite hotel — London's Connaught. The Connaught is not the most ornate or opulent, but, to my taste, it is the most elegant. Favored by discriminating Americans and English gentry from the shires (in my next life that's the gentry to which I plan to belong), it radiates discretion. There is no "Mr. and Mrs" on the bill, no signing of bar chits. You whisper your name to the waiter and the next time he — and his colleagues — recall it.

Nor is a signature required for room service, sometimes leading to unexpected complications. Once, I received, weeks after my return to Montreal, a letter from the management. It said that due to an oversight on the hotel's part I had not been charged for a bottle of Moët et Chandon and a carafon of red wine at breakfast. Could I please remit?

I wrote back, in feigned indignation but in truth, that on the morning of the alleged crime we had departed in haste for a visit to Bath, with hardly time to sip even our wake-up tea. But, more to the point, I said my dignity was injured. How could it even be suggested that at one and the same moment I would order for breakfast a fine bottle of champagne and a lowly carafon of red wine? The next letter from the Connaught was filled with apologies and the admission that the floor waiter had erred and the real culprit had been located.

From a journalistic point of view, my most memorable hotel experience was at the Havana Libre, previously the Havana Hilton, where I stopped during visits in the early 1960s. Fidel Castro was consolidating power, with the help of the Soviet Union, and one of the prices was a deterioration in service and comforts such as air-conditioning. Still, the Havana Libre was the place to be — filled with *compañeros,* comrades from around Latin America, and bright-eyed young Cubans, fresh from the countryside, exposed to their first look at a big hotel. I had an entire floor to myself, not quite sure why, until I heard that the Russians were about to open their first embassy in Cuba — in the Havana Libre. This might be their floor, but it seemed inconceivable that a foreign journalist would be permitted to remain in close proximity.

It was not inconceivable. It was simply sloppy bureaucracy or lax security, for one day I found corridors on the floor loaded with filing cabinets and electronic equipment. Men carted the material into rooms all around me. What made the situation particularly tantalizing was that the new Soviet ambassador was a man named Sergei Koudriavtzev.

I knew him. Koudriavtzev had served as first secretary in the Soviet embassy in Ottawa when I was stationed there in 1943. Along with other members of the Press Gallery I attended several receptions at the Soviet embassy. What none of us knew, of course, was that, though we were allies, Koudriavtzev headed a Soviet spy ring in Canada. This fact emerged only after the war, when a cipher clerk, Igor Gouzenko, defected and told all to the Mounties. Koudriavtzev, meanwhile, had skipped town.

My room, No. 1825, at the Havana Libre was part of a suite. The rest of it was unoccupied — that is, until Koudriavtzev arrived. It was unbelievable but in effect we were sharing quarters. He was in Nos. 1821-23. I could swear I heard him gargling in the bathroom. This small western island in a Red Sea was obviously an oversight, and some poor Cuban or Russian security officers were going to have to do a lot explaining. Apart from the fact that I could have planted a microphone on Koudriavtzev, I received phone calls intended for the embassy. Once, a hotel switchboard operator asked, "What are you doing up in that den?"

Finally, after a few days, I decided it was time to exploit my luck, or commit a foolhardy act, and I slipped a calling card under Koudriavtzev's door suggesting a neighborly drink. The next morning I received a phone call from someone who said he was the ambassador's secretary, and while Mr. Koudriavtzev would very much like to say hello again — yes, he remembered Ottawa — he was awfully busy, and would I be free next week? Ten minutes later the phone rang again. It was now the manager, to say my belongings would be picked up immediately; a room awaited me on another floor.

Later my favorite switchboard operator pacified me by saying I was much safer in my new quarters. Only the night before, two bombs were detonated outside the Havana Libre in Koudriavtzev's honor.

It was on that trip that I interviewed Ernesto "Che" Guevara. Castro may have been leader, but Guevara was the dynamic figure of the Cuban revolution. He went on to animate young revolutionaries throughout Latin America and much of the rest of the world. I had sent him a cable from Montreal, saying I was heading for Cuba to write a series; I would appreciate a meeting. It was a pro forma request. I hardly expected an answer, let alone acceptance. Cuban chieftains at that stage were suspicious of the foreign press. Surprisingly, I received a reply the next day: "When in Havana come and see me." It was signed "Che Guevara."

We talked for an hour. I asked him to comment on what I thought was an apocryphal story — that Castro, in appointing tasks to members of his first cabinet, asked if anyone present was an "economist." Guevara, the story went, thought Castro said, "Communist," and announced he was one. That's how he was placed in charge of economic planning. Guevara chuckled and said the story was not apocryphal. It was true; he had indeed misunderstood Castro; after all, he was not an economist; he was a physician.

Guevara, a handsome, reflective person, expressed sureness about Cuba's future and waved aside his own future as unimportant. (Six years later, training guerrillas, he was killed by soldiers in Bolivia). But his current status turned out to be crucial to me and a few of my fellow reporters.

I finished my work in Havana and set out for José Marti airport. My shoulder bag was loaded with film and reports by other foreign journalists, anxious to avoid scrutiny and censorship. I passed through customs and immigration easily enough, without a search. Relieved, I started to walk across the tarmac to my plane. Then, out of nowhere, two plainclothes security men fell in beside me, demanding to examine the shoulder bag. I protested, more out of fear than principle. They persisted. Suddenly I remembered Che Guevara's cable; it was still in my pocket. I said, "Entende inglés?" They shook their heads. "If you don't understand English, maybe you understand this," I said, hauling out the cable. The security men stared at the signature, and in unison said, "Por favor....please." Without another word, they bowed me aboard. It was a very stiff drink I gripped on take-off.

My hotel in Seoul, the Westin Chosun, was comfortable enough, but otherwise undistinguished — except for a bit of logistics. It was a short cab drive to Itaewon Yong San, a shopping street favored by the U.S. military. Mr. U.S. Kim, tailor, derived his initials logically enough. His establishment in Itaewon carried walled photographs and testimonials of American admirals and generals, and even a few sergeants.

Mr. Kim measured me for a couple of suits, delivery guaranteed the next day. It happened that Mr. Kim was also President Ronald Reagan's tailor. I must be careful how I tell that story; usually I simply say that we shared the same tailor. In any case, Reagan, on an official visit to South Korea, had Mr. Kim go to the U.S. ambassador's residence, where he was staying, to measure him for a couple of suits. Now Reagan's cheque, uncashed and framed, adorned a wall of Mr. Kim's tiny shop.

It reminded me of a tale about George Bernard Shaw who supposedly paid his tailor by cheque, deliberately. If a bill came to £20, Shaw signed four cheques for £5 apiece, knowing the tailor would sell them to memorabilia collectors who would never cash them. Mr. Kim asked for my American Express card.

Stretching up from Chile, the great *cordillera* of the Andes forms a massive barrier between Peru's coastal desert and the eastern plains of the Amazon River. The loftiest Peruvian peaks are almost as tall as Mount Everest, and the canyons are tremendous — some nearly as deep as the Grand Canyon. In many places the rivers pass through narrow gorges with vertical rock walls. Roads, a few built by the ancient Incas, are carved like winding shelves on these awesome parapets left by Nature.

The Incas were a clever people, and well advanced in civilization. Five hundred years ago they performed intricate brain operations. The only trouble with the Incas is that they never invented the wheel, so that no matter how marvelous were their engineering feats in hacking roads on the face of perpendicular rock they did not visualize humans in speedy locomotion. The Incas, who possessed good nerves, went by foot around the steep and blind curves, or used llamas as beasts of burden.

There is a modern version of the llama, and it is called a *colectivo*. A *colectivo* is a kind of taxi: that is, an old sedan boasting four wheels, a motor of sorts, and a horn. The name comes from the connotation that it is a pool operation; the driver takes off for a journey up into the Andes when he has collected four or five passengers.

I started out in good faith for the community of Vicos, high in the *sierra*. It was four in the morning, hardly an ideal time to vacate a hotel room in Lima, the comfortable and sophisticated capital of Peru. But I was anxious to visit Vicos because of an experiment conducted there by Cornell University — an experiment to prove that the fatalistic attitude of the backward highland Indians, many of whom had never even heard of Peru, could be altered by proper guidance from the white man. This was 1962 and I was collecting material for a newspaper series and a book on Latin America. The Cornell representative in Lima, Dr. Henry Dobyns, assured me it would be a pleasant and scenic trip.

Now, I should not malign my friends from Cornell. The scenery for five hundred kilometres was indeed varied and picturesque. As first my *colectivo* driver, a *mestizo* (a person of mixed blood) whose name was Garcia, pointed out, the smooth surface we were on belonged to the Pan-American highway, which runs a good length of the continent. This felt like a fine flat road, and we clipped along it merrily in the dark.

And then, in the first glimmering of dawn, I saw that we had reached the coastal desert — a pretty sight, except that on the right side of the road shifty sand dunes spilled a bit over our path, and on the left there was nothing but a clean drop of several hundred metres directly into the Pacific Ocean below. Garcia disapproved of vehicles ahead of him. So, with the precipice and sea to the left, he passed a few cars at seventy miles an hour. I had to estimate the speed; the speedometer, which had known better days ten years ago, was not functioning.

Suddenly, Garcia, coming around a curve, jammed on the brakes. The car rolled but finally stopped. A hill of sand had cascaded right across the highway. If we had hit it the sand might have acted like a cushion; or maybe it would have resembled a billiard table and we would have bounced into the sea. For a moment I thought of asking Garcia's opinion, but decided instead I urgently needed fresh air. Waiting for a bulldozer to clear the road, I made my way to the edge of the cliff, and it was then that I noticed for the first time the white crosses. There were three of them, in a neat row, planted on the roadside and confronting the sea.

I retreated to the *colectivo*. Two of my fellow passengers were Indians who spoke only the Quechua language of their Inca ancestors and no Spanish (I boasted the rudiments of Berlitz Spanish). The fourth occupant was an agriculture student from Lima en route to visit his family in the town of Carhuas. "What," I asked him, dreading the answer, "is the meaning of the white crosses?"

"Cars," he said. "Cars that went over the edge. One cross for each car. It is a nice kind of remembrance."

He glanced obliquely at me with an amused gleam in his eye. "Nervous?" he asked.

"Not at all," I protested.

"We Andeans," he said, "are quite used to this kind of driving and living."

For the next hour or so I was able to forget the white crosses and the fact that I had foolishly examined our tires and found them pathetically bald. The barren desert with its treacherous sand was gone, and we were driving through the richly green landscape of tropical valleys. Cotton plantations intimately nestled between quiet streams; and, even though the road had a dirt surface, it was straight and clear.

It occurred to me after a while that where you have valleys you usually find mountains, and here they were — breathtakingly beautiful — all around us, complete with snowcaps. We then began to climb, higher and higher. It was only after we were on the Andean road for about twenty minutes that I realized that the surface was still of dirt but the width was cut down to a single lane. The beauty of the mountains vanished. The road twisted and wound in an endless series of S's, except that the bends were shaped like Z's. Garcia honked his way past the fearsome corners without slackening his pace.

On one side a rocky mountain wall rose straight up; on the other side was an escarpment straight down, a sheer plunge in places of about half a mile, with no bushes to break the view — or the fall. Garcia was a man of aesthetic spirit; he kept peering over his shoulder at the spectacular scenery, guiding the ancient Chevrolet at fifty miles an hour by instinct and horn. At one particularly steep decline he thought prudently enough to shift into second; but the gear refused to hold, and slipped into neutral.

The car gathered speed. Garcia steered with his left hand while he continued to wiggle the lever with his right hand, until the gear clicked into position.

I found myself stammering in my Berlitz Spanish: "Are you sure your brakes are good?"

Garcia swung around to answer. "We used them on the Pan-American road. They worked, didn't they?"

Since there were devious curves every fifty metres or so and Garcia insisted on answering by looking at me instead of the road, I withheld further questions. A few white crosses flashed by. I leaned toward the agriculture student and said, "What happens if a car comes from the opposite direction?"

He grinned, shrugged and said, "There's no room for two cars."

Actually we did encounter a few *colectivos* and trucks coming the other way. I am still not sure of the rules of the Peruvian road, whether the car on the ascent or descent is expected to give ground. But Indian drivers must have a code of signals of their own. After a few honks and a toot we backed up until we reached a patch wide enough for the other vehicle to go by.

This was an interesting operation. In order to get better vision while he twisted and navigated backward, Garcia opened his door. I got then a much clearer view of the toy-like bottom of the ravine. The open door also provided a magnificent frame for photographs of the white crosses.

By the time we had gone twelve hours and risen to five thousand metres I felt I was in a rarefied and almost holy atmosphere. I thought: if I have to commit suicide I would prefer it by my own hand and not the hand of a stranger named Garcia whose Inca blood gives him courage but not necessarily a knowledge of the wheel.

Garcia, as though reading my mind, murmured something about having to be on the lookout for *huaycos,* avalanches; this was the height at which they sometimes occurred, and there was no telling when boulders might tumble on the road. I said to the agriculture student: "When a car goes over the side, can they ever find the wreckage in the depths below?"

Gently he patted me on the shoulder. "There are far more accidents on the Pan-American highway; it is wide and people drive faster." Then, noticing the numb expression on my face, he said in what was intended to be a reassuring tone: "These mountain drivers are very experienced." What he did not mention, and what, unfortunately, I remembered from incidental research, was that the life expectancy of the average Andean is thirty-two years. Garcia was thirty-five years old — and at least three years overdue.

At the end of the line, in Vicos, I was greeted by two young Cornell archaeologists, Gary Vescelius and Nicholas Asheshov. They asked me how I had enjoyed my trip. I told them that not even wartime shellfire had left me so terrified and shaken. The Cornell men promptly decided I needed a drink, a large bourbon.

"You may wonder," said Vescelius, "how we managed to get ice."

I had not wondered.

"Remember," Vescelius said, chidingly, "there are no refrigerators in this part of the world."

My mind, I made it clear, was not on refrigerators or ice.

"Glacier ice!" Asheshov announced, undaunted. "That's million-year-old ice in your drink, sir. We've an Indian who chops a chunk for us once a week."

"Under no circumstances," I said, "will I return to Lima the way I came."

The two archaeologists considered this amusing. Could I suggest an alternative?

A few days on the shoulders of the Andes, living with stoical and simple Indians, can be wonderful for your nerves. You know you are in a distinctive world when you see a painting that dominates nearly an entire wall of the tiny local church. It is a Quechua interpretation of the Last Supper. Never mind that the Last Supper was a *seder,* celebrated on the eve of the first day of Passover. Never mind the Judaic dietary rules. Here are Jesus and the disciples, dark-skinned, awaiting carving of the meat in the centre of the table: a suckling pig.

Perhaps the thin air affects your reasoning. In any event, the decision abruptly appears very simple: either you stay there or you go back. My driver this time was much older than Garcia. He was at least thirty-seven, and therefore more mature and experienced. But he had more Indian in him, and his eyelids gave the impression of being half closed. I was not really certain whether he was awake at the wheel.

As we started out, shrouded in the clouds that grace the heights of the Andes, he confessed that he had just driven the five hundred kilometres from Lima and had managed to snatch only an hour's siesta. His breath also advertised the stale odor of *chicha,* the devastating corn liquor brewed by the Incas for hundreds of years. But he was resourceful. He stopped at a stream and dipped his head in the icy water. This enhanced his ability to manoeuvre the car through a herd of llamas clogging the road. Every once in a while he repeated the performance at another stream, returning to the driver's seat wet but revived.

We underwent only two near misses. The first occurred just outside a quaint village where adobe huts clung to the mountain ledge. We were proceeding toward a curve at the leisurely speed of forty-five miles an hour, with nothing between us and the chasm but a feeble horn. Honking! Screeching of brakes! A car from the other direction! We halted two inches apart. As I glanced at the scenic wonders about a quarter of a mile underneath us I choked and said to the driver, "Would you kindly drive a bit more carefully?" Those may not have been the exact words. Still, there is nothing more effective in a foreign country, if you want to establish rapport with the people, than to speak their language.

The next time around a turn we touched bumpers with an oncoming car. It was one of the few points in hundreds of kilometres where the outside rim of the road was protected by jutting rock. In the slamming of brakes, our car skidded on the dirt surface; the rear end jammed into the protuberance and held fast. Visualizing what otherwise would have been a swift drop into the abyss, I again used my "impeccable" Spanish.

The driver shouted back, "But I honked my horn, didn't I?"

When I made Lima I reported immediately to the Cornell office and asked Dr. Dobyns why I had not been warned about the shattering adventure that befalls anyone ignorant enough to scale the Andes. Dobyns, a rather shy professorial type, beamed and said: "If I had told you, would you have gone? We want publicity for our project."

He settled back slowly in his chair and reminisced. "As a matter of fact," he said, "I made the trip to Vicos myself two weeks ago in my station wagon. I would never trust a colectivo. And do you know, as I was coming around one of the bends I saw a crowd on the road. A policeman stopped me. He asked if I wouldn't mind taking four bodies to the nearest mortuary. A car had gone over the cliff, landing, fortunately for the next of kin I suppose, in a place people could reach. Anyway, I couldn't argue. They loaded the back of the station wagon with the bodies."

Another car, another white cross.

Thirty years later I set out to examine the effects of Latin-American terror of a more calculated nature — the lingering impact on the families of *los desaparecidos* (the disappeared ones). Thousands of mothers and fathers in Argentina faced agony and the hell of the unknown when their young sons and daughters were swept up by military death squads. I concentrated on the story of one such set of parents, Angélica and Emilio Mignone, whose daughter Mónica vanished fifteen years ago.

I met the Mignones in 1991, days after they returned from one of their frequent drives to the seashore, one hundred and seventy-five kilometres from their home in Buenos Aires. The excursion was not to seek the pleasures of a beach but to sprinkle flower petals into the lapping waters of the south Atlantic. It is possible, even probable, that Mónica's body was disposed of in this ocean by soldiers during Argentina's reign of terror. The Mignones may never know, for records have vanished, along with the remains of other murdered young people.

Still, the aging couple continued the hunt not only for truth but as a kind of insurance against a recurrence of the nightmare that lasted from 1976 to 1983. Emilio Mignone, in his early seventies, a lawyer and educator by profession, is recognized in his own country and around the world as Argentina's leading human rights activist. Material rewards are neither required nor part of his life. Five feet nine inches tall, weighing one hundred and seventy-six pounds, with thinning, barely combed grey hair, he looks like a rumpled college professor. Usually he wears baggy trousers, sweaters and odd jackets.

On March 24, 1976 the most recent — and most ferocious — of Argentina's military juntas seized power. The excuse was that the country was being wrecked by labor strife, inflation, bombings and other acts of violence by terrorists demanding a new social order. The armed forces imposed their own form of "stability " — new repression. Every university rector, every senior academic chosen during the previous government's tenure, was automatically fired. Two hundred soldiers occupied the National University of Luján. Mignone, its rector, was replaced by an army major. "At that moment," he says, "I took the decision to fight the junta."

The phrase *los desaparecidos* had not yet crept into common use in Argentina, but soon because of it the régime would attain international disrepute. At five a.m. on May 14, 1976 five men, wearing mixed military garb and carrying grenades and automatic weapons, burst into the Mignone apartment. "I thought they had come for me," says Mignone. Instead, it was for twenty-four-year-old Mónica, the second oldest of the five Mignone children. But why Mónica? An educational psychologist at a local hospital, she also spent several hours a week working with two priests in a slum area. At her own expense she paid for an operation for an abandoned five-year-old boy, Julio Miranda, that saved his vision. She was hardly a terrorist.

Emilio Mignone, recovering from his initial shock, demanded to know why and where the strangers were taking Mónica. "We just want to talk to her about a friend," said the leader. "She'll be back in a few hours." It was the last the family saw of her.

I spent several days with Angélica and Emilio Mignone, much of the time in their apartment on busy Avenida Santa Fe — the same apartment with memories for them of the tragic, inexplicable intrusion. A small black-and-white photo of Mónica adorned the living room mantlepiece. Otherwise, there were few physical reminders. Emilio's four thousand books, many of which Mónica had read, still covered wall after wall. For the most part we talked, not about her personally, but of injustice generally and the decline in Argentina of ethical values and creature comforts.

It is known now that executions were carried out largely by colonels and majors, and other regular troops; draftees, who might have rebelled, were not used. It is known, too, that at least eight thousand, nine hundred and sixty-one young men and women were executed without legal process, many of them after torture. But to this day, not much more is known. Emilio Mignone believes the figure must be much higher. But he is as frustrated in arriving at some basic facts — for instance, how many bodies were buried on land, how many deposited in the sea — as he was immediately after Mónica's seizure.

In those days, seeking information, he raced from one government office to another, meeting only shrugs, rebuffs or hostility. In the summer of 1979, with a U.S. government grant of $40,000, Mignone established in Buenos Aires a human rights organization, the Centre for Legal and Social Studies. One goal was to restore Argentina's moribund legal process, particularly the protection of habeas corpus. Another was to handle individual cases of missing people where evidence existed of military complicity. And, always, there was the hope of one day bringing to trial the tyrants who had imposed their own laws.

Meantime another group, Angélica Mignone at the forefront, generated a poignant appeal to the world. One Thursday afternoon in May 1977, several mothers, bereft of word about their children, made a spontaneous appearance in Plaza de Mayo, the square in front of Casa Rosada, Argentina's White House — the president's residence and seat of government. They circled the plaza in silence, holding aloft photos of *los desaparecidos*. Television camera crews from several countries caught the drama of the *Madres de Plaza de Mayo* pleading for information. The generals did not provide any. Nor could they dare halt the quiet but devastating force of the women.

Much has happened since then. The generals and admirals have gone, trapped and discredited by another event for which they were responsible — the Falklands war against Britain in 1982. After

Argentina's defeat, members of the junta resigned en masse. An elected civilian government took over, and the former military leaders were brought to trial. But the mothers — many of them elderly or infirm now — still take their places on Plaza de Mayo every Thursday at three thirty p.m.

Angélica Mignone, though not in good health, continued to make it most Thursdays. So occasionally did Mrs. Renée Epelbaum. Widowed in her mid-forties, she had brought up two sons and a daughter. Students in medicine, law and psychology, the three disappeared in 1976. Alone in the world, Mrs. Epelbaum, in her late sixties, must still work and found it difficult to take off Thursday afternoons. "But like survivors of the Holocaust, we are not going to forget or forgive," she said. "It is impossible to forgive torturers and murderers."

A score of other mothers kept up the ritual. For an hour they plodded in a circle, a few with faded pictures of sons and daughters dangling from chains around their necks. What I discovered touching also was the sight of a couple of hundred other citizens — ordinary men and women, many in their twenties — who joined the procession. "Why?" I asked a twenty-one-year-old woman. She said, "It is the least we can do." Her purpose was threefold: to perpetuate the memory of the disappeared ones; to make certain it will never happen again; to protest the leniency of punishment for the junta members.

After receiving prison sentences, all the officers were pardoned by President Carlos Saúl Menem, along with the leader of a terrorist group, on the eve of 1991. He said it was necessary to reconcile Argentine society, to start a new page with the new year. Later Mignone confronted Menem and said, "I am a civilized person, but you put me in a position where I should look for a machine gun and kill these officers because they killed my daughter." Menem said, "You are a Christian. You would never do that."

Indeed, such is Mignone's probity that he sees nothing sinister in Menem's pardoning of the generals and admirals. It was not, as one might imagine, submission to a threat from the remaining military — but largely, Mignone says, because that establishment is so weakened it is barely effective today: "Menem is sincere and serious in what he says and believes about beginning again. But I think it is a great mistake. If you erase justice you revert to the primitive."

Mignone estimates that no more than five per cent of *los desaparecidos* were terrorists: "The worst feature is that the military decided who was guilty or innocent, without a trial. What they said was, 'Any person who thinks against Christian and Western civilization is a subversive person.' With this definition, half the country could be killed. The junta used against the state the same weapons the subversives used — bombing, torture, kidnapping. 'It was a war,' they said, 'and in a war some innocent people get killed.' But in a war prisoners are not executed."

The emotional misery may not show its scars for years, as it did in Europe after World War II, when many people were impelled to seek therapy. Meanwhile, Emilio Mignone says he has found peace within himself: "I suffer sadness at the disappearance of my daughter — not knowing how she died, or what were her thoughts when she was alone. I will never know, and when I think of that, I start to cry. That is my heart. But in the context of history and politics my head is satisfied. I discovered in the human rights movement a reaffirmation of my religious feelings and also of my political beliefs and my human experiences. The movement in human rights is succeeding."

Some of the warmest stories develop in the least expected way. Take, for example, the story of the soldier and the nun. This began as a standard kind of assignment. The fiftieth anniversary of the Dieppe raid was coming up, and I suggested a piece for *Reader's*

Digest. The magazine accepted the idea, but none of us, at the start, was too clear about the approach. It was a vast subject. Many books had been written about the raid, which was intended simply to test the strength of German defences along the French coast but turned into one of the most controversial actions of World War II.

We decided to start with the basics and see what evolved. The basics were these: On August 19, 1942, more than six thousand Allied soldiers took part in a landing in and around Dieppe, on the coast of Normandy. Included were one thousand British and fifty U.S. Rangers (commandos). But the main force was Canadian. Of 4,963 men who embarked on the operation, scarcely one in three got back to England. There were 3,367 casualties, including 907 dead and 1,946 taken prisoner. It was a disaster. Allied leaders insisted the lessons learned did contribute to the successful invasion of Normandy two years later.

I started by talking to a dozen veterans across Canada. All had harrowing episodes to relate. But nothing that I could see would make the telling of a complex story digestible in a relatively short magazine article, or at least a departure from the standard anniversary account. One veteran whom I met in the town of Woodstock, Ontario, Ed Bennett, said that when I visited Dieppe I should look up a nun, Soeur Agnès-Marie Valois; she had nursed his wounds. Other Canadians gave me the names of other French civilians.

One approach, I thought, might be the interplay between soldiers and ordinary French men and women that terrible day so long ago. In Dieppe I ran into fascinating sidelights. The Germans had marched out some of their prisoners. Fourteen kilometres to the southeast of Dieppe, in the village of Envermeu, seven-year-old Jean-Claude Robillard, spotted a barefoot Canadian hobbling on the flint road. He clutched the hand of his father and whispered, "Give him your shoes, papa." Paul Robillard pulled off his shoes, and tossed them to the Canadian. The Canadian put them on and looked back gratefully. German soldiers seized Paul Robillard. Jean-Claude, now fifty-seven, shared his memories with me, and said, "It was a day of bravery — for the Canadians and for my father."

Soeur Agnès-Marie recounted almost endless examples of the courage shown by her patients, and unwittingly by herself. Many were dead, many badly wounded when they arrived at her hospital in Rouen. Some lay on the floor, before beds could be found, "and they were very dirty — covered with sand and mud and grease." Soeur Agnès and other nursing sisters cleansed the faces of the soldiers with butter. But before there was even a chance for surgery, ten died that night.

Surreptitiously, when no German guards were around, the nuns carried the bodies to their garden in the hospital grounds, and covered them reverently with earth. "We did not want them to lie next to German soldiers," Soeur Agnès said. A few days later townspeople came secretly with horses and carts to move the Canadians to the Saint-Sever cemetery in Rouen.

The incidents of the people of Dieppe piled one upon another, just as had those of the veterans. It was astonishing how clear, in 1992, was the memory of 1942. Obviously August nineteenth was a day no survivor could forget. Still, the question vexed me: How to put it all together in a few thousand words?

I walked along Dieppe's beach, pondering the question and stumbling over stones the size of grapefruit. It did not require a knowledge of engineering to see how the terrain would sabotage vehicles disgorged by landing craft. But what shook me was the sight of *les falaises,* the cliffs. Nothing I had read prepared me for the awesomeness of these cliffs. They made my mind flash back and try to imagine what it must have been like for Ed Bennett, almost blind in a crippled tank, and for the infantry staring up at the impossible height that confronted them — one hundred metres of perpendicular chalk, atop which Germans in concrete blockhouses poured fire over open sights. That is, they could see their targets distinctly — and hardly miss. What terror did the attackers endure? How were French men and women, themselves trapped for the last two years by an occupying force of Germans, able to help these young Canadians?

I decided this was the kind of story that could only be told in the starkest terms, shorn of any fringe elements. One of the most difficult disciplines of journalism is to discard material you think is engrossing. But unless it is absolutely essential to the story, most of the time it must go. I have learned to play tricks on myself: for instance, even if I have taken lengthy notes about a particular incident, I later pretend to myself there was no such incident — if it does not fit the overall story — and throw out the notes. Or, I scrap a good interview — again if it doesn't blend with the whole — by telling myself the person I was supposed to interview failed to show up for our appointment.

Ultimately, everything possible must be learned about a subject for the writer to know what portion to cling to, and what to abandon. Good and tough editing by a dispassionate editor can help. But the first and only responsible authority of an article is the writer himself. Here — the result of two months' travel, research, scores of interviews — is how the piece on Dieppe's fiftieth anniversary appeared in *Reader's Digest:*

Lieutenant Edwin Bennett of the Calgary Tank Regiment was wounded before he even touched the beach at Dieppe. A German shell punched through the side of LCT-7, a Royal Navy landing craft, and hit a hydrogen canister just as the twenty-eight-year-old tank commander was about to climb into his Churchill Mark III. A sheet of fire lashed him, badly burning his face and hands. Shrapnel from the blast took the sight out of his right eye, and when he reached up, his hair was crisp.

Bennett slapped a field dressing over his wounded eye and scrambled up into his tank. His left eye was swollen from burns, but he could make out the columns of seawater thrown up by the furious enemy barrage. The LCT finally scraped the beach. Its ramp splashed down, and Bennett's tank, the nickname *Bellicose* painted on its side, roared out.

Squinting into his periscope, Bennett could see tanks from the first attack were bogged down on the incline of the stony beach. Shells and mortar fire threw up deadly pillars of shrapnel and rock fragments amid the ear-shattering din.

The men of Canada's 2nd Division, caught in a murderous cross fire, were being massacred as they landed.

Keeping to the waterline where he could manoeuvre, Bennett charged along the beach until he found a low spot on the seawall and swung through barbed wire and over the wall. But *Bellicose* and the other tanks that were able to get over the wall were stopped from entering the town by concrete roadblocks. They could only roar up and down the promenade, firing at the German positions. The army engineers who were supposed to blow up the blocks, their equipment destroyed by enemy fire, watched helplessly.

At 11 a.m., some five hours after he had landed, Bennett heard in his headset the order to pull back. As *Bellicose* neared the water's edge, a shell blasted off the tank's left track. Bennett and his four crewmen scrambled out and took shelter behind a stranded landing craft. Some troops had been evacuated, but everywhere men were struggling to burrow into the shingle away from the sleet of gunfire as they waited for more boats. Shortly after, with no boats coming, a senior officer gave the word, and white flags of surrender went up along the beach.

* * *

Defying German orders, a fourteen-year-old French lad named André Amourette ran to the cliffs at the east end of the beach to watch the tremendous air battle overhead. Later he made his way to the railway station, where he saw hundreds of Canadian soldiers waiting dejectedly for the trains that would take them to prison camps. Some were barefoot, some wore only their underwear. One caught the boy's eye and held two fingers up in a V-for-victory gesture.

* * *

Ed Bennett lay on a stretcher in Hôtel-Dieu hospital in Rouen, his face swathed in bandages. His good eye closed from burns, he hadn't been able to see a thing since he was taken prisoner on the beach several hours earlier. His wireless operator had led him by the hand, under German escort, to a hotel where the wounded were temporarily collected. That night he had been loaded into a railway car with other casualties for the fifty-kilometre journey to Rouen.

The voices around him were all male, all speaking German. Suddenly he felt soft hands holding his and heard a female voice speaking to him in French.

The woman spoke slowly, clearly, precisely. With his high-school French, Bennet understood when she said: "Everything will be all right....I am a French nurse....I am going to take care of you."

Sister Agnès-Marie Valois felt a sentimental attachment to Canada, a country she had never seen. This wasn't unusual in the ancient province of Normandy. Samuel de Champlain had set out on his voyages to New France from Normandy. In 1639 three Augustinian nuns sailed from Dieppe, home of the order, to establish Quebec City's Hôtel-Dieu, the first hospital in Canada.

Now young men had come from Canada to strike at the German occupiers. The fifty Canadians brought to Hôtel-Dieu were placed in the care of six Augustinian sisters. Many of the men were seriously wounded. The sisters washed them, tended their wounds and prepared them for surgery.

Though Sister Agnès spoke only a few words of English, she and Bennett managed to communicate. With help from French Canadian soldiers, they spoke a little of their childhood — his in Woodstock, Ont., hers in Rouen. Other Canadians told him she was petite and very pretty. But he didn't realize she was a nun.

As he was being moved to a bed, Bennett managed to remove from the inner pocket of his battle dress a small photo of a young woman. He felt a table beside him and propped it there. "Your sweetheart?" Sister Agnès asked.

"Yes," Bennett said. "My wife." Her name was Lee. She was in Canada, he said, but before long she would be in England as a Red Cross driver.

He kept next to him this picture that he could not see, and Sister Agnès understood why. It's as if his wife were beside him, she thought. It gives him hope. He touches the picture as if he's saying, "I will see you again."

Bennett underwent a five-hour operation — from midnight to five a.m. The German surgeons could do nothing about his right eye, but they were able to reduce the pain and swelling in his left, which would eventually heal.

Sister Agnès was there when Bennett was brought back to his bed. She stayed with him many hours, changing the dressing, nursing him. When he regained consciousness, she said in English: "Good. Only good."

A week later Bennett was told he would be moved to a prisoner-of-war camp in Germany. His eyes still covered, he said to Sister Agnès, "Maybe one day I will see you."

"God alone knows that," she said.

* * *

The next time André Amourette saw Canadians was two years later, at 10 a.m. on September 1, 1944, when khaki-clad soldiers marched into Dieppe. They were the vanguard of the rebuilt 2nd Division, coming this time as liberators.

The same month Ed Bennett was freed in a prisoner exchange and reunited with Lee in London. In June 1945, mere weeks after the end of the war in Europe, he visited Dieppe. While there Bennett met Amourette, now a tall, slender youth of seventeen. It was the start of a great friendship. Over the years

Amourette and his wife twice visited the Bennetts in Woodstock, and they entertained the Bennetts during their several visits to France.

In 1982, on the fortieth anniversary of the raid, the Canadian ambassador held a reception in Dieppe. Amourette was there. At one point a nun approached him and asked, "Are you a Canadian?" It was Sister Agnès.

When Amourette responded, "No, I am Dieppois," Sister Agnès sighed and explained that back in 1942 she had nursed a Canadian soldier with wounds to his eyes.

"I pray for him." she said. "Maybe he is dead. But I am asking Canadians here if they know of him." She didn't know his name, but she remembered him well among all the soldiers she had cared for. He had had a young wife in the Red Cross.

Amourette was stunned. This is the nurse Eddie told me about! This is the nurse he couldn't see. "One minute, Sister!" he said excitedly.

Only a few metres away, Bennett was standing in a group, champagne glass in hand. Amourette strode over and said, "Eddie, come with me." Bennett followed.

"Hello, good afternoon," Sister Agnès said in her limited English. Bennett stared. He knew her voice at once, but he was unable to speak. Finally he broke the awkward silence. "I am Ed Bennett," he said gently. "You took care of me in Rouen."

"Mon petit soldat!" the sister cried. "Is it possible?" They hugged each other. She touched his face, whispering, "You've recovered."

Bennett called to his wife. "I want you to meet Sister Agnès," he said. "She is the one. It's because of her I can see you." The two women embraced.

* * *

Over the next ten years, the Bennetts and Sister Agnès kept in touch, exchanging gifts and corresponding regularly. Sister Agnès became an active member of Association Jubilé in Dieppe, a grass-roots organization formed to plan the observance of the fiftieth anniversary of the raid the Allies called Operation Jubilee. Some one thousand Canadians — four hundred veterans with family members — showed up. The Amourettes were again hosts to the Bennetts, for whom a highlight of the anniversary was once more a reunion with the nun who took such good care of her "petit soldat."

* * *

In April 1993 Soeur Agnès arrived in Canada, wearing on her breast the ribbon, and carrying in her purse the medal, of the *Chevalier du mérite nationale,* the high French honor recently given her in recognition of service to France and Canada in the aftermath of the Dieppe raid.

It was her first trip to Canada, the gift of an Air France ticket arranged by the Jubilé committee. She flew from place to place. On hand to welcome her were members of her order in Quebec City, Bennett and his wife Lee in Woodstock, and veterans in Toronto and Montreal. Several of the wounded, apart from Bennett, remembered how she had nursed them a half century ago.

For Soeur Agnès it was all a dream come true. "Canada — it is as much my home as France," she said. In Montreal she was received by dignitaries at city hall, fussed over, and asked to sign the register of distinguished visitors, preceded over the years by General Charles de Gaulle and Queen Elizabeth II. In June, Soeur Agnès would observe her eightieth birthday, and who — she said — could have imagined such an affectionate, overwhelming demonstration at this stage of life?

We had lunch at the Bonaparte, a quiet little restaurant in Old Montreal, and she celebrated with a half glass of wine — watered down. This was an exuberant lady, tiny in size, magnificent in character. She still worked part time, caring for the sick. She said she would stop only when the good Lord told her to stop.

10 Moscow: Then And Now

ON MY FIRST TRIP TO MOSCOW, IN 1953, I was met at Vnukovo airport by the Canadian embassy's second secretary, Jim Barker, who handed me a book an instant after we stepped into his car. Barker, driving to my hotel, the Metropol, was aware that I was exhausted after a long flight from Montreal — passenger planes in those days were still propeller driven — but he insisted that I read at least the first few pages before falling asleep.

The book, written by a French journalist who spent three months in Russia, describes how he was careful in his conversations, assuming these were monitored. He watched what he wrote in his letters home and carefully guarded his notes, never leaving them unattended in his hotel room. "The diplomatic corps and Westerners in general have always been considered by this government, with its Byzantine spirit, and by Russia as a whole, as malevolent and jealous spies," he observed. "There are no cafés where one comments on the newspapers — indeed real newspapers do not exist. If people speak about grave and, consequently, dangerous subjects, it is only in a whisper and that in private. The government dominates everything and gives life to nothing. Secrecy — administrative, political, social — presides over everything."

The Frenchman, the Marquis de Custine, concluded that the Russians are different from other Europeans because completely different social and political conditions have shaped their lives and perceptions for hundreds of years. He called their inscrutable ways "Oriental." The Kremlin? "A masterpiece of despotism." The reason for Jim Barker's insistence that I stay awake long enough to dip into the book was quickly apparent. He wanted me to understand a fundamental lesson: the basics do not change. The book was written, not in 1953 but in 1839, during the régime of Czar Nicholas I.

Stalin had been dead only six months when I arrived in 1953. But his methods, whether classified as Stalinist or Czarist, lingered. I quickly learned that the main difference between the security of 1839 and 1953 was one of technique. No longer did secret police simply listen at hotel doors. Electronic microphones were far more effective. But today's journalists were perhaps more nonchalant than was the Marquis de Custine.

Eric Downton of London's *Daily Telegraph* was the first, but not the only, correspondent to give me some simple advice: Discretion may be important at times, but in general the only way to function in the Soviet Union is to presuppose that if they consider it important enough, the MVD or KGB will know everything there is to know about you and your contacts. With that in mind, I relaxed, but I still went through an exercise I learned from the Royal Canadian Mounted Police. To test if your room is searched, you arrange your ties neatly in a bureau drawer, one stretched on top of another. You make a mental note of the sequence of colors, knowing that no hasty examiner could restore the pile precisely.

After a week, when nothing happened, I abandoned even a cursory check of my ties. I assumed I was followed. But in fact I was aware of surveillance only twice. The first time was in Tbilisi, the capital of the Soviet republic of Georgia, when a big, florid-faced man, his white shirt open at the neck, stood out in the crowd as he kept close to me block after block; I surmised that was deliberate and other followers were less obvious. The second time, my last day in Moscow, a carload of men and women kept tabs on every stop I made. I gathered from other Westerners this was routine, the MVD simply checking to determine who, if any, were the Russians I might have met during my stay, interesting enough for me to bid farewell — and therefore for them to interrogate. I had learned no state secrets, nor sought any.

I paid another visit in 1955, and again in 1960 — and thirty years later, 1990, as the old Soviet Union crumbled. I anticipated the changes would be enormous. But I was not quite prepared for my arrival at Sheremetyevo airport. This is not modest Vnukova airport of 1953 (the main entry point then, still used today for domestic flights). Sheremetyevo is a huge, teeming, international terminal, with individual baggage carts bearing an advertising label of Samsung, the South Korean electronics maker. The foreign influence includes a duty-free shop proclaiming in English, "The lowest prices anywhere." How capitalism has caught on!

One of the display counters featured Soviet-made watches — "the same as those used by Soviet infantry commanders" — for $99. My mind flashed far back to the last days of World War II, to April 1945 and the ecstatic link-up I witnessed on the Elbe River between American and Soviet troops. Few of the Russians possessed watches, and the trading with American owners was spirited. The Russians judged the quality of a watch by its tick — the louder the tick the better the watch. Mickey Mouse watches, which cost in the United States $2.98, brought forth vast quantities of vodka. In turn the Americans then shared the vodka with slightly drunken Russians who produced fish by the simple device of lobbing mortar shells into the Elbe.

The biggest impact now at Sheremetyevo, however, was the sight of Russians close up. I had seen them often over the years, individually and on television — parading or competing in sports — but I had never realized until now what a difference a generation or two would make physically. Here at the airport were many tall and lean young men, some in neat uniforms — not short, squat, unkempt Slavs. They could have been Canadians or Americans. Better nourished than their parents whom I first encountered? More exercise? I don't know, but it was an intriguing first impression of change.

The Canadian ambassador, Vernon Turner, who was on hand to greet me, also bade farewell to a four-man delegation of the RCMP led by its chief, Commissioner Norman Inkster. The RCMP contingent had been in Moscow for a week. How long ago was it that Mounties were busy rounding up suspected Soviet spies in Canada? Now here they were, in the heartland of the old Soviet Union, at the invitation of agents of the once dreaded MVD, (*Ministerstvo Vnutrennikh Del)*, Ministry of Internal Affairs, which, until 1954, formed the umbrella for external as well as internal intelligence work. The MVD, in trying to transform itself into a modern police force, had turned to the highly respected RCMP for suggestions and cooperation.

The cooperation included a war against drug smuggling. Indeed, it was the MVD that in 1987 tipped off the RCMP about a large shipment of hashish on a Soviet freighter bound from Odessa for Montreal. Until that time Soviet authorities never admitted drugs were moving through their country. But once the admission was made, along with a decision to collaborate with the Canadians, arrests took place at both ends. It was an early "joint venture."

The MVD's fresh objective was to operate efficiently without violating new rules of law that were coming into effect. Ironically, the Mounties were startled to hear MVD officers say that in today's Russian climate they could no longer engage in wire-tapping in the investigation of criminal cases such as drug smuggling. In Canada, the police could, and still can, with a judge's consent. If the Russians were anxious to question the Canadians, it worked the other way, too.

Wire-tapping remained in the purview of the KGB *(Komitet Gosudarstvennoy Bezopasnosti)*, Committee for State Security. But even the once secretive and impenetrable KGB was now open to some scrutiny. Turner, with other ambassadors, received during my stay an invitation to a briefing by the KGB's chairman, Vladimir Kryuchkov. Spy novels abound in CIA-KGB escapades, and Kryuchkov acknowledged that no state can do without "special services," a euphemism for intelligence and counter-intelligence. But the KGB, he said, was loyal to the concept of Gorbachev's *perestroika* (political, social and economic restructuring). Turner asked about the KGB's role in economic intelligence.

"The question is asked by a skilled diplomat," replied Kryuchkov, who then proceeded to admit that Soviet business enterprises, because of their inexperience, were "vulnerable." The KGB would protect them, in the current drive for joint ventures, against foreign predators. It would provide data to fill the gap in Soviet commercial expertise — a tacit admission that economic spying would go on.

There was an Alice-in-Wonderland atmosphere to the briefing, accentuated by the presence of television cameras. On the national newscast, at nine that night, excerpts were shown to millions of Russian viewers, with cameras panning periodically on Turner. His face was becoming familiar, because he accepted many ministerial invitations. Turner was under no illusion. He knew that these occasions were sometimes used by the authorities to communicate with the public at large. He also knew that they could provide snippets of information and degrees of nuance in shifting government policy. It was part of an ambassador's job to analyze them.

Turner was experiencing history in the making: "We, the diplomats, all felt we were seeing in Gorbachev a new type of leader. But nobody ever anticipated how far the changes would go." The spirit of *glasnost*, or openness, was real. It took a sinister Alice-in-Wonderland turn when a few hard-liners attempted a coup against Gorbachev. Kryuchkov, one of the conspirators, was arrested.

I was back again in 1993, during a profound transformation toward democracy. Boris Yeltsin had replaced Gorbachev as president. Russian bureaucracy remained virtually intact, but basics had changed. Much of the Marquis de Custine's description no longer applied. Though some older people feared a return to the past, and Yeltsin had to order in troops to suppress a revolt by members of parliament, the younger generation looked on the world with new openness.

Alexandre Mironov, nineteen years old, in the Russian merchant marine, worked for a former state company, now privatized, that operated ninety-nine vessels. I met him when he was on his way with seven companions to the United States. They were chosen from among four hundred candidates to spend a year at the U.S. Merchant Marine Academy in Kings Point, N.Y. Alexandre, like the others, wore an American summer white naval uniform.

"Does this feel strange?" I asked him.

"Yes," he said. "Strange, but good."

So much for old antipathies, so much for decadent capitalism. Alexandre hopes one day to own his own shipping company. It is all strange. But is it all good? For part of the answer one does not need to go farther than the Metropol. In 1953, if I had carried a copy of *The Wall Street Journal*, it would have been confiscated at the airport. Now the paper, printed the same day in the Netherlands, awaited any taker at the front desk of the Metropol. So did *The New York Times* — in Russian. Good.

It used to be said that "old women don't retire in Russia; they become floor-ladies." The alert and vigilant *dezhurnaya* was a fixture in almost all Soviet hotels. She sat in a commanding position on every floor of the Metropol, a box of room keys on her desk. These she dispensed with a sharp eye on the recipient and any unregistered companion, who must be out by eleven p.m. Why Russians did not concern themselves with possible activities before eleven p.m. remained a mystery. But the power of the *dezhurnaya* was absolute. It was not impelled by a post-revolution need for security; it went back at least to the time of the Marquis de Custine.

In 1993 the *dezhurnaya* was gone from the Metropol, victim of a drive for modernization. Good? Yes, but.... Five doors down the hall from my room three plainclothes security guards maintained constant vigil, day and night. One, in shirtsleeves, marched up and down, pistol visible from the holster dangling at his belt. A few doors beyond this fortress another team watched over another occupant. These were today's guests in a Moscow hotel: Russian gangsters fearful of extermination by rivals, or foreign businessmen aware of dangers of kidnapping for ransom — payable in hard currency, not rubles. The crime rate in Russia had risen at a rate of fifty per cent a year since 1991, when Gorbachev's central government in Moscow collapsed. "The structure was destroyed, and nothing replaced it," is the way Alexandre explained the phenomenon.

It was a sensible explanation, amplified in a document Ottawa circulated to Canadians who enquire about conditions: "Russia is a high-risk market with a degree of lawlessness reminiscent of early capitalist industrial development." The Wild West! A Canadian oil company, Fracmaster, whose operation I looked at in Western Siberia, hired a private security firm to protect valuable equipment offloaded at docks in St. Petersburg. To thwart hijacking, men armed with submachine guns rode shotgun all the way to Siberia.

Alexandre believed that in ten years Russia would be fine — stable and prosperous. He was not resentful or jealous of North Americans. "I think it is good to see how well they can live," he said. "It makes me feel that one day perhaps I can also live as well." I heard much the same sentiment from Alexandre's peers, young waiters at the Metropol. In my induction there, forty years ago, I met only ancient, sloppy, bored, unprofessional types. This led to adventure. On my first morning I made my way to the dining room for breakfast, to discover there was neither a menu nor a waiter dealing in English. Smartly I drew a picture of the only item, fried eggs, I thought I could depict — a circle enclosing two moons.

My waiter nodded grimly — smiles were hard to come by — and returned with a platter of six eggs. Belatedly, I learned that the standard order, at least in those days, was three eggs; he simply thought I wanted a double order. I also learned that menus for room service included an English listing. I memorized my room number, 468, in Russian and next day cheerily telephoned, "Shetteree, shest, voosem — menu." Eventually a waiter arrived with a stained menu, and finally with breakfast. The process cost a couple of hours, so I then fell into the habit of ordering the night before. It was a successful gambit, the meal rarely more than a half hour late. For lunch, if I was pressed for time, I opened, in my room, a tin of Russian crab meat. Good.

But it was much, much better this time, 1993. The old guard had vanished, replaced by a battalion of youthful waiters, smartly attired in fresh white jackets, eager to please, trained, proud, and obviously intent on making a career in this field. Andrey, twenty-two, speaks good English. Inevitably I ask him how he feels about what is happening today and what he expects tomorrow. He says in effect that the best time to have lived in Russia, judging from what his mother, in her forties, says, was during the leadership of Leonid Brezhnev (1977-82). Then people were paid equitably and enjoyed security without the terror of the Stalin era.

Still, real freedom was lacking even in Brezhnev's time. Would Andrey relinquish that freedom for a return to the Russia of a few years ago? "No, of course not — never," he says. Then, almost pityingly, he looks at me and says the wisest words I have heard from anyone on this trip: "Don't try to understand Russia. Russians can't do it."

He is optimistic about the future when he completes his institute studies in hotel management. But he finds it difficult to rationalize the destruction of an orderly society. Racketeers abound, and inflation, at a monthly rate of twenty per cent, impoverishes pensioners and ordinary workers. Andrey's mother, an engineer, makes twenty dollars a month. As a waiter, Andrey is paid more: twenty-five dollars. How does he feel when a guest like me spends on one meal what he earns in two months?

"It never occurs to me," Andrey says. "These are the prices people pay in their own countries, so why not here?" I try to knock down that peculiar logic of market economy by pointing out that Moscow hotel prices are exorbitant, much steeper than abroad. Andrey is not deterred. "You are paying for this," he says, looking up at the exquisite stained glass ceiling high above us.

How well I remember this dining room from 1953. Dinner was a free-for-all. The band, ensconced on the stage at one end, was dominated by three trumpet and three saxophone players who leapt up regularly in unison to blast out a couple of bars, in the style of U.S. orchestras a decade earlier. Russian women deserted their partners, usually party bosses or senior functionaries, to ask men at other tables to dance. Everyone smoked, and the strong penetrating odor of Russian tobacco clung to everything. The cloud rose to the ceiling.

Now? A sedate quartet plays chamber music (at breakfast a harpist is on stage) but, more important, you can appreciate the amber delicacy of the ceiling. The Metropol underwent major renovation in 1990, and Russian craftsmen peeled a layer of nicotine, one centimetre thick, from the surface of the stained glass. No one had bothered about such cleanliness before, in the seventy-three years since the revolution. It was enough that history resided in the Metropol, beginning in the early 1900s. Grigori Rasputin, the mystic monk, held his notorious "tea parties" here. Chaliapin sang here. Isadora Duncan danced here. Lenin gave speeches, from a balcony here. If he were at the Metropol today, I'm sure an outraged Lenin would berate the hotel for its ultra-capitalistic price of twenty-six dollars for a continental breakfast.

My room 468 contained a lumpy, narrow, cot-like bed covered in the ubiquitous and hideous red satin material of Soviet hotels of the time. The dominant feature was a grand piano. Why I was given that room I had no idea, except that it was probably kept in reserve for foreign journalists, microphones in place for the benefit of the KGB That was a routine assumption. My thoughts were on the incongruous grand piano and visions of a Czarist officer chasing a poor serf girl around it.

Now, in 1993, my room, on the fifth floor, having been restored by Finnish and Italian contractors, was tastefully decorated in a pleasant floral pattern, the bed king size. Instead of microphones there were telephones — made in Canada — that worked, including one in the bathroom. But no grand piano. Irina Krevetz, the guest relations manager, assured me that it still existed — but now it was in the presidential suite. I confirmed this personally, except I could hardly believe the tone; it was now tuned. The suite rented for two thousand dollars a night. (My room was *only* $475).

Who usually occupies the presidential suite? A twenty-seven-year-old banker from Georgia, one of the breakaway republics, who claims he puts together big financial deals. There are hundreds of such "bankers" floating around. The Georgian owns no credit card (few Russians possess one) and in the habit of Old Russia pays in cash — hundred-dollar bills. The Metropol, like other leading hotels, posts all prices in U.S. dollars and accepts no rubles. The hotel is a bit queasy about the Georgian; he has run up a big bill. But his white Rolls Royce sits outside. Collateral?

Such is the New Russia — on the surface. In some ways I prefer the Old Russia. The people were better dressed than now, even if dully, and better fed. Everyone had enough money to spend, but there was little in the stores to buy. Now no one — except a so-called "businessman"— has any money, and there is plenty to buy. Businessman? The word does not exist in Russian. It is derived from the English and holds vague meanings. For older Russians it connotes capitalists and exploiters. For others it marks a behavioral change: you buy bananas from a distributor and sell them for more than you paid. This basic stage will be overshadowed one day when you own the plantation abroad growing the bananas. Meanwhile you are a "businessman," whether it involves bananas or working for the "mafia," the generic term applied to racketeers and gangsters.

But wait. On the pavement outside my hotel saunter a group of four young men. They wear strange-looking uniforms. Cossacks! Even as late as 1990 Cossacks were banned, reminders of Czarist days. Now anyone can wear anything, and do anything, and say anything. You could call it "verbal anarchy." In parliament, deputies label one another "criminals," failing to realize they are all products of the same system. They must yet learn to debate without demonizing opponents for holding differences of opinion. They also need to crack down on organized crime — a serious threat to what the government is trying to do. Democracy used to be a crime — that is, preaching democracy. Now democracy is seen as fostering crime.

A plane marked "Azerbaijan Airlines" stands on the tarmac of Moscow's Domodedovo airport, a reminder that the Union of Soviet Socialist Republics once consisted of fifteen "republics," until Azerbaijan and others broke away in 1991 and 1992. But Siberia is still part of Russia, and it is from Domodedovo that you fly if you want to cross the Urals and head eastward.

In 1993 I set out to do a piece for *Reader's Digest* on Canadian specialists working to restore the Siberian oil fields. Despite the end of communism, the same old red tape and bureaucracy persisted. In 1990, before the Soviet Union collapsed, the Canadian embassy sponsored my visa application. Now a Canadian oil-extraction company, Fracmaster, sponsored it.

By good chance I sat next to a Russian helicopter pilot, Ilya, who spoke four words of English — three more than my Russian. Hospitality is a Russian byword that needs no translation. Ilya insisted I join him and two mechanics at the rear of our Aeroflot TU-154. Aeroflot provided no food, but Ilya brought his own. He sliced thick slabs of bread, broke off chunks of cheese, poured tumblers of vodka, and thrust it all into my hands — along with bunches of shallots. That was how we spent a good part of the long trip. Then Ilya lured me to the flight deck where the captain, a Kazakh, hearing I was Canadian, grinned and said repeatedly his one word of English, "Gretzky, Gretzky." Marquis de Custine, were the Russians in your time as generous and warm as in my time?

It was in the Siberian town of Nefteugansk that I saw an illustration of the deterioration of Russia's infrastructure. Faxes exist, but Fracmaster veterans know that messages to their Moscow office, over Russian land lines, often end in limbo. It is faster and surer to transmit to headquarters in Calgary, via satellite, for refiling backward, also by satellite, to Moscow — instead of three thousand kilometres, an expensive stretch of twenty thousand kilometres.

From my notes: Today (May 9, 1990) is a holiday — observance of Soviet triumph over Nazi Germany in the Great Patriotic War. Ambassador Turner and his wife Beryl, with me in attendance, are watching the military parade in Red Square. Gorbachev and other leaders stand in their familiar spots atop the Lenin Mausoleum in front of Kremlin ramparts. Previous slogans I recall, about Communist superiority, are gone. Instead, a four-storey high banner proclaims, "Victory in the Name of Life on Earth."

Thousands of soldiers march past with impressive timing, hundreds of tanks roll by in formation. "They do this so well," comments Turner. "If only they could apply it to their civilian economy." Church bells from within the Kremlin are pealing for the first time since Stalin in his anti-religious mania stifled them. Now they sound the tolerance of religious expression.

But everything here touches on incongruity. Can that be Bob Hope ambling by? What would he be doing in Moscow? In Red Square? Impossible. From Red Square we proceed to a garden party at the home of a veteran American correspondent, Edmund Stevens, who for fifty years has written about the Soviet Union for such publications as *The Christian Science Monitor* and *Sunday Times* of London.

Who stops by for a few minutes? It is Bob Hope, his arm around the shoulder of his "old friend," Stevens. Hope is in Moscow to tape a television program, and he was indeed in Red Square and saw the military display. "It was quite a show," he quips. "I hope the Lithuanians were convinced." But there is also serious conversation, for no Moscow gathering these days is free of it. "Would you say that this revolution is as great as the one in nineteen-seventeen?" I ask Stevens. He says: "Nineteen-seventeen was a disaster. This is a hopeful revolution."

I go off on my own, on a hunt for McDonald's, for I know that since it opened, a few months ago, it has become a Moscow landmark, with the addition of branches anticipated in many of the republics. While ethnic tension marks the many conflicts among members of the old Soviet Union, it is the lowly American hamburger that offers a common link. A taxi driver, as we pass a liquor shop where several men wait to get in, snorts: "Vodka, perestroika." In two words he is telling me his scorn for the campaign to cut down on the use of alcohol and to restructure the economy.

We swing through Dzerzhinsky Square, where KGB headquarters are located, and circle the statue of "Iron Feliks" Dzerzhinsky, founder of its forerunner, the Cheka, immediately after the 1917 Bolshevik revolution. The line-up outside McDonald's is incredible, running three-four-abreast four or five hundred metres — longer, I estimate, than the line-up at Lenin's tomb. Does this symbolize the lure of capitalism over communism? Too simple. But it does represent Gorbachev's desire to improve life for consumers, and a complete reversal of Soviet propaganda.

I proceed along the queue, chanting a prosaic journalistic refrain: "Does anyone here speak English?" Quickly I fall into conversation with two twenty-four-year-olds, Boris and Vladimir, economics and language students. We reach the battery of twenty-seven cashiers in about a half hour, and as Boris starts to munch on a "Beeg Mek" he says, "If people can't go to America, they get a sample of it here." McDonald's is fashionable among Muscovites, especially the young.

Boris and Vladimir like Gorbachev, but criticize him for not moving fast enough. "We need radical changes in the economy," says Vladimir. What kind of system? "Something we can evolve ourselves, between a market economy and socialism." Boris and Vladimir debate this, and finally conclude that social democracy of the order found in Sweden and a few other countries might be the answer.

I mention the counter-argument I have heard, particularly among older people. Of Moscow's population of nine million, two million are pensioners (women retire at fifty-five, men at sixty) living on seventy rubles a month (a hamburger at McDonald's costs two rubles). They are terrified that extreme changes might cause prices to leap fivefold. "One way or the other," says Boris, "there must be dislocation."

We talk about subjects ranging from the military to the black market. I am surprised to hear Vladimir, a former soldier, say he has little regard for the once revered army. Afghanistan was the turning point. The generals today are suspect for wanting to hang on to their power and resources. Vladimir approves of Gorbachev's demand for a trim in military spending, and says there is too much waste on parades.

But what about recognition of the veterans who participated in the Red Square march past? They are among the valiant survivors of World War II, when twenty-seven million Soviet soldiers and civilians — more than the entire population of today's Canada — perished. One of the more sombre remembrances of my visit to Moscow in 1953 was the sight of many one-legged men and women hobbling along the streets. So sensitive was the government to the fact that not all the disabled — eight years after the end of the war — had yet been fitted with artificial limbs, that press censors cut the reference in one of my stories. "I have respect for what the veterans did, the fight they made, but...." replies Vladimir. And he recalls that when he was a school child there was a cult about those veterans, poems written to them, gifts prepared for them...... "but now I want to get on with the future."

The future begins with the urgent task of purging the "mafia," the epithet Russians apply to party bosses, who still live in luxury, as well as to black marketeers who run Russia's underground economy. Boris cites the example of the small Lada car. It costs nine thousand rubles legally — and you have to wait at least five years. But you can get one immediately on the black market for thirty thousand rubles. I say I am shaken by how much more prevalent the black market appears than on my last visit, 1960. Trading in hard currency, except in authorized places like banks, is illegal and subject to severe punishment. There are three rates of exchange. In payment for a hotel room, or a meal in a hard currency restaurant, one ruble costs U.S. $1.50. Otherwise, the legal tourist rate is six rubles to the dollar. Black market operators, openly soliciting on the streets, will give fifteen rubles for one dollar.

In a restaurant, a waiter carries a container of scarce caviar under a napkin and tries to swap it for dollars. A taxi driver requests cigarettes — preferably Marlboros. A pack will take you almost anywhere in Moscow. In Germany after World War II, I recollect, one cigarette was the usual tender. A pair of nylons in Berlin got you a woman. In deference to changed styles, in Moscow it requires panty hose. I mention these things to Boris and Vladimir, and say that I am terribly depressed to find Russians in such degradation, suffering such indignity. "At least the Germans," I say, "had an excuse. They had just come through six years of war." Vladimir, in reference to the 1917 Bolshevik revolution, says softly, "We have come through seventy-three years of war."

Boris and Vladimir are aware and pleased that people abroad regard Gorbachev as a great man because of *glasnost* and the lifting of the curtain around Eastern Europe. But they concede that he fails at home. I say, "But now there is freedom — freedom to talk to me, a stranger. Freedom to criticize the government. Freedom to say what you want. Freedom to travel."

A young woman at the next table, overhearing our conversation, intrudes. "What is freedom?" she asks, and answers her own question. "Freedom is to have the means to travel, not just the permission."

On every visit since 1953 one common denominator hit me: the use of the words "them" and "us." In 1953, with Stalin's shadow still omnipresent, ordinary Russians, brave enough to speak to me informally, alluded to the régime as "them," a kind of unseen amorphous group of people dictating from somewhere on high. The dictation, obviously, was to "us." It never changed, even as late as 1990 when a benign government under Mikhail Gorbachev, though Communist, introduced and attempted to establish, gradually, a market economy. In 1990 the "them" included foreign workers — Finns, Poles, Germans, Hungarians, Italians — brought in to handle the rebirth of old hotels and other buildings because Russian workers were slipshod and apathetic.

A Russian woman, Elena Korenevskaya, deeply distressed by the Russian loss of pride and quality, pointed to the flawless, sixteenth century St. Basil's Cathedral in Red Square. "That was built by Russian craftsmen," she said. "No foreigners were imported." With her husband, Zinovy Yuriev, a novelist and former staff writer on the satirical magazine *Krocodil,* Elena Koreneskaya owned and edited a new English-language monthly magazine, *Soviet Culture.*

A contemporary of Gorbachev — they were at Moscow State University at the same time — she is strikingly handsome, a stunning dresser who looks as though she might portray a Hollywood version of an exiled Czarist countess in the 1920s. In fact, she comes from an old family of Bolsheviks. Her father, a member of the Communist party's central committee, was purged by Stalin, and executed; her mother spent seventeen years in a *gulag* labor camp.

"Obviously," she said, "I hardly have any affection for Stalin. But I must concede that the country under him possessed dignity. There was a belief by many in the system. There was stability and security. People knew they would be fed." When did deterioration set in? She believed it began under Nikita Khrushchev (in power from 1958 to 1964) and intensified during the régime of his successor, Leonid Brezhnev: "People said, 'If you in the system insist on cheating us, we'll cheat you.'"

I mentioned that my overriding personal feeling was one of sadness. Here was a long-suffering people on the promised threshold of a great new life, yet I sensed no exhilaration. I reminisced about my first visit in 1953, when I walked from the Metropol into a chilly November morning. Russian passersby — strangers — motioned to my bare head and said in unfamiliar but understandable language: "Put on a hat or you'll catch cold." Now, in warm weather, I encountered mainly unpleasantness — from clerks in shops, waiters in restaurants.

I told Elena Korenevskaya how yesterday I embarked in search of a restaurant, armed with a scrap of paper bearing the name and address in Russian. Lost, I stopped a policeman, and showed him the paper. Instead of aiding me, he berated me. A woman stepped forward and said in English, "May I be of assistance?" She directed me while the policeman stomped off. "Why is he so angry with me?" I asked the woman. "Everyone," she said, "is angry with everyone else." It was "them" and "us" in different guise.

Elena shrugged and spoke of the frustration that permeated the country. She cited a favorite aphorism: "We are optimists — not by choice but by circumstances." Then she said, "I love my country so much. It's like a sick child. You suffer with it in its illness, and love it even more on its recovery."

We met again in 1993 — Elena, her husband Zinovy and I. Now their magazine was renamed. No more "Soviet" on the cover. Now it was *Inside Russia Guide.* Now the "them" were the criminals making fortunes, the "us " the simple Russians still clinging to bureaucratic jobs or venturing, in small numbers, into free enterprise of their own. They ran kiosks at street corners, selling cigarettes or sneakers, Wrigley's chewing gum or tape recorders, whiskey or Coca-Cola, once the arch symbol of capitalist exploitation. New billboards abounded, advertising Mars bars, Sanyo electronics, products from around the world — even a Turkish bank.

Elena did not recant any of her judgment of three years earlier. But I modified something I had noted back then. As a foreigner, I had found it required major haggling to get a taxi driver to accept rubles. He wanted dollars, or at least American cigarettes. American cigarettes in 1993 were plentiful and inexpensive, burying one tool of the degradation. The black market in dollars had also evaporated, the government realistically permitting open trade in currency exchange shops.

Nonetheless, Elena picked up the question of dignity. "It is still not back," she said. "We had a big, mighty country. Now we have our hand outstretched for charity. It destroys our dignity." We discussed the variations in the Russian mood I had noticed over the years: in the 1950s, a proclaimed self-esteem with the launching of Sputnik I, the first space ship in orbit, beating the Americans. This was followed, in the 1960s, with cosmonaut Yuri Gagarin's pioneer orbiting of the earth. And still later the insistence that life in the Soviet Union was superior to life in the West. But now? I found general demoralization.

"You have to remember," said Zinovy, "that with our Russian character we are either boastful or engaged in self-doubt. Russians were told from the day they were born that they were at the height of achievement — with the best system in the world, the highest standard. Now they see that all their lives were spent in meaningless lies, that the emperor wore no clothes."

Yet both he and Elena were optimistic about the future. "We must face agony now," said Elena, "but in twenty years we will be a great country again. With Russian intellect, it will work better. Society will improve because of all the experience we have gone through." Her main question was what kind of a democracy would evolve. She was against copying the United States: "It is far from being a paradise." Zinovy: "Our development will be closer to the Canadian model. In a way we are a new nation."

There are memorable moments from every visit. In 1955 another reporter, René Lévesque — twenty-one years later premier of Quebec — and I accompanied Canada's Lester B. Pearson, the first NATO foreign minister to visit the Soviet Union since the start of the cold war. Pearson would become prime minister of Canada, but now, at a reception at the Canadian embassy, he was surrounded by five Soviet vice premiers — Malenkov, Molotov, Kaganovich, Pervukhin, Saburov — trading opinions about international relations. Suddenly Malenkov said, "Our conversation is being recorded." Lévesque had moved in quietly, his *Radio-Canada* tape recorder at his side, a microphone deftly thrust into the midst of the group.

"Don't worry," Pearson assured the Russians blithely. "We have freedom of the press in Canada. They'll print anything I tell them to." There was barely a chuckle.

Someone in Ottawa had suggested that, for public relations and color, Pearson should take with him a scarlet-coated Mountie. Pearson supposedly said, "Haven't they enough police of their own?" In fact he was accompanied by a Mountie and other security people. Unwittingly, however, he performed his own detection. He returned early one evening from a concert, and walked into his bedroom in the Soviet government guest house — to spot a startled

Russian working on what Pearson assumed was a recording device. Marquis de Custine, are you there?

In 1990 I had lunch in a "private" restaurant — one of the first truly individually operated enterprises in Moscow. The restaurant, the White Swan, was two blocks from the Canadian embassy — in the basement of an apartment building. It was put together by two women and a man, and very simple in decor — six kitchen tables and chairs, holding a maximum of eighteen people. A wall featured a reproduction of a pre-1917 magazine advertisement, in Russian, for German confectionery. Shabby decor, but edible food — salad, hearty *borscht,* pot roast, and a jug of strawberry squash.

I returned in 1993. The place was unchanged, and so was the menu. The price, doubled, came to only four dollars a person. Still, this represented almost two days' wages for the average Russian. Scores of restaurants similar to the White Swan now operated in Moscow. As Elena Koreneskaya pointed out, there was a substantial difference between 1990 and 1993. "In the past," she said, "what was important was your contact in the Communist party. This applied to writers, composers, intellectuals — everyone. Today, for the first time, you find that neither the party nor the KGB can do anything for you. You are your own boss."

Elena and Zinovy introduced me to another restaurant, the Imperial, as an example of how entrepreneurial initiative was taking hold. "If these people can do it," said Elena, speaking of the proprietors, "this country has a future." There were myriad handicaps, financial principally, when Roza and Daniil Suk-hachykov, decided they wanted to open a restaurant in the old, Czarist style. Daniil, now forty-three, a farmer originally, managed a state restaurant. Roza, forty-one, worked as an interpreter at the Australian and U.S. embassies. It was at the U.S. embassy that Roza made a discovery — how proud Americans were of their history.

She realized that she knew little of her own history; school books had emphasized the 1917 revolution and its aftermath.

Roza, reading U.S. magazines such as *House Beautiful* and *House & Garden,* learned that pride extended to the way Americans enjoyed lovely settings. She remembered how her grandfather would show her a goblet or piece of fine dinner ware and explain these had been crafted by Russian artisans of the past. Roza and Daniil, encouraged by Gorbachev's sense of enlightenment, opened a small café in 1988 with their life savings. Fantasizing that one day it would become something grander, they questioned friends and searched country stores to locate remnants of the past. In a Moscow antique shop they stumbled on what became the centre piece for their dream restaurant — a large, wooden, double-headed imperial eagle of Czarist times. The shopkeeper said it had been hidden in a loft, covered in rags. Exposure in Communist times would have cost its owner twenty-five years in a Siberian *gulag* camp.

The Imperial restaurant, which opened in January 1993, is located on Ryleeva Street, in a turn of the century building that once housed Orthodox priests. Roza and Daniil spent months of their own labor plastering the ceiling and walls. Lovingly they collected furnishings and added touches of the old style as they unearthed them. The Imperial is a stunning tribute to nostalgia. Seventy dollars a head is about right for a superb dinner. Half the patrons are foreigners, half Russians. "Mafia" types are not welcome, limiting — at least theoretically — local clientele to entrepreneurs who succeed legitimately.

The prosperous patrons of the Imperial hardly represent the typical Russian dentist who must work a half hour to earn the rubles necessary for a loaf of rye bread, or nearly two hours for a litre of milk, or a full day for a kilo of beef. But the Imperial exists as a hopeful augury for the future. So does GUM, the ageless and huge department store facing Red Square. On every visit to Moscow I have always dropped by GUM to get an idea of what goods are available to Russians. From year to year the quality and styling hardly changed — shoddy household items, garments of uniformly drab gray or black or brown, all turned out by state factories.

Now? A merchandising revolution took place in 1992 and 1993. GUM, becoming a private corporation, was loaded with foreign boutiques such as Christian Dior. A lineup of men and women waited to get into Galeries Lafayette of France, which featured hundreds of exclusive and costly items, including Lacoste tennis shorts and shirt at $120. A German chain, Karstadt, the equivalent of K-Mart, offered men's suits at $180 and women's suits at $155 — eye-openers to Russians for the superiority of style and quality to anything they ever made.

Most revealing was Botany 500, the line of popular men's wear in the U.S. A sports jacket cost U.S. $225, the same as in the United States. Tuxedos? Here they were displayed in batches, in a country immersed in proletarianism for three-quarters of a century. "Who buys tuxedos in Moscow? Foreigners?" I asked a saleswoman. "No," she said, "only Russians." For 350,000 rubles or U.S. $350. (Three years earlier one ruble cost $1.50; such was inflation that now it took one thousand rubles to buy one dollar).

When Botany 500 opened in Moscow it expected to sell two suits a day. The Saturday I was there it sold fifteen — plus shirts, ties and accessories. Eighteen clerks worked two shifts, from eight a.m. to eight p.m. As far as I could judge, the only demand was from their own compatriots. In SoapBerry, a Canadian-owned boutique selling skin-care products, a Russian woman one day put down one thousand dollars cash to pick up an assortment of facial cleansers and cosmetics.

In Escada, a German haute couture shop, I spotted a beautiful black silk suit with a price of 4,732 Deutsche marks (roughly $3,500). "Why don't you buy it?" I said to the salesgirl, a lively blonde in her early twenties. As soon as I said it I realized how insensitive was the question. But she was not annoyed. "Who, me?" she said, her blue eyes wide in astonishment, as though I was serious. Then she saw the irony and laughed.

"How long would it take you to work to buy it — if you didn't eat or pay for rent or anything else?" I asked. She made a quick mental calculation and finally said, "About twelve years."

Who shops in GUM? "Business" types? "Mafia?" Undoubtedly some came by money through slick or unsavory means. But others are obviously honest Russians splurging, in terms of their income, to sample the fruits of the West. GUM not only features the latest in Western fashions and products. It is a civilized oasis for Russians brutalized by the bureaucracy that still dominates traditional Russian stores. In GUM you select what you want, you pay for it, and someone wraps and hands it to you. In Gastronome Smolensk, also in the centre of Moscow, you line up to determine what food item suits you, then you wait while it is weighed and priced. You line up again, at the cashier's counter, and, after unbounded delay, you put down your rubles and pick up a receipt. You return to the food counter to collect your five hundred grams of cheese. The selection of cheese did not require any great decision-making; only one kind was displayed.

This was the system in 1953; it remained intact in 1993. But there was a major difference compared with 1990. Three years ago, regardless of how many rubles you carried, you could buy *no* cheese; much of the time there was none. Nor is it any longer a question of ability to buy if you have the right contacts. Now goods are available if you have the money. The frustration of everyday shopping undoubtedly will be eased as more and more state establishments become cooperative or privatized, or introduce check-out counters. The example of a transformed GUM stands out. Only by such modest but significant gains is material progress marked in Russia.

Meantime, in the most meaningful advance, the statue of "Iron Feliks" Dzerzhinsky, the old Cheka chief, is gone from its pedestal near the once notorious Lubyanka prison. It was toppled by demonstrators celebrating new freedom in 1991. Now it rests in a kind of symbolic stillness in front of the Museum of Modern Art. Next to it, lying on its side is a statue of Stalin, its granite pedestal smashed.

The museum is located across the road from Gorky Park. I spent an afternoon in the park, introducing myself to strollers, finding the odd person who spoke English. In 1953 two kinds of opinions were expressed — official and personal. Official simply meant a parroting of the party line. Rarely did you hear anything "personal" — a frank opinion, and then only in the safest surroundings. There is no "official" line today. Everything is personal — freedom of expression, freedom of action. Even the crime that flourishes is a reaction to the former regimentation and endless check-ups. The release from restraints led to an ignoring of rules of honesty, an abandonment of dread of interrogation. The types who drive a Mercedes in Moscow — masses of these expensive cars navigate downtown streets — do not yet tremble over government questioning of where the money came from.

That is a likely step in the future when the drive to halt criminal activity gains momentum. But that would not threaten political freedom, the stifling of which was assured by the KGB. In Gorky Park I spoke to Anna, seventeen years old, a student, who hoped to become a lawyer. Did she fear the KGB might come back to power? "I do not think it is possible," she said. "Democracy has made its roots."

I sat on a bench and relaxed. A girl, perhaps sixteen, came up to me, curtsied, and said, "I hear you are a journalist from abroad. I just want you to know we are going to be all right. We are going to come out of our difficulties." Then she made another curtsy and left. Old World charm had returned to New Russia. However, one of the gravest quandaries of the day remained: How to offset the cynicism, the lethargy, the corruption, the bitterness, the demoralization that undermine what began as *perestroika* and culminated in *demokratizatsiya,* democratization.

In previous trips to Moscow I emerged invariably, like travellers before me, with a sense of relief. The Marquis de Custine likened it to the joy of a bird escaping from its cage "or coming out from under a vacuum bell." He said, "I can speak, I can write what I think, I am free!" Both in 1990 and 1993 my departure was with a feeling of sadness rather than relief. The Russians are a warm, extremely likable people with few affectations. I still think of how total strangers stopped me outside the Metropol on a cold November morning in 1953 to tell me to put on a hat. There was a simple *mouzik,* or peasant, quality to the gesture, and I believe that deep down it remains despite any surface atrophy. What saddens me is the indignity to which a good people have been subjected — their forfeit of pride in work or achievement.

At least Russian humor remains alive, illustrated by this tale: Two friends meet on a Moscow street, and one says to the other, "I've some fantastic news, and some bad news. Which do you want to hear first?" "Tell me what's fantastic," says the friend. Says the first: "I've just met Lenin's mother. She's still alive!" "That is incredible," agrees the friend. "Now tell me the bad news." "The bad news?" echoes the first. "The bad news is, she's pregnant."

By contrast, a visit in 1992 to Czechoslovakia left me buoyant. Here was an Eastern European country that, unlike Russia, was emerging from the stagnation and oppression of communism with a sense of optimism. Its federation, like the old Soviet Union's, was breaking apart. But there was little rancor and no bloodshed, such as blighted Armenia, Azerbaijan, Georgia and other former Soviet republics. Slovakia was going its way in peace, and so was the Czech Republic.

A different history and economy formed the bedrock. The Russians had never known the meaning of democracy. The Czechs like to quote a saying, "Socialism is the most complicated road from capitalism to capitalism." Uniquely among the residents of what were once iron curtain countries, they can invoke the saying from their own experience. For twenty years — between the two world wars — Czechs savored the luxury of independence and the challenge of an open economy. Then came the Nazi occupation, and soon after it the Communist takeover.

In 1989 the Czechs threw out their authoritarian rulers in a "velvet" revolution. It was a perfect description of a bloodless act of history. The road back, while still gentle, is hardly as smooth as velvet. The Czechs are undergoing a transformation that might well shatter a lesser people. But the point is that they are confronting it — and moving ahead.

Reader's Digest wanted to tell the story of the transformation, with the emphasis on the present, as much as possible through the eyes of one family. The question was: What kind of family would be appropriate? We decided on a young family — that is, parents in their thirties or early forties, because we wanted a generation straddling the old era and the new. We also favored a medical background, because it symbolized the nation's advanced standards.

The rest was easy. I asked a few doctor friends, and Dr. Richard B. Goldbloom, professor of pediatrics at Dalhousie University in Halifax, provided a candidate. Through a Czech colleague in Halifax, he heard of a husband-wife team in Prague. That was how I met Dr. Jiri Procke, a surgeon, his wife Eva, an ear, nose and throat specialist, both thirty-nine, and their thirteen-year-old son Michal. They proved ideal — spirited and informed.

The Prockes live in Southern Town, a Prague suburb of 150,000 people (the city's total: 1.2 million). It is an ugly complex of plain, high-rise apartment buildings, indistinguishable in style from those in East Berlin and parts of Moscow. The inhabitants suffer from what they call "panel disease," an allusion to pre-fabricated walls that keep breaking into their original sections. But Eva and Jiri are lucky. They had to wait only seven years to get in; meanwhile they lived with Eva's widowed mother. Michal occupies a tiny bedroom. His parents' is not much bigger — about the size of a walk-in closet in the homes of many Canadian doctors. A wall hideaway bed emerges as a double-decker to save space. Jiri made it. The living room measures about four by three metres. The whole area is sixty square metres.

But there is charm and warmth, thanks largely to Jiri's hobby and skill in furniture making. Deeply stained wooden wardrobes, bookcases and trimming are his creation. The bathroom is a tight squeeze since it contains a washing machine. There is a refrigerator, but no dishwasher. Eva and Jiri share all household chores, including cooking and cleaning. They cannot afford a cleaning woman.

Yet their combined income places them among the more affluent Czechs. Jiri's salary as a surgeon amounts to seven thousand koruny ($280) a month, after taxes five thousand koruny ($200). Eva's take-home pay is $180. The apartment is a cooperative and in theory will belong to their heirs in one hundred years. But, like so much else in Czechoslovakia, that is changing. No one is sure whether occupants will stay on as tenants, or who is going to own what — and when. Outright purchase now of anything equivalent in size and location would require an impossible sum of three hundred thousand koruny ($12,000).

Savings? When I asked, both Jiri and Eva looked at me not so much in embarrassment as bewilderment. Who could save? At the end of a month they feel lucky if the equivalent of sixty dollars is left over. This goes into hoarding for immediate purchases. Right now Eva takes delight in a freshly acquired telephone answering machine — needed to screen night calls from patients — that consumed three months' savings. It took them seven years, and a generous gift from Eva's mother, to accumulate one hundred and thirty thousand koruny ($5,200) for a 1990 Czech-made car, a midget Skoda.

Though Jiri occupies a senior position — chief of emergency services at Chirugicka Klinika, on Londynska Ulice in the centre of Prague — he rarely drives there. No parking space is available. Instead, he rises at 6.20 a.m. to travel by foot and subway, to start work at 7.30 a.m. I spent a day with him, having walked a good stretch from Charles Bridge. Jiri was upset when I mentioned that en route I paused to watch street vendors hawking Soviet knickknacks to tourists. The last of the Russian soldiers pulled out of Czechoslovakia a year ago, but some of their garb was on sale: wide-crown military hats (twenty dollars); army greatcoats (thirty dollars); badges and insignia (four dollars).

"I hate these peddlers," said the gentle Jiri with uncharacteristic vehemence. "I'm ashamed of them because they are typical of today's new rich. Books? Yes, sell books on the streets — but not Russian uniforms. It is not dignified. It doesn't represent the image of Prague."

That image is of a beautiful city, now receiving a facelift after decades of neglect. Many buildings, scrubbed for the first time, reveal ochre or natural stone complexions. It makes me think of a woman's aging gown that is frayed but shows exquisite detail in the quality of material and workmanship. The woman herself? The anxiety of long strain and illness cannot hide her tenderness and charm. The pride has returned. Namesti Antonina Zapotockeho, named for a former Communist president, is replaced by Winston Churchill Square.

The most visible change, however, is in the reappearance of emblems of a market economy — the big and brightly illuminated signs on Vaclavske namesti, the main boulevard, proclaiming products from around the world: Fuji film from Japan, GoldStar electronics from Korea, *Time* magazine from the U.S. The Czechs like it. These are more than advertisements. These are emblems of a world the country knew before propaganda mechanisms — Nazi, Communist — took over.

The sign that undoubtedly evokes the most nostalgia — and special pride — is Bata's. In 1939 Thomas J. Bata left his native Czechoslovakia rather than work under the Germans. He moved to Canada to build Bata into the world's largest manufacturer and marketer of footwear. Now, in March 1992, he was back, at the age of seventy-seven — for the ceremonial re-opening of a factory and forty of his stores. The huge Bata logo dominates Wenceslas Square, competing for attention with the statue of good King Wenceslas astride his horse. Czechs do not seem to mind.

Jiri even approves of the ads on street cars — blue camels on a big yellow background promoting U.S. Camel cigarettes. Eva disapproves, asking, "Would you like Michal to start smoking?" Jiri says: "I'm excited that we now have variety and color and life — on the buildings and on the side of street cars. Under the Communists, everything was painted red."

Through the Prockes I met a fair representation of contemporary Czech society. To start, there was Mrs. Vilhelmova Bozena, who runs a neighborhood restaurant, the Prazanka. The Prazanka, the first private restaurant in Southern Town, is the simplest of establishments, seating one hundred and fifty people at plain wooden tables. It had been a state beer hall. Now it provided an example of what it means to establish one's own business in a country breaking from a Communist mold.

Vilhelmova had long dreamed of fleeing from her drudgery as a hundred-dollar-a-month clerk in a food stall. She obtained the Prazanka for two and a half million koruny ($100,000) in an auction, against five other bidders. The state bank granted a four-year loan of two million koruny, and the other five hundred thousand she raised among a sister and four other relatives. All now worked as cook and servers. Vilhelmova's husband had to retain his job as a construction laborer for extra income. But he contributed by installing new wall board to make the place at least look revitalized.

Vilhelmova appeared exhausted and older than her thirty-nine years. "Our new life in Czechoslovakia is great, but no one realizes how hard it is to make a start," she said. The Prazanka was almost always filled, but Vilhelmova had not anticipated two problems: first, most of the patrons were in their twenties and did not want to eat — just drink inexpensive beer; second, it was tough to deal with state suppliers who retained the monopolistic habit of serving or ignoring state and cooperative restaurants.

"Perhaps when there is more private business, private suppliers will start up, and it will be easier," said an uncertain Vilhelmova. Meanwhile, she must rely on state agencies for eighty per cent of her supplies. She must also pay cash because of the poor credit record of new operators. Recently, Vilhelmova decided to turn part of the Prazanka into a food store. The "food store" is two metres wide, two metres long — "the smallest supermarket in the world," Vilhelmova calls it whimsically. But it does help her meet her loan repayment and bring in a modest monthly profit.

There is, however, a new problem: recruiting staff. Most waiters she finds incompetent or lazy; they prefer to work for cooperatives. The good ones quit to start their own restaurants. I tried to lighten Vilhelmova's anxieties by asking, "What will you do when you become a millionaire?" She shot back, "Put all my money in the bank and live off the interest." I said, "A true capitalist." Vilhelmova loved that. Meantime, our bill, for traditional Czech braised beef and dumplings, had come to one dollar a person — a working person's meal out.

I learned other exercises in current Czech economics when we visited a clothing shop managed by Mrs. Bohuna Frybortova, one of Eva's former patients. The shop, operated by the Prague Dresses and All-Wear Company, a state enterprise, was due for privatization. Mrs. Frybortova, forty-nine, earns a good salary — three thousand koruny a month — enjoys merchandising and works long hours. Would she like to be the owner? "Everyone has this kind of dream," she says. "But I have no chance. Only a foreigner could afford it." The cost will probably run to one hundred million koruny ($400,000).

Under foreign ownership, she could hope to stay on as manager, with an increase in pay and incentive bonus. Immediate issues, however, preoccupy her. She has difficulty finding a good staff — thirty salaried clerks, and twenty-five unpaid learners. In the days of communism, everyone worked — at least in theory.

One of the more dubious joys for many Czechs, in their introduction to democracy, was the discovery that it wasn't always worth while to hold a job. Unemployment insurance paid only a few hundred koruny a month less than a clerk's wage. Hence Mrs. Frybortova was always short-handed. The Czech government solved the dilemma, after a year's exposure, by limiting unemployment insurance to six months.

Now the challenge for Mrs. Frybortova is to keep the people she's got. Hers is a "big" shop — defined by its number of employees. Only a few have been privatized so far because the government concentrated at the start on "small" shops (up to fifteen employees). Three-quarters of these — two thousand so-called boutiques — are now under private ownership, luring clerks with offers of higher wages. They also attract customers like Eva, who prefers to browse in boutiques because the clerks are more pleasant than in the old state or cooperative shops; try-ons are permitted, and prices are not necessarily higher.

We visited one of the most successful operations, run by two people with daring but no previous experience in merchandising. In 1990 Ms. Iveta Svarcova, now twenty-six, worked as a secretary in the Intercontinental Hotel. Jiri Malik, now forty, a state building engineer, knew construction values and what space was available for rental in Prague. The two raised twenty thousand koruny ($800), between themselves and friends, to register as a company. In 1991 they rented a store called "Adam." A famous and expensive men's wear establishment back in Austro-Hungarian times, it had stumbled during the Communist régime. Czechoslovakia still knew how to produce good woollen fabrics, but failed in linings. Able now to import lining material, Svarcova and Malik restored Adam's old reputation for quality in men's suits. On the strength of Adam's prosperity, they obtained one hundred and seventy-two million koruny ($688,000) in a state bank loan to buy on auction "Dum Elegance," a state-run men's and women's wear store. Today it is the most fashionable boutique in town.

Svarcova and Malik plan to open a third exclusive shop, with gowns selling at eight hundred dollars and up. Who can afford such tags? Svarcova claims that apart from many foreign visitors, there are thousands of new millionaires in Czechoslovakia, beneficiaries of privatization and restitution of old property confiscated by the Communists. The biggest problem, she says, is hiring staff with the right attitude and mentality: "Clerks were so used to seeing a line-up of people waiting to buy whatever the store had to offer, all they bothered to say was, 'Next, please,' usually without the 'please.' Now a clerk must learn to sell, to accommodate a customer, to smile."

Jiri would like to be part owner of his hospital, along with other surgeons. But they are not yet sure of a loan from a state bank — money is scarce — or how to raise it themselves. Even if he becomes a co-owner, Jiri intends to continue on a salary during a transition period — maybe five years — while a scale of fees can be worked out. Nobody knows yet the value of any surgical procedure. "But one thing will improve," Jiri believes. "A better surgeon will have more patients and will earn more than an unsatisfactory one. Now everyone receives the same salary, regardless of how hard he works or doesn't work." Jiri's seventy-hour work week, partly voluntary, is not matched by all his colleagues. That imbalance permeates every field.

Jiri's most gratifying reward has already come: appointment as surgical consultant to the president, Vaclav Havel. The letter from the president's office arrived while I was there. It was Eva who showed it to me. Jiri's modesty prevented him saying anything until I confronted him. Yes, he conceded, it was an honor — not only acknowledgment of his resistance to membership in the Communist party but recognition by his peers of his professional skills.

Eva, who still works in a state clinic and sees between sixty and seventy patients a day, says she hopes to become a private practitioner. What she has in mind is to join with nine other doctors and buy a small building in Southern Town. A former state nursery, the building is now closed because of a drop in the birth rate.

A friend of Eva and Jiri, Miloslav Francu, a fifty-four-year-old chemical engineer, came by their apartment one Sunday afternoon. Francu works for a large state company, CKD. His division, with three thousand employes, makes semi-conductors, and was kept busy when thirty per cent of the production went to the Soviet Union. But that ended in 1990; CKD no longer was compelled to sell through a central state agency, and Moscow lacked money for open orders. CKD failed to fill the gap elsewhere. There was no market in the West.

"We were five to seven years behind the West in production methods," says Francu. "That was typical of socialist countries, especially in high technology. We made illegal copies of computer parts from Motorola or Intel. Then, when we had the opportunity to purchase original components, we lacked the money." CKD decided its only salvation was to sell its six divisions separately. Francu's division will probably become a subsidiary of a French company. This will enable it to obtain modern computer hardware (CKD's own software is good) and become — at least theoretically — more competitive.

"We'll benefit, and so will the French," says Francu. "We are good middle men. There are some advantages to having been trade partners with Russia, Bulgaria, Poland, and the others. Those markets can open again." Still, Francu anticipates difficult conditions for several years: "We enjoy political independence, but we have not yet found economic independence. It is very important that we receive foreign capital and the help of joint ventures. There are many problems. But I am an optimist. We will solve them."

"What about the problem of the Czech worker? " I asked.

"We are not Russians," said Francu sharply. "They are lazy." The Czech worker, despite forty years of communism, still has much of the desire and capacity for hard work as his father had, Francu argued. Then he paused and said softly, "We are bent, but not broken."

It was a judgment I heard confirmed by foreign businessmen in Prague. Whether the influence is subliminal, or the lessons are handed down from one generation to the next, the Czech worker remains industrious. The principal hurdle is psychological, an unwillingness to make decisions, the effect of central command exercised by the Communist party. Even today's cabinet ministers sometimes display a fear of committing themselves in business negotiations. The penchant is to refer decisions to another department.

The revival of free expression has caused an eruption in book publishing, with two to three hundred operators, mostly small, willing to express a wide assortment of opinions. Eva and Jiri invited Zdenek Volny, forty-six, to share with us a bottle of wine. They knew him when he was exclusively a novelist — author of seven books. Volny did well enough to live off his writing when the state was in rigid control. This meant he complied with rules of the ten state publishing houses. The system kept out foreign competitors. For instance, Ian Fleming's James Bond books were forbidden, since these dealt with Western security people in deadly combat with the KGB.

After 1989 Fleming thrillers were snapped up by eager readers who hadn't enough money left to think of natives like Volny. He was forced to start translating from English to Czech for business periodicals. He also formed a partnership with three colleagues to found Bonus Press. Its first book, in 1991, was titled *Black Cobra Conspiracy*— a spy story about the CIA versus Arab secret services. The author? Alex Scott. That happened to be a pen-name coined by Volny. It's his book, a shameless attempt to cash in on the popularity of foreigners such as Fleming and John le Carré. *Black Cobra Conspiracy* reached an impressive sale of fifteen thousand copies.

"What does democracy mean to the literary world of Czechoslovakia?" I asked Volny.

"It's freedom to write and publish as we please," he said. "But it's also freedom of the market place, which means that British and American publishers at first may be more successful than Czech houses and authors. There's a big demand by people here searching for novelty, for fresh entertainment."

Bonus Press expected to publish only four or five titles in 1992. Instead, it came up with thirty-five on its list. "This is a great success story," says Volny. "It's a message to the whole country that it is possible to do well in a new enterprise." It also reflects the popular mood today. After five decades of censorship and political indoctrination, Czechs crave relaxation. Most of the books by Bonus Press are Star Trek novels. In their choice of films, Czechs place Arnold Schwarzenegger's at the top.

Introduction to the ways of the West gave Eva and Jiri a taste for the stock market. Like all Czechs, they become beneficiaries of joint ventures. Through investment vouchers they can claim an indirect share of Volkswagen's payment of seven billion dollars for acquisition of a seventy per cent interest in Skoda. The investment voucher is a cornerstone of Czechoslovakia's privatization program involving large state companies. In 1992 Eva and Jiri bought, for thirty-seven dollars each (the figure was nominal, to cover the cost of government book-keeping), their allotment of vouchers. Part they transferred to an investment corporation. The rest they are holding until they can themselves decide what to invest in. A chocolate factory? Beer? Bohemian crystal?

"We are quite stupid about finances," says Eva of herself and Jiri. "We have no experience in this." They are not alone. Most Czechs do not yet understand details of a "capitalist" technique that enables them to trade in the free-market place. "We are the first people in the world to engage in a transition this way," says Jiri. "But I don't want to spend time looking at money charts. It's not the most important activity in my life."

Meanwhile, Eva and Jiri know only that free enterprise brings some strange results. Their great indulgence is the opera, to which they go twice a month with Michal. Under the Communists, tickets cost only eighty koruny ($3.20) each; the state paid a heavy subsidy. Leading singers — or actors in the theatre — were often chosen because of Communist party membership. Under the new government the subsidy was lowered. The price of liberty? Two hundred koruny ($8) a ticket. "It's worth it," says Jiri. "Now the artists are chosen because of merit."

Jiri no longer has to warn Michal not to repeat the anti-Communist discussions that used to take place at home. Jiri's own childhood was filled with admonitions. His father, Jiri senior, now sixty-nine, had a hard life. He could not go to university because the Germans, during their occupation, shut down universities. Instead, he was sent to Germany in forced labor — to haul rubble from the streets of Berlin. His generation underwent the most vicious period of communism — the execution or imprisonment in the early 1950s of Czechs accused of contacts in the West because they had served with British forces in World War II. I remember a visit to Prague in 1956, when three writers met with me in my hotel room. I listened to them until four in the morning, to their frustrations, to their inability to express themselves publicly, to their fears for the future. We drank, and we wept in common understanding. Now life was so different, so refreshingly open.

The Prockes took a vacation in the summer of 1991 in Holland. They carried their own food, mostly spaghetti, drove in their tiny Skoda, and camped out. All they could afford, it was hardly lavish by Western standards. But the family thought it the most luxurious happening in the world. They had been able to leave Prague without an exit permit — impossible under the old Communist régime — and no one at the Dutch end demanded a visa. This was freedom.

Perhaps even more gripping, at least for Michal, was their experience on a side road. Lost, they stopped a Dutch car and asked the driver for directions. "It is too complicated," he said. "I'll lead." He swung his car around, and drove eight kilometres out of his way to their destination. "Maybe I will see you one day in Czechoslovakia," he said. "Bye, bye." Michal was awe-struck. He could only think that in his country people, still getting over the effects of communism, were suspicious of chance encounters with strangers.

11 Spies and Adolescents

WHAT IS A REPORTER'S RESPONSIBILITY in exposing — or not exposing — a delicate issue of national importance?

Early in 1967 I made a swing through several countries in Southeast Asia, to describe what they felt about the war in neighboring Viet Nam and how they were affected by it. Laos turned out to be one of the more delightful stops, its people among the most stoical and appealing I have ever met. Quickly, I learned a key word in Laotian, *bopigman.* Probably the most casually expressive in any language, it means several things: What's the hurry? Nuts! *Mañana, tant pis, nichevo,* don't panic, take it easy, so what?

It was really not a word; it was a philosophy. When the Mekong River rose, flooding the streets of Vientiane, the capital, men and women still sat at sidewalk cafés, water above their ankles, and said with a shrug, *"bopigman."*

Vientiane was the base for a Canadian military detachment of the International Control Commission. The ICC, composed of Poles, Indians and Canadians, had been established in 1954 to monitor the truce that ended the French-Vietminh war, leading to transition of French Indochina into three independent countries: Viet Nam, Laos and Cambodia. Peace hardly existed. Apart from the fighting in Viet Nam, and an increasingly heavy U.S. involvement there, tiny Laos was engaged in its own civil war.

Still, the ICC maintained a presence, clinging to the vestiges of truce supervision through its missions in Viet Nam, Cambodia and Laos. To connect them, and allow members to move from one post to another, the ICC operated the only air service between North Viet Nam and the western world. In a weird phenomenon of the Viet Nam war, a chartered old Boeing 307 Stratoliner, flown by pilots of a French company, made the rounds every Friday and every other Tuesday, going from Saigon in South Viet Nam, to Phnom Penh in Cambodia, to Vientiane in Laos, and finally, in a two-hour flight, to Hanoi in North Viet Nam. The last leg, of course, was the crucial one, for it permitted a rare light on activities of a Communist state at war.

Vientiane was also a base for Air America, an airline not required to show a balance sheet. There was no secret about who owned and operated Air America. It was the Central Intelligence Agency, which, peculiarly enough, functioned with a minimum of cloaks and daggers. The local Air America manager was a short, bouncy, fifty-one-year-old Texan named Frank Dunn. I met him simply by taking a taxi from the Lane Xang Hotel, in the centre of Vientiane, to nearby Wattay Airport.

Dunn, wearing a Stetson, greeted me cheerfully in an operations shack reminiscent of the Yukon or other bush-pilot locales. There may have been tall palms outside instead of snow caps. But the same kind of men — rawboned, garrulous — wandered in to check on weather, to examine charts, and to see what lay between them and their drop zones in the hinterland. Air America's task was to supply munitions, medicines and food to isolated Royal Lao forces and loyal tribesmen in combat with the communist Pathet Lao and their North Vietnamese allies. Thirty-two aircraft, some vintage C-46s, were in service. Most of the pilots and "kickers" — the sturdy types who shoved or booted crates from an aircraft's open hatch in flight — were U.S. air force veterans.

In the evening the American fliers, and others employed by the CIA, repaired to the Canadian officers' mess. The Canadians of the ICC operated the best and busiest bar in Vientiane. "Happy hour" began at eight a.m. and never ended. The ringing of a cowbell signified that someone was buying a round for all present. "*Bopig-man*" led in popularity such salutes as "cheers," "here's how" and all other known alcoholic good wishes. It was a friendly, animated atmosphere, appropriate to a far outpost.

One evening I sat reminiscing with a Canadian captain who matched my wartime stories with his ICC experiences. Hanoi, a principal target of U.S. bombers, was hardly a place to tarry, he commented. The Canadian and other ICC members were happy to get their work done and fly out. Then, casually, between sips, the captain remarked that the real beneficiaries of those ICC excursions to Hanoi were the Americans. How so? With hardly a pause, he went on to explain that Canadians acted as informants for the Americans, passing on first-hand intelligence they gathered in North Viet Nam.

I asked no more questions. I simply listened, dumbfounded. Here was an open admission that Canadians serving in supposedly a neutral, apolitical agency, the International Control Commission, were spying for a belligerent.

The captain was in a monologue mood. Without prompting, he detailed the way it worked: they came back from Hanoi and relayed principally to CIA officers — and he waved a hand toward a couple of men at the bar as representative — their observations of the accuracy of bombing raids, the effect on civilian morale, and other intelligence items that would otherwise be difficult, if not impossible, to collect.

At this point I intervened to ask the captain: Didn't he think this activity was a violation of the ICC's mandate? He simply shrugged and said the commission was far from a harmonious organization. The Canadians disliked the Indians for their preaching. They also accused the Poles of being dour and doctrinaire Communist party types, more concerned about reporting data on Laos and Cambodia and South Viet Nam to the Russians than doing an objective job of handling complaints about border violations and other tasks of the ICC.

The Canadians themselves? I repeated: Weren't they breaching a trust? I expected a vague answer. Instead the captain said, "We're really Americans, aren't we?"

The revelation or confession of espionage was understandable in a sense, since it suggested the age-old meeting of military minds — in this instance, Canadian and American military minds. Yet this was a shocker, a contravention of Canada's image of itself as a peacemaker. Now I asked questions of myself: Could I report the story without jeopardizing the career of the captain? Would I be accused of poor ethics, abusing the hospitality of a mess, or, worse, of lack of patriotism? For several days I mulled over what to do.

This was a not unfamiliar quandary; it confronts every reporter at some time. The question of protecting the source was easily settled; I simply would not use his name, or pinpoint Vientiane or the officers' bar. But the bigger issue embraced old alliances and affections between Canadians and Americans. Still, we were not at war; nor, officially, was the United States. At risk was Canada's well won reputation as an "honest broker," a trustworthy and non-partisan referee in the international arena.

Only a decade earlier, Lester Pearson had earned a Nobel Peace Prize for initiating the United Nations peace-keeping force which kept combatants apart at Suez. Even now, Paul Martin, external affairs minister, was preaching at the United Nations that Canada, "by virtue of our membership in the ICC," could exert great influence in bringing together the warring sides in Viet Nam. Such influence might face ruin if Canadians continued to serve as informants and aroused Hanoi's suspicions.

I'm not sure how much of this I consciously added to my decision to tell the story, but it was a strong element. More simply, I felt it would be wrong not to tell it.

The Star played the report on page one under a sober headline, "Canadians Abuse Viet Role." News agencies picked it up, and almost instantly opposition members stood up in the House of Commons and challenged the government. Paul Martin stiffly denied the report, saying that Canadians "are not engaged in any clandestine or spying activities." It was, for the normally cautious

Martin, an oddly instantaneous and unequivocal rebuttal. Martin was known in the press gallery for his ability to obscure the meaning of a statement. But now he was loud and clear. It would have been more judicious to say: I doubt if such activity goes on, but I will look into it.

That, in fact, is what Prime Minister Pearson did say the next day when John Diefenbaker, Conservative leader, called for an inquiry by Parliament. Pearson termed it an "interesting sugges-tion." By now a second reporter, Tim Ralfe, had followed up, contributing to the uproar — and uproar it was, with front page headlines in *The Toronto Daily Star* and other major newspapers across the country. Ralfe, a CBC television and radio correspondent who had spent six months in Viet Nam, added details to my report. He disclosed that Canadian members of the ICC took photographs and made tape recordings of a U.S. raid on oil dumps near Hanoi, passing these on to the Americans. Pearson said that Ralfe and I might be called before a parliamentary committee.

The story was a forty-eight-hour wonder, not much more, at least in terms of headlines. Bill Wilson, *Montreal Star* bureau chief in Ottawa, sent me a message saying, "It seems perfectly clear that the last thing in the world the government wants is to ever let you and Ralfe get within a mile of that committee." He was right. The government dropped further public references to the issue. But questions remained. Did instructions now go out from Ottawa to Canadians on the ICC to desist from clandestine operations? Did Canadians on the ICC stop treating Americans as comrades in arms? I have no way of knowing, but I doubt it. I am, however, sure they practised discretion before bragging in a bar about extracurricular activities.

Some philosophic debate continued over the obligation of a reporter — whether it is to serve the state or society. Almost unanimously commentators and letter writers supported my dis-closing the Canadian breach, and also my paper's decision to publish it. James Eayrs, a political scientist, wrote in his syndicated column:

"It is hard to be both a good reporter and a good citizen, but I think the verdict of history will be that Clark, on this occasion especially, served both his masters with distinction."

A couple of times in my newspaper career I was asked to engage in a little spying. I presume this is an occupational hazard. The reporter gets around, is expected to examine places and situations, and to ask questions. Therefore, in theory, he is less suspect than other snoopers.

My first exposure to the ways of the clandestine world came in 1958 when I departed from China via Hong Kong. Communist China was very much a country of the unknown in those days. I was not surprised when Canadian external affairs people in Hong Kong invited me to meet for lunch with a small group of men to recount my impressions. About a dozen were present, and they asked penetrating questions. I had little doubt some worked for British and American intelligence agencies. But since I had no proof of it, I did not mind. I didn't feel I was acting as a spy, first because I possessed no military information, but mainly because it was the kind of debriefing I would offer fellow journalists. I was not violating any professional code of journalism — a code, incidentally, written by the individual, since no other exists.

The second occasion, a few months after Hong Kong, smacked of a scene from a ludicrous play. I was in Toronto, on a visit from London, enjoying dinner with friends in the main dining room of the Royal York Hotel. I heard my name called. A page boy led me to a man seated in the foyer, black homburg in lap. He rose and identified himself as a major in Canadian military intelligence. "When you left China," he said in low voice, "did you happen to take with you a timetable of China Airlines?"

I could have been polite and simply said, "No." But my dinner had been interrupted by an unnecessary and clumsy attempt at data gathering. I felt perverse. "I haven't got one," I said, in equally low voice, "but I tell you what. Have someone go to the office of the New China Travel Agency on the Kowloon side of Hong Kong. There's a stack of timetables on the counter." It was the truth, and I didn't mind underlining the ineptness behind the question.

The third time — an attempt to recruit me — was the most serious and disturbing from a journalistic point of view. I had just returned from Czechoslovakia and other East European countries, in 1967, and Expo 67 was about to open in Montreal. I received a phone call from the Royal Canadian Mounted Police. An officer would like to visit me in my office. I had no idea of the purpose, but of course agreed.

The next morning a young man presented himself. He said: If, in the next several months, I spotted at Expo, or anywhere in Montreal, anyone I had met in Czechoslovakia or the other countries of Eastern Europe, would I call him immediately? I said I would not call him. We were not at war, with Czechoslovakia or any other country. I was a reporter. If I hoped to continue functioning as a reporter, especially abroad, I could take no chances of becoming identified as an intelligence agent or an informant.

The RCMP officer left without another word. I wonder if my name went on file as an uncooperative citizen, or worse.

Unanticipated sights or sounds sometimes stir up a bygone image, not necessarily of great significance but of value as an insight into human nature. Not long ago friends of mine returned from a visit to India and regaled us with a description of village life. My mind immediately leapt back to a trip I made in the nineteen fifties.

India was in the midst of one of its recurring birth control campaigns. Instead of condoms or pills, costly and requiring constant replenishing, the government distributed millions of strands of inexpensive beads, each strand with a variety of colors. Women, instructed in the rhythm method, were told how to move the beads to keep track of periods of safer sex.

I was impressed to note how many of these lengths of beads hung on the inside walls of mud huts in the most remote villages. Then disaster — unexpected, unpredictable — struck the government's valiant intentions. Men, coming in after a day's work in the fields, would glance at the beads, and mutter to themselves: the hell with this, tonight's the night. And they'd jiggle the beads.

At another time in India I finally met in person a man, Chester Ronning, with whom I had spoken on the phone several years earlier. Then he had been Canadian chargé d'affaires in Chungking; now he was high commissioner to India. Ronning held a theory that the main reason why the Chinese were much more energetic than the Indians was diet. The Chinese, he pointed out, ate anything and everything that crawled; grubs, included, were high in protein. The Indians, dominated by religious practice, avoided much nutritious foodstuff. The Chinese cooked over a quick flame, retaining vitamins. The Indians used dried dung as fuel, searing over a slow fire, thus destroying much of the remaining value. I've mentioned the Ronning theory to doctors, and have not heard it rebutted.

Perhaps these splendid but useless vignettes do not constitute history, but they add to the entertainment value of journalism. The mind jumps in a potpourri of tidbits and unanswered questions. What is there about the seats in a jeep that seem unchanged from decade to decade? In the many times I have ridden in army jeeps in Israel, the biggest common denominator I found is the inevitable oil stain impregnating the seat covers. The current generation of Israelis might get some solace feeling their fathers and grandfathers probably shared the same blemished vehicles.

When I think of Israel, I think of El Al, the Israeli national airline. Probably more tales are told about El Al, sometimes in frustration but almost always with affection, than any other airline in the world. An Israeli diplomat once told me of his typical experience. He had survived a rough day at the foreign ministry, starting with a mix up over some important papers. At home, he got into a row with his wife. Then he hastily gulped his dinner because he had to pack a bag. On his way to the airport to catch an overseas flight, he sideswiped another car.

Finally the distraught diplomat settled into his seat on the plane, motioned to a stewardess, and sighed, "Please, a double whiskey." The stewardess glared at him. "It's midnight," she said. "Why do you want to drink?"

The clash between women passengers, especially North American Jews, and El Al stewardesses is notorious. The foreigners like to chide the flight attendants for not staying home and raising a family. The Israeli women, predictably, snap back — an absolute mother-daughter relationship in capsule.

Jewish clannishness at one time presented the airline with problems. El Al's New York office had to appeal to the International Air Transport Association in Montreal for help. A friend of mine, Ralph Cohen, IATA's public relations chief, took the call. Did the association, asked El Al, have any big signs that clearly stated that passengers must pay extra for excess baggage? It did, indeed. El Al passenger agents at the airport, explained the caller, faced a battle whenever they told a passenger that his luggage to Tel Aviv was overweight; there would be an additional charge. "Why do you bother me this way?" the passenger usually cried. "As one Jew to another....."

Cohen promptly shipped a batch of appropriate signs. A few days later he phoned New York to inquire about the results. "Ah," said El Al, "we didn't need them, after all. Somebody in the office came up with another idea." Every passenger agent now had a name plate in front of him at the check-in counter. Mr. McDuff, Mr. Reilly, Mr.....

Why does airline travel remind me of trivia? In the early 1960s, I was stuck in Lima, with a forty-five-day excursion ticket due to expire. I needed another couple of days to complete my work. I stopped by the airline office and asked a girl behind the counter if an extension was possible. No, she said, unless I paid the difference between this and full fare — several hundred dollars more. I was crestfallen, because I was researching a book on Latin America at my own expense.

The girl stared at me for a moment, then said, "Are you feeling all right?" "Fine," I said. "You don't look well," she persisted. I tumbled, and asked where I could find a doctor. She told me, just down the street — a very fashionable street. I followed directions, saw a building with several brass plaques. I chose the most impressive — a physician with degrees from Berlin, Vienna, and a few other big medical schools. Only the best for me.

Upstairs, a receptionist greeted me in a tastefully decorated office with many fine paintings adorning the walls. Several patients waited, but a nurse ushered me, a gringo, straight to the doctor. A distinguished looking man in his sixties, he asked what he could do for me. I said, "An airline sent me." Without another word, he said, "How much longer do you want to stay?" I told him. He scribbled a note saying I was unfit to travel for another week, and I gave him his fifteen-dollar fee. The airline clerk beamed when she extended, without further charge, the validity of my ticket.

I have learned since that little has changed, in Latin America and elsewhere. Travel agents regularly make deals on behalf of clients. Many airlines look the other way.

Soon after my return from London in 1960, a colleague at *The Montreal Star,* David Legate, took me as his guest to the University Club. Instantly I liked the club, with furnishings, including a hammered brass table top in the tiny lift (and it was a lift, not an elevator), that looked like transplants from England. The University Club was a private, very low key establishment unconnected with McGill, though many graduates were members along with professionals from other universities. Humorist Stephen Leacock, an early pillar, was enshrined in a portrait that hung in a corner of the Leacock Room, a lounge.

The Leacock Room — indeed much of the club — was a male preserve. Typical of the day, the University Club did not admit female members; moreover women guests were required to enter by a special entrance. This, too, was in the London tradition; in fact, the press club in London, just off Fleet Street, proclaimed proudly that it held "ladies' night" once a year. If there were males who objected to this sexism, you never heard them. But when it came to my turn to seek "admission" to the University Club I was jolted into a reminder that discrimination against males also existed — if they happened to be Jews.

Apart from covering such stories as the entry into Buchenwald, the death camp, and the trial of Adolf Eichmann, I don't believe I had ever thought, in personal terms, of anti-Semitism since McGill days. I had never felt held back in journalism because I was Jewish (maybe, as I discovered in conversation with Mrs. David Ben-Gurion, it sometimes carried an advantage). I asked Legate if he would propose my membership. He mumbled something about doing what he could do, but warned there was a terribly long waiting list — several years long.

That was the first hint. In my naivete, I had not realized there still existed restrictions. I confirmed this quickly through easy checking. No Jews were members of the University Club. Nor were there more than a token number of French Canadians. The Anglo "establishment" (fading as it was) appeared oblivious to its anachronistic clinging to old ways; this myopia applied to many branches of the establishment.

Eight years later, as editor of *The Star,* I encountered no difficulty gaining entry into the University Club. I don't doubt that my title helped. But more significantly, several Jews had by now preceded me, among them Phil Vineberg, an old *McGill Daily* mentor and more recently *bâtonnier* of the Montreal Bar. I'm not sure why I recall this phase of history, except as a pointer that many prejudices have undergone positive transformation. Not only are Jews members of the University Club. One hears as much French spoken as English. And, horror of horrors, not only do women use the main entrance; they are members on an equal basis with men.

The most crushing blow to any of that dying band of oldtimers who resisted Jews, francophones, and female members, must have been the sight out of nowhere of a *woman* sitting under Leacock's picture, smoking a cigarette, wearing slacks — and speaking French. God knows, she might even have learned her French in Morocco and migrated here as a Jew.

This is a nice story I am telling. It ends well. I relax frequently in the same huge and comfortable leather easy chair occupied almost daily in his time by Leacock. I don't know how many drinks he consumed, but I am happy with a martini and a newspaper. One day I was joined by John Humphrey, the distinguished international jurist who taught law at McGill when Leacock was an economics professor.

Humphrey said his favorite anecdote about Leacock was one the humorist himself related — about a trip he had taken on a cargo ship that carried a few passengers but no physician. Leacock, called "doctor" because of his PhD, was approached unexpectedly by a crew member who asked if he would mind examining the pretty stewardess who had just banged her knee. "I rushed," said Leacock, "but I was beaten to it by a doctor of divinity."

What attracts people to newspaper work? There are, obviously, lofty explanations, some idealistic. But one of my favorite commentaries comes from Sander Vanocur, a graduate of the old school of reporting — print and television — in the United States. "Journalism," he wrote, "is the world's most prolonged form of adolescence."

Newspaper work? It's a natural outlet for a dilettante, at least for someone unwilling or insufficiently motivated to devote a lifetime to an uncertain career — in the sense of not loving it at first sight. I might have turned into an acceptable doctor, but I doubt if I would have been a happy one. In newspaper work, I've been a doctor. As a neophyte reporter, I spent days riding ambulances in Montreal and watching the hectic pace in hospital emergency rooms.

I've also been a policeman, driving with detectives on night patrols and listening to their exciting yarns and even witnessing the results of lurid crimes. I've served as a lumberjack, leaping from raft to raft on northern Quebec rivers, and eating heaps of marvelous buttermilk pancakes at six a.m. In Kimberley, B.C., I've descended deep into the shaft of a hard rock mine, completely geared as an intrepid miner. In Toronto I was a firefighter, experiencing all the child-like delights of whisking through the streets with sirens screeching and following men who plunged into smokey buildings. In Hollywood I became an actor, portraying (as an extra) a fierce pirate. I even played myself, a newspaperman, interviewing Bob Hope (in a movie trailer for *The Great Lover*).

"Child-like," of course, may be the key. But "adolescence" is better, reinforcing the public impression that reporters, at best, merely collect impressions, that they possess no expertise. Even that is not accurate. It may be that a reporter is an observer, rather than a participant. But I've discovered that a good reporter becomes a master at what he or she is doing — gathering information. A good reporter strives for proficiency in assessing that information. That is real participation.

At still another level, one learns to anticipate reactions and events on the strength of having studied how past reactions and events developed. It is a great field for self-education, ever demanding. The satisfaction is believing that other people may pick up some knowledge from what you relay to them.

It is not always an easy mental process, as I verified when I interviewed Marshall McLuhan, the "medium is the message" guru. I listened intently for four hours. Spotting my bewilderment, McLuhan referred to Margaret Mead, the anthropologist, and said:

"Don't worry if you don't understand me. Margaret Mead spent four days with me and she didn't understand me either."

The challenge of translating complexity into relative simplicity is awesome, yet gratifying. That challenge has never left me. Even after I became editor of *The Star* it was with the understanding I would continue also as a reporter, free to get out when, and to where, the story warranted. That, to me, is the dividend of the ego trip on which you embark when you step into your first newspaper office.

My saddest day in journalism burst when my beloved *Montreal Star* collapsed. We had endured a long, demoralizing strike, and it appeared we were on the way to recovery. But nothing was the same, just as nothing had justified management's mishandling of the strike. It was a tragic end to what had been a great success story — the creation of a newspaper in 1869 by a young entrepreneur named Hugh Graham (later Lord Atholstan), the takeover by a self-made business tycoon, J.W. McConnell, and the insistence on quality by the son who succeeded him as publisher, John McConnell.

John was dedicated and superb in work. His private life was less fortunate. accented by a faltering marriage and chronic uncertainty of personal worth. His health suffered and he was frequently unavailable for important decisions. The time eventually arrived for a change in leadership.

There was never any danger of the paper failing financially. Its profits, along with those of the family's sugar refinery and flour mill, contributed to the McConnell Foundation; with an estimated value of $600 million, it was the biggest foundation in Canada by the late 1970s. But direction was needed at *The Star*. Both of John's brothers, Wilson and David, were dead. None of the dozen of J.W. McConnell's descendants were capable of, or interested in, operating a newspaper. John's own adopted son, Royden, became a playboy who liked to race around town in the ambulance which he operated as a public service.

The only candidate was a member of the family by marriage — Derek Price, whose wife, Jill, was Wilson's daughter. Price had worked briefly for a bank and for Wilson in the sugar refinery, and then moved over to *The Star* , serving in various departments, including editorial, to develop a feel for publishing and what was required of it. A decent, likable, handsome man, he had the proper motivations including a sense of duty. His father, Brigadier John H. Price, who had led Canadian soldiers trapped by the Japanese in Hong Kong during World War II, maintained into his eighties an office to care for any of his veterans who needed help.

Derek Price, in his early forties, never felt at home after he became publisher of *The Star* in 1969. In particular, the editorial process, which had been John McConnell's great forte, baffled and bothered him. He found it difficult to accept criticism of editorials from friends or family members who would call over trifling matters of headlines— standard hazards for any publisher. Price was honest enough in his own analysis to realize he lacked the kind of stamina or fire to carry on, and within eight years decided to resign as publisher. The problem that had driven him into the post in the first place remained: who, in the family, could take over? There was no one. Thus, a great community property, with profits ranging from $6 million to $8 million a year, became part of an impersonal organization, FP Publications, based in Toronto.

The deal was straightforward. In relinquishing ownership of *The Montreal Star*, members of the McConnell family acquired twenty-five per cent of FP Publications, which included Toronto's *Globe and Mail, The Winnipeg Free Press, The Vancouver Sun* and five other papers. The man chosen to serve as publisher, William Goodson, had started at *The Star* as an office boy at age sixteen, and proved over the years to be a shrewd businessman, converting the plant of *Weekend* into such a commercially viable property that it even printed the opposition magazine, *The Canadian,* and several other journals. FP Publications also hired a new president, George Currie, who, fresh from a management consultant firm, possessed no newspaper background. Less than three months after Currie's appointment, *The Star* was shut down by a strike. Price, who served as the McConnell representative on the FP board, told Currie to keep out of it. Goodson would know how to cope.

The strike, which began on June 15, 1978, was seemingly over a simple issue — the number of men who would be engaged in the press room, to keep the presses rolling. The union had already won long and nasty battles with *Le Soleil* in Quebec City and *La Presse* in Montreal. Members of Goodson's own staff argued that the union could hardly be expected to yield to an English-language paper when it had succeeded against French-language papers. Goodson ignored the argument, saying it was time to stand up to unions. He had served as a fighter pilot in World War II, and, before long, union members felt he was trying to fight the Battle of Britain all over again. He, and *The Montreal Star,* lost. After eight months, with a relatively feeble *Gazette* picking up lucrative *Star* advertising and circulation revenue, Currie and the directors settled. They also named a new publisher, Art Wood, a competent and veteran *Star* editorial hand.

It was too late. On September 25, 1979, a Montreal institution ceased to exist. We didn't even have a chance to say good-bye to our readers. The first edition of the paper had come out, when the news of the end was delivered. There was no other edition for us to thank Montrealers for one hundred and ten years of loyalty.

Later, after the folding of other Canadian papers, the government set up a commission on newspaper ownership. George Currie testified: "You know, being a Quebecker myself, I should have realized that there was just no way that *The Montreal Star* was going to get those unions to agree to a settlement with *les anglais* which was any less generous than the settlement they had with *La Presse*. But I did not. We took the strike." It was a devastating confession, and did not console an anglophone community that felt increasingly beleaguered.

When the paper folded, I wept. So, I am sure, did two hundred other editorial people and one thousand additional employes on the *Star* premises. Some of my grief found an outlet in *The Globe and Mail*. "Death? Breakup? Loss?" I wrote. "How does one evaluate the end of a newspaper? It cannot, obviously, be as meaningful as the termination of a life. Yet it is all of these things to me: the abrupt and unchosen halt to a love affair. A living creature that performed a remarkable service, representing human frailty and maybe greed at times, but most often generosity of spirit, and, more important, a pride of dedication, has gone."

Rereading that piece now, I realize how trite it must have sounded. Still, I am proud of the last paragraph: "I can only say that I am sad, so sad that a doctor friend of mine calls it 'a separation anxiety.' But he is only partly right. I am separated from a long-time mate and home but I won't be separated from journalism. Somehow or other I, as an individual, will continue in this greatest of fields until I encounter a story situation which I have never met before."

The last sentence, of course, is the clue, for nothing is new. Everything in journalism, as in life, is a repetition of the past, only in different form. The catch is how to remain alert to detect that difference. This means a constant kind of self-renewal through acceptance of fresh contests. In ancient times, Japanese artists fought the threat of boredom by changing, every twenty years, their styles of painting, their locations — even, sometimes, their names.

I wasn't prepared to go to the extreme of altering my identity, or even my residence, but the burial of *The Star* propelled me into writing a book — my fourth — and taking on assignments from the Canadian edition of *Reader's Digest,* published in Montreal. The connection with the *Digest* proved to be a lifesaver. Basically I continued to do what I had most enjoyed doing for *The Star* — travelling for stories, sometimes in Canada, but more often abroad. And, despite my years in the profession, I learned a good deal about journalism. I had never before witnessed such meticulous checking by researchers. Every fact, every date, every quotation, required verification, often from three sources. No other magazine that I knew of, certainly no newspaper, came close to this respect for accuracy.

On one occasion, in 1985, I flew to Ethiopia to do an account on the exodus of Ethiopian Jews for Israel. These were blacks, like other Ethiopians. But other Ethiopians still called them *falashas*, "strangers," even though they traced their origin in Ethiopia to the time of King Solomon. Now they faced enslavement as victims of a civil war. I learned that it was Mossad, the Israeli intelligence agency, that organized the odyssey code-named "Operation Moses."

In trickles of a family or two, or sometimes in groups of one hundred, the *falashas* set out by foot for Sudan, hundreds of kilometres away, across mountains, grassland, and desert. The trek — made in the darkness of night to escape detection — was hazardous. Soldiers were on the lookout, bandits and rebels roamed the countryside, disease was prevalent, food was scarce. But the urge to "return" to Jerusalem, a place forebears had left two thousand years earlier, was powerful.

Mossad agents, among them a forty-year-old *falasha* recruit whom I knew as "Baruch," awaited them in Sudan. Baruch had helped plot their escape route. Now the more than seven thousand refugees were loaded in charter planes and taken to Israel. Baruch's description of his own earlier decamping from Ethiopia resembled fiction: disguised as a Moslem traveler, he was smuggled by camel caravan through Chad, made his way by rowboat at night across the Logone River, into Cameroon, bribed officials to get into Nigeria, where a Greek sea captain took him to Singapore; finally, he was able to hop a plane for Tel Aviv.

Maybe it was fiction. Maybe a cover story. It is impossible to confirm with certitude, for Mossad did not exist — at least officially. Almost any taxi driver in Tel Aviv could take you, without hesitation, to Mossad headquarters, on the road to Haifa. But Mossad, the spy factory, the source of true espionage tales, was a myth. That, at least, was the formal line.

Nonetheless "Operation Moses" turned out to be an intriguing story and *Reader's Digest* researchers had to go through the routine of corroboration. They faxed my manuscript to an Israeli correspondent in Jerusalem. He promptly sent back a message, possibly to placate censors, along the line: What is Mossad? In any event the researchers were able to satisfy themselves, after expurgating a few minor points, that the account was sound.

There was a postscript. A little later I ran into an acquaintance who was active in Canadian-Israeli affairs. He had just returned from Tel Aviv, where he dined with an old Mossad hand. The Mossad man said that he and his colleagues had enjoyed reading the *Digest* story — long before it appeared in print. Somehow — I wonder how — the faxed version had reached "Mossad Tower."

My continuing relationship with *Reader's Digest* reinforces what I have always felt about journalism: there is no substitute for on-the-spot reportage or face-to-face interviews. You pick up sounds and scents of a situation that no computer or fax machine can provide; you read a person's body language unobtainable in a telephone conversation. Sadly, more and more reporters must rely on collecting information by remote control; their publications plead economies imposed by time or budget.

Recently I returned from Lake Chapala, Mexico, where I visited a school for deaf children who came from poor, remote villages. The school, humble but effective, offered their only opening to a productive life. Operated and financed mainly by Canadian retirees in the Chapala area, it had been founded by two Canadian school teachers now living in Victoria, B.C. One of its benefactors was the bishop of the Roman Catholic diocese of Mackenzie-Fort Smith in the Northwest Territories. I mentioned to Alex Farrell, editor of the *Digest,* that I would call these contacts in Victoria and Yellowknife. He immediately said, "Why don't you go there?"

So I flew eight thousand kilometres for two one-hour interviews; the airfare alone cost more than three thousand dollars. But with what result? As I was leaving the bishop's study in Yellowknife, my coat donned, he casually mentioned that he was returning soon to Paulaktuk, an Inuit village of two hundred and fifty people on the Arctic coast. Several Inuit had contributed two dollars each and a storekeeper gave two thousand dollars for the deaf children far to the south in Mexico. That link between native peoples made only a sentence or two, but enough to add an extra, touching ingredient to the story. I would have missed it on a telephone.

What are the tricks of the trade? What shortcuts can be found in journalism? Amazingly enough, despite very long experience, I don't know many tricks of the trade. I can think of a simple rule in drawing an advance on expenses: always get more than you know you can possibly use; it looks good to return money, not so good to ask for more later. But I'm not sure that's an exclusive journalistic secret.

I do have one tip I relay to young writers: Whenever possible, stop writing when you most want to go on — that is, if you are working on a book or a long series of articles and are not pressed by an immediate newspaper or magazine deadline. Set a daily quota, whether it is five hundred words or fifteen hundred words, and when you are near reaching it, halt at the point the flow is best. There is nothing more conducive to delaying a day's work than to know a leftover problem confronts you. In reverse, resuming writing is a relative pleasure when it marks an easy continuation of the day before. I sometimes stop in mid-sentence or even mid-word. Then I can hardly wait to pick up.

Such is the kind of trick you learn to play on yourself. The final result — the feeling that you have achieved a goal — can be highly satisfying, though I don't believe the actual act of writing is pleasurable.

I tend to take many notes during an interview, except when I sense the subject is nervous and it would be more prudent to forgo the written word and rely on memory. If we are in a restaurant, and it is something I must remember word for word, I excuse myself to get to the men's room where I can scribble the words before they are lost on me. I will accept it is time to quit working when I can no longer remember what it was I wanted to jot down between leaving the table and getting to the washroom.

Rarely do I use a tape recorder — usually in dealing with an official whose business it is to stay on the record. Despite reassurances from a subject that he or she will not be inhibited, I think most people do tighten up when they sense their thoughts are engraved.

The foregoing doesn't add up to a huge list of tips on how to ease a work load. I haven't a huge list. But what about shortcuts? Again I am unschooled. I am not familiar with any way to get information other than to dig, dig, dig. I have yet to acquire a technique that lets me sit down at a keyboard, whether it is a typewriter or a computer, and dash off a report without confidence in my information.

I like immediacy, in the sense of dealing with current, rather than bygone, events. Still, unlike many other reporters of my generation, I've never been drawn particularly by "hard news" — that is, the fast-moving, urgent story. Rather, from the start I tended to gravitate to "features" — background pieces that either placed a perspective on the headlines or attempted to anticipate why a general condition might take a specific turn. I've covered hard news when necessary, but never with a feeling of comfort and usually with a sense of awe the way colleagues were able to sit down amid terrible confusion and noise, and rattle off readable copy.

Simultaneously I've never felt any special compulsion to go after big names in the news. I've preferred to look for social or political trends through people on the periphery of power, those who could spare the time to pass on their knowledge or whose personal case histories provided insightful examples of what was going on. It was always pleasing to dress up an article with an exclusive quote from a Golda Meir or an Anwar Sadat, but it was more important, I thought, to put together bits and pieces from many sources, in an effort to create a whole picture. Print journalists today are doing a better job at this than reporters of a generation or two ago. For one thing, they are better educated and more interested in discerning social trends. For another, television has robbed a "news" paper of any claim, or ability, to show real speed in describing events as they happen. I wish I were starting my career today. My kind of journalism would be more in demand.

Still, I am not complaining. On the contrary, I have been fortunate to observe some major events and learn, constantly, something about the world and about myself. I've never considered myself very brazen, but occasionally, if I feel provoked by perversity, I respond perversely.

Early in the 1960s, the U.S. state department banned American reporters from travel to Castro's Cuba. The Canadian government, believing it was important to maintain contact, imposed no restriction on the Canadian media, and I made three trips to Havana. As a result, I was invited to address the Committee of One Hundred. The Committee of One Hundred, while maintaining a low profile, constituted the most powerful group of business people in America. Members were not merely presidents of such corporations as General Motors and IBM. They were chairmen of the boards. Now they wanted to hear about Cuba; at a black-tie dinner, at their private club near Miami, I told them. I think they expected a hackneyed condemnation of Castro's seizure of U.S. property. Instead, I related, as I had done in newspaper articles, a bit about the history of the Cuban revolution and how

Washington had pushed Castro into communism. I sensed a growing hostility in the audience.

American businessmen, like newsmen, were prohibited by their government from any dealings with Cuba. They did not object; they regarded this as appropriate. The questions that followed my talk indicated high conservatism. Finally, a man stood up and demanded, "Why do Canadian businessmen still do business with Cuba?" I shot back, "The Canadian government believes in free enterprise. It does not believe in telling business people where, or with whom, they should do business." The dead silence signalled an end to the meeting.

The most satisfying groups to address are young people. They listen usually without prejudiced preconceptions, and they know no inhibitions in asking questions. Once, at Glebe Collegiate in Ottawa, I spoke about China. Good questions followed. A teen-age student accused me of saying one thing at one point, then another at another point: "Why did you contradict yourself?" I muttered, "China is full of contradictions," and tried to muddle through. But he had me cold.

My preferred work, luckily, is not on the lecture platform. It is out in the field, observing, reporting — and always learning. The bizarre twist to a story, the unpredictable ways of the human race — the lure is to find these. In Australia, twenty years ago, the trade union movement could hardly have been classified as radical; it was not much further to the left than the business community. Yet, strongly unionized construction workers refused to build an underground parking area for the new and exciting Sydney Opera House. To have done so would have meant demolition of three fig trees — trees that were brought down from the tropical north by an explorer in the nineteenth century and had grown to tremendous size. As self-appointed conservationists, hardhats thus found themselves in an unholy alliance with youth.

The hardhats also spurned a request to build an extension to a jail, arguing that in a modern society there was no further need for imprisonment. I asked a young academic, "Doesn't this attitude suggest anarchy?" He admitted, "Yes, it does. But a little anarchy is better than rampant apathy."

The learning process in journalism is fascinating because you never know when or how an unusual occurrence will bring with it new insight into human behavior. In 1969 Montreal police went on strike. The grievance may have justified some kind of dramatic action, but a strike by law enforcement officers was almost inconceivable — so much so that *The New York Times Magazine* asked me to write a long article about it. With the thin blue line of public security removed, masses of normally peaceful, law-observant men and women roared out on a rampage, smashing downtown shop windows and looting everything from pocket radios to fur coats.

I spoke to a German-trained psychotherapist, Dr. Paul Fircks, about the phenomenon. He cited a book that became a classic, *The Crowd: a Study of the Popular Mind,* written in 1897 by a French psychologist, Gustave Le Bon. The crowd — the mob — is amoral, and if the law relaxes, the people in the crowd act out their impulses. Morals and ethics are externalized by the presence of the police; if the police are not there, the mob does as it pleases. It is the believer in individuality who stands back, who refuses to join the mob, who rejects looting, who behaves in a civilized fashion. "But the majority of people," said Fircks, "join mobs when given an opportunity. Germany has shown this. Hitler was a genius who created out of supposed individuals in a crowd, a mob."

The story did not end there. Fircks, a widower, lived alone in a large home in a high-income residential district where burglaries were frequent. Shortly before midnight he prepared to retire; but having heard the late news about the strike and the troubles downtown, he decided on precautions. He remembered that in his office in the basement was a .32-calibre revolver that he had taken from a patient. He fetched it, climbed upstairs to his bedroom, bolted the door and slipped into bed — the revolver on the table next to him. When he awoke, it was to the sound of someone jimmying the bedroom door.

Fircks fired three times. He found at the foot of the stairs the body of a man who, it turned out, was a habitual burglar. What was Fircks' reaction? "I went through two world wars and the Nazis. No burglar is going to frighten me," he exclaimed. But shooting and killing even a burglar? "I looked at the man lying there, and I cursed him. I thought: How does he dare? Who does he think he is to threaten me, to come into my home this way?" That phrase — "Who does he think he is?" — has stayed with me ever since. So have the lessons of that story, written a quarter century ago, helped me understand human behavior a bit more acutely.

The traditional dictum by realtors is that the three most important elements in a successful real-estate investment are: location, location, location. I say about journalism: preparation, preparation, preparation. In July 1992 I proposed to the *Digest,* a story on United Nations peacekeeping, pegged to the current stationing of Canadian troops in Sarajevo, Bosnia. Their mission was to open up and guard the airport, long closed to any commercial traffic, so that UN relief planes could bring in food and medicines to the 300,000 besieged inhabitants of Sarajevo.

The question was how to get there; this was before the arrival of a stream of media people, when facilities, though still rugged and uncertain, became more plentiful. Even department of national defence officers in Ottawa could offer little more than broad suggestions. They told me simply to report to Canadians at the airport in Zagreb, Croatia, the jump off point for Sarajevo. I was assured that they would arrange on the spot a lift for me on a Canadian Hercules running the shuttle between Zagreb and Sarajevo.

I hate vagueness of this sort. No one had a name to offer me, or anything more precise than "Get to the airport at Zagreb, you'll find someone to set it up." Before leaving Montreal, however, I got through on the phone to Sarajevo, thanks to national defence people, and spoke to Captain Doug Martin, Canadian spokesman with the UN contingent. It was a clear and sharp line, making it hard to believe that mortar bombs and shells landed all around him.

After Martin briefed me on what little he — or anyone else — knew about specifics of my entry, we chatted casually for a few moments. I told him I had been a correspondent in World War II. He asked, "Do you play cribbage?" I didn't get the connection but I thought maybe he needed a cribbage set, and I offered to bring him one. "It's not that," said Martin. "My grandfather was also a veteran of the Second World War and as a kid I loved playing cribbage with him."

At that point, having established I was of venerable age, and unwittingly making me feel it, Martin called me "sir." I repeated the question: What could I bring him? Liquor? No, said he. Then what? After a long pause, he finally said, "You could bring me a bag of sunflower seeds."

What? I said. He repeated, "Sunflower seeds....in the shell...salted." So that's what I prepared for, laden on take off in Montreal, not with a bag but four bags of sunflower seeds. I figured that anyone who held to simple pleasures while machine gun bullets and artillery rounds crashed around him, deserved no fewer. Later, I mentioned to Maj.-Gen. Lewis MacKenzie, the Canadian commander of UN forces, that oldtime soldiers would have leaped at any offer of booze. "I'm surprised," he said, "that Martin didn't ask for peanut butter. That's what the young soldiers go for these days."

"Why must you go?" my sister Ruth said when I told her I was going to Bosnia. "Haven't you done enough? Haven't you taken enough risks?" Ruth, now in her eighties, was the one for whom Dr. Norman Bethune, so many years ago, had promised full recovery from a grave illness — promised it in a spontaneous dance of exuberance with my startled mother. My daughter Bette didn't ask the question. She knew me well enough, and perhaps by now understood my absences from home when she was a child. Barbara, my wife to be — I had been married and widowed twice — didn't ask. Barbara knew me, too.

My sister's kind of question is valid and difficult to answer in terms that don't sound banal. I won't say that you go because that is where the story is. That is so simple. Nor will I accept the amateur psychologist's analysis that you are trying to perpetuate youth. There are other ways of pretending you experience such a non-existent state.

To me the overriding answer is that I was doing a story on peacekeeping. How could I not visit a place where peacekeeping was undergoing its gravest test? How could you do a roundup, referring to the many past peacekeeping missions, now dormant, and the perennial ones like Cyprus, but also relatively inactive, without trying to capture the flavor and fears and problems of men and women dealing with minute by minute reality and decisions affecting life and death?

Maybe there is more. Maybe there is the rudimentary need to smell a place, the air, the dust, to hear the rattle of equipment, the pitch of human voices, to assess, in part, what kind of situation really prevails. In theory you could wait until soldiers come out of the line, back to a sheltered base, and talk to them there. But that would be like a doctor examining a patient for the first time — after the patient has recovered.

Long before China opened itself to foreign visitors, I argued that it was far more revealing to walk down a street in Peking for twenty minutes than to sit with China watchers in Hong Kong for twenty days. You never know when you are going to unearth the elusive nugget that helps to lift and make understandable an intricate story.

In Sarajevo airport I spotted a Van Doos (Royal 22nd Regiment) corporal, behind his sand-bag emplacement, fingering the chain around his neck on which dangled the sniper's bullet that got caught in his flak jacket a day earlier. How can you discover that kind of sharp vignette without going there? More intangibly, but no less important, in a combat zone there is a sense of identification between reporter and soldier that comes with the sharing of dangers. No matter how passing or ephemeral the sharing is for the reporter, it carries incalculable weight.

My flight from Montreal, on Lufthansa, took me to Frankfurt, with a connection to Zagreb — only it wasn't precisely Zagreb. Western airlines were not going to Zagreb, since Croatia was considered a war zone and insurance rates were too high. So we landed at Ljubljana, in another former Yugoslav republic known by its own name of Slovenia. From there Lufthansa transported me — and a dozen others — on a three-and-a half-hour bus ride to the Intercontinental Hotel in Zagreb.

I had a booking at the Intercontinental, but I also had a name provided by an external affairs officer, Guy Archambault. That was hardly a master stroke. It was routine, but it's what I mean about preparation, preparation, preparation — as much as possible ahead of time, even to small details. The name was Sam Hanson, External's representative in Croatia — a formal exchange of ambassadors was not yet in place. His phone number, it turned out, was the Esplanade Hotel. Before checking in at the Intercontinental I asked the receptionist to make the call.

Instantly I was speaking to Sam Hanson. He had received a fax from Archambault about me. A promising start! Did he, I asked, by any chance know who I was to report to if I wanted a lift to Sarajevo? He did indeed: it was Squadron Leader John Barrass, and Barrass was also staying at the Esplanade.

It was a short taxi ride, and within minutes, by four thirty in the afternoon, I had checked into the Esplanade (there was no problem about getting a room, thanks to the reluctance of tourists and business people to travel to a war zone). At five o'clock I was enjoying drinks with Hanson and Barrass. Barrass, a Royal Air Force officer on exchange with the Canadian armed forces, told me to meet him in the lobby at five forty-five the next morning. He was going to be flying a Hercules C-130 transport, and I'd just tag along with him to the airport, and on to Sarajevo. It was all so simple. Having gone without sleep the night before on the Atlantic leg, I felt relieved and at repose this night.

The UN shuttle base was at the far end of the Zagreb airport, and I don't know how I would have reached it on my own through Croatian security. But now, trailing Sqn. Ldr. Barrass and his Canadian crew, I boarded the C-130 without delay or formality. The air distance between Zagreb and Sarajevo, two hundred and ninety kilometres, should have been covered in little more than a half hour. But hostile Serbs had warned that planes, even UN planes, would be endangered if they passed overhead. So our route was indirect, hugging the Adriatic coast and then swinging inland for Sarajevo airport, a flight of an hour and a half.

Barrass handed me a flak jacket. I had never before worn one. It was heavy — sixteen pounds — and uncomfortable. But I learned to appreciate it when I saw and heard of the encounters of troops on the ground. I scribbled a note to retain for my own use: "Sometimes I feel awkward in the company of young men who could be my grandsons. Then I realize that they don't deal with me — or talk to me — as they would a grandfather. I'm one of them, even to their calling me by my first name. Maybe it is communal participation, the implicit hazard that embraces everyone regardless of age. But I also have a sense that to these youngsters, seeing an oldster who still insists on exploration and movement, there's a positive message of encouragement for their own futures."

Captain Doug Martin liked the four packs of sunflower seeds. Other soldiers appreciated the fresh newspapers I brought from Canada. Long ago I learned that the best gift anyone can receive in an isolated place is news in print that is barely a day old. General MacKenzie, who said he had resumed smoking only after he was posted to Sarajevo, thanked me for the four packs of Marlboro cigarettes I happened to have with me. On the Lufthansa flight I'd bought a carton, knowing Marlboros denoted treasured symbolism in former Communist countries.

A few weeks after Sarajevo, and after MacKenzie's return to Canada, *Reader's Digest* suggested that I write, in addition to an overall report on peacekeepers, a profile on the general. Within minutes after I made my first contact with the public affairs office at national defence headquarters in Ottawa, my phone rang. It was MacKenzie on the line. "I'm still coughing," he said, "from the Marlboros."

MacKenzie, a highly intelligent, educated, professional soldier, a composite of dedication, efficiency, bravery and irreverence, was barely known outside military circles though he had shared in eight UN operations. Then Canadian peacekeepers arrived in Sarajevo. CNN, the BBC, and other major television and print agencies showed up, too. Almost overnight MacKenzie became a global media figure — articulate, personable, outspoken, charismatic. His bluntness was biting, yet imaginative and appropriate. Serb gunners shelled Sarajevo. A British reporter asked MacKenzie, "Why don't you do something about it?"

"What do you want me to do?" shot back MacKenzie. "Go stab them with my ball-point pen?" It was telling the reporter he should have known the limitations of the UN mandate and equipment. But, more cogently, it was a graphic way of conveying the same message to an uninformed public.

I like to think that Canadians can attract international attention because they can be colorful as well as useful — a Lew MacKenzie, a Pierre Elliott Trudeau. I admire Trudeau enormously — his intellect, his breadth of vision. Eighteen months into his premiership, I described him in *The New York Times Magazine* as an intensely individualistic person, "a complex mixture, a man to himself and comparable to no other political figure. He can be patrician, autocratic, cold, self-protective and mysterious — but also charming, warm, carefree, open, modest, and shy."

Trudeau in the past managed to escape periodically to a mountain retreat, Thoreau-style, to meditate alone. In public life, the best he could do was to walk alone from one parliament building to another — without security escort. The man who on occasion wore an ascot and open sandals in the House of Commons, also, attired in white tie and tails, slid down the banister of Lancaster House, a British government mansion in London.

Trudeau showed, and still shows on his return to private life, little patience with the press, especially reporters who throw at him trivial questions. Was he, he was asked on becoming prime minister as a swinging bachelor, going to give up his Mercedes? "Which one," he replied, "the car or the girl?" But mostly his observations were serious and trenchant. I remember what he once told me when he was still a law professor at Université de Montréal. Referring to separatists who talked blandly of a "viable" Quebec carrying on economically, as in the past, in a customs union or common market with Canada and the United States, he said: "It doesn't occur to them for one minute that English Canada would be so hostile it would rather go barefoot than buy shoes made in Quebec — or that Washington might not be at all sympathetic to a new country on its border."

The thought is as pertinent now as it was thirty years ago.

Why do some names and episodes continue to haunt? I can still see Tony Ladas, lieutenant with the Chaudières, climb into his landing craft on June 6, 1944. Why does that incident, considering the many incidents I have experienced since then, stay alive? Because I stayed alive, to write about Ladas? Because I know I replied to his parents when they sent me a letter asking about those final moments before he died? Because I haven't the vaguest idea what I said to them? I can't answer the question about why certain images never disappear, any more than I can anticipate exactly the behavior of mobs, even though I picked up some clues from Dr. Fircks.

It took me nearly fifty years to learn the true meaning of "objective reporting," and that was not in a western environment, with its incessant and often boring analysis of the influence or evils of the media. It was in Ramallah, the West Bank — on land claimed by Arabs and occupied by Israelis. The color of my car's licence plates (yellow) designated its origin in West Jerusalem — thus my driver and I were legitimate targets for Palestinian youth hurling stones. Then the Palestinians moved on to a road block, and tried to dismantle it. Moments later an Israeli patrol roared up in a jeep and fired off canisters. My driver and I, caught in the middle of the fury, were engulfed in tear gas. It was a bloodless vignette, a sad reminder of how completely and effectively neutrality can be thrust on a visitor.

A few months later I witnessed more ugliness. But this time it was on television, and I sat in the safety and comfort of my Montreal home. The TV setting was the South Shore of the St. Lawrence River, as Canadian soldiers prepared to take down barricades erected by native people, Mohawks demanding sovereignty. Since bullets might fly, a convoy of cars, carrying women, children and the elderly, set out from the Kahnawake reserve. These were refugees, seeking security. But whites demanded revenge because Mohawk warriors had blocked the Mercier bridge and direct access to Montreal. The whites stood there and methodically heaved rocks at the cars and the defenceless occupants. The hatred, the malevolent expressions on the faces of grown men reminded me of other scenes. There was Sharpeville 1960, with white South African police brutally rounding up blacks. And of course there was the West Bank. Canadians pride themselves on their "tolerance," but racism or bigotry here, as elsewhere, takes little to make it emerge.

I am not sure whether I can enunciate, even after a long and happy career in journalism, the credo that fashions a long and happy career. I'm not even sure if I can spell out the rules that must go into the decent practice of journalism. Perhaps these are very simple and few in number: never to underestimate the intelligence of the public, never to assume it knows too much. A fatal flaw in many reporters is to write, consciously or otherwise, with disdain for the audience. Or, conversely, to omit basic information on the assumption that the reader already is in full possession of all that is relevant. The bigger the story, the greater the elucidation required. This does not imply preaching or imposition of the reporter's own ideas. It means what it says: inform, rather than advocate.

A great American journalist, Walter Lippmann, once described the task of the professional reporter and observer as finding out what is going on, under the surface and beyond the horizon, and what this meant yesterday and what it could mean tomorrow. "In this way," said Lippmann, "we do what every sovereign citizen is supposed to do but has not the time or the interest to do it for himself." In the end, it is not a reporter's employers or colleagues who sustain him quite so much as the public. "And I have found," Lippmann concluded, "that the public applies only one consistent test — not agreement with one on substance, but the perception of honesty and fair intent. There is, in people a tough, undiminished instinct for what is fair."

Every serious reporter, at some time or other — and sometimes very often — asks himself the question: Have I passed the test? Have I played fair? I hope I have, and I think I have. One measure is that I have continued to practise my profession long beyond the years when most men yearn for retirement. I have done so because I have believed in journalism and in myself. I do not think such longevity of career would have been possible without such belief. The more you enjoy what you are doing, the less likely you are to want to stop doing it. And you enjoy it largely because you have won acceptance. I will stop when my legs give out — or, also practically, when I am no longer in demand, by an editor or a reader.

Does this mean that the audience expects "objectivity" in the person who brings the news with all its uncertainties and barely definable lines? I doubt it, any more than the audience, or anyone else, expects properly to define "objectivity." There are other catchall, common phrases: "even- handed" or "balanced" reporting. These, too, are only perceived, they are not physically laid out so a count can be taken of the number of words for or against an issue or a belief. Back in 1960 I covered part of the U.S. presidential campaign — of the Republican candidate, Richard M. Nixon, and the Democrat, John F. Kennedy. How could the public feel sure that political commentators and columnists were unprejudiced when they predicted a Kennedy victory, especially since the professional analysts and pollsters refused to commit themselves one way or the other? In other words, in forecasting Kennedy for the White House, were the reporters being influenced by wishful thinking?

I said in a CBC radio broadcast at the time, "I know in my case, after following Nixon for a week and wondering about his sincerity, I would vote against him if I were an American. At the same time, after a week with Kennedy, I was so impressed that, frankly, my copy was biased in his favor. I imagine that other newsmen, going from one campaign train or plane to the other, reacted the same way." So much for "objectivity." Still, leaving aside any personal preference, I think the forecasts of a Kennedy victory were based on some solid indications. For one thing, the crowds drawn by Kennedy were much bigger than Nixon's. They were much more enthusiastic, even in areas normally considered Republican. Kennedy established rapport, a warm personal touch lacking on Nixon's part. And since the election was not going to be won on an issue, but rather on the impression that each man made, I think the average reporter's reaction could almost be considered the reaction of the average voter. In simple language, Kennedy was going to win.

If that is the test, relaying a sense of fairness in forming a judgment, I want always to make it. And if there is a perception that I have retained fairness, my medal for it will be worn with clear conscience.

So, after all this, what is the role of the reporter? It remains, as it has always been — to provide eyes and ears on the world. But the media at large can also become a propaganda tool, a delicate issue in the Gulf War when CNN was able to keep a correspondent, Peter Arnett, in Baghdad. As far as I know, this was the first war in history in which a representative of the enemy appeared nightly in the domain of the other belligerent. Thanks to television, Iraq's Saddam Hussein or one of his spokesmen received immediate attention on millions of U.S. screens.

In 1992 I attended my first meeting of the Canadian War Correspondents Association in thirty years. Most of my old colleagues were long since gone, and the generational gap became apparent when eight young reporters, veterans of the Gulf War, were welcomed as members.

A neophyte, Tim Naumetz of *The Toronto Sun*, described the difficulties he encountered in Saudi Arabia — not so much the physical dangers, which exist in any war, but the obstructionism by the military. The conclusion was simple: in World War II correspondents held the official approval of the army, a blessing handed down from General Eisenhower and others below him. The press — radio, too, in those days — was regarded as an important adjunct of the military, to be provided with facilities for functioning and communicating.

Thus we wore uniforms, though we were civilians, and we had access to information; most important we could count on the use of jeeps and other vehicles to get around, on press camps to bed down, on mess tents to offer sustenance, even on tables where we could prop our typewriters.

Naumetz and his peers encountered major obstacles trying to reach the action, and almost always failed. The U.S. army saw to that. The attitude was that the media was the enemy, and needed to be kept in check, an attitude that originated in Viet Nam, sharpened itself in later U.S. actions in Grenada and Panama, and infiltrated the mentality of the British in the Falklands war. Naumetz benefitted from fast electronic communications — a fax transmitted instantly by satellite, and not submitted in advance to military censors. But if the authorities — in this case Saudi Arabian as well as American — decided there had been a violation of privileges, or undefined security rules, correspondents were thrown out of the theatre.

We, the oldtimers, believed that correspondents could function better when they knew that professional military people scanned their despatches to ensure that nothing of security value to the enemy was inadvertently included; it was much easier than a civilian correspondent making such judgment himself. I remembered how, when we entered Paris during the liberation, and censors had not yet arrived, some reporters sent stories from the Eiffel tower, where radio transmission linked up with London for re-filing from there. Invariably, in censoring their own copy, reporters were more rigid than experienced military censors.

I asked Naumetz if he would have felt comfortable working under censorship. He didn't have a clear answer. I sense that the word "censorship" connotes different meanings to different generations. Those of us covering World War II accepted it as logical and necessary — not as an attempt to stifle opinion, which we could express even during the war, and certainly amplify with military facts if warranted after the war. Today's generation of reporters equates "censorship" with "suppression." Bill Boss, who covered the Korean war in the 1950s, holds a theory that this fear is a flashback to old church doctrine of banning discussion of certain subjects under grave threats of punishment.

Whether the wars or the events of peace happen in the 1940s or the 1950s or the 1990s, some factors remain constant. Journalism demands the loyalty and dedication of a soldier. General MacKenzie told me not long ago: "The soldier basically is a very selfish person. If you train to be a surgeon for twenty years and you never operate, you become frustrated. It is the same for a soldier. When opportunity, like a UN mission, comes up, you go, you volunteer." The same kind of compulsion and obligation — and selfishness — must dominate the reporter's life.

I returned to Normandy in 1994 — the big anniversary for anyone of my generation. It is difficult to believe that fifty years elapsed since young men reached the shores of Normandy to assure the liberation of Europe. Some died doing it, and more than half since then. But of the remainder, many thousands arranged to get back, if only to pay respects to those who did not get back.

I thought back to a couple of weeks before D-Day, and the briefing Montgomery gave war correspondents — warning of possible defeat and disaster. I think that we today forget the realities of so many decades ago. Perhaps it explains the abysmal insensitivity and ignorance of some modern film makers and television producers — the Brian McKennas of *The Valour and the Horror* — who overlook the key ingredient of the history of World War II: It was fought by amateurs on one side and professionals on the other. The professionals had prepared and trained many years for combat. Still, here, at the cemetery of Bény-sur-Mer, are some of the amateurs who stood up to the professionals: the Tony Ladases. Only on this 1994 occasion did I learn from other Chaudières what happened to Tony Ladas in 1944.

Lionel Langlois, the Chaudière who on the vessel Prince David wondered what slit trench he would sleep in during his first night ashore, found out soon enough. The Chaudière objective was to capture and hold the high ground before the village of Colomby-sur-Thaon, eleven kilometres inland. They achieved the objective. Lieut. Ladas and other officers, knowing a counter-attack was inevitable, exhorted their men to "dig, dig, dig fast." Langlois says he did not need the spurring: "We dug, no one had to tell us to dig fast." There was no sleep. The Germans did strike that night. Ladas held a grenade in each hand, ready to throw, when a bullet hit him between the eyes. He died instantly. The Chaudières held fast.

As a result Caen, the pivotal Norman city, was eventually taken. Eighty per cent of Caen was destroyed. My lingering image of it from 1944 was of piles of rubble — only rubble. Now, in 1994, I saw a rebuilt city that still prized historic landmarks: the Abbaye aux Hommes, the Abbaye aux Dames, le Château de Guillaume le Conquérant, and other structures that had survived from medieval times. There are some new street names: Avenue du 6 Juin, Avenue de la Libération, Place du Canada, Esplanade Brillaud de Laujardière. The last is in memory of the city's chief architect whom I had met in 1944. Brillaud de Laujardière lived long enough to see Caen emerge, as he had predicted, a city of the future, its population doubled.

I thought: Is there any vocation other than journalism that makes possible such a reliving of history — and reminds one of the importance of hope?

The life and world of the foreign correspondent have undergone drastic changes in the last thirty or forty years. No longer is the public dependent on the newspaper reporter setting the scene of a momentous development in a faraway place. Television takes the public there instantly. The television reporter, however, whether or not he wears a trench-coat on camera, has hardly supplanted the old-style foreign correspondent. The camera is the dominant feature, matched by satellite time. The depth of coverage comes in a distant last.

The fact that the huge majority of television viewers receive most of their information in this fashion, and sporadically turn to newspapers, has been deplored long before I made these observations. But I believe that long afterwards there still will exist a brand of journalists — some even on television — who will function the way serious newspaper reporters always tried to function: to help the reader or viewer or listener understand what is happening in the world. It will go on this way, not only because of some public demand but because of the men and women who continue to enter journalism with a dedication and conviction that theirs is a satisfying and gratifying and responsible service in an ever complex society.

We all have a sense of purpose — at least that is the presumption. Many of us never know the good fortune of realizing it. I am one of the fortunate ones, to hit not only on a profession I loved from the start, but to be able to carry it on to the end. I must qualify the last phrase. I am able to continue in journalism so long as physical afflictions remain so contained as to permit travel, and seeing, and hearing, and touching a keyboard.

These, of course, constitute many qualifications, but at least boredom is not among them. I cannot imagine a dull moment ahead. I have encountered them often in the past, when time seemed boundless and I could afford to feel bored. Now my time is distinctly limited, and I am more than ever grateful for a profession that allows me to function much as I did when I began it. Every moment is exciting. Can a surgeon, who must put aside the scalpel because his fingers are unsteady after many years of work, say the same? Can a steel worker summon enough strength to do arduous physical labor after even half that time?

I am a writer. I am a reporter. I like to write and report, as I discovered the day I entered university. To me no punishment would have been greater anywhere along this path than if someone had removed my typewriter. Can you imagine — even in wartime to be blessed with the continued use of a preferred instrument while others must shoulder arms? The only change, basically, is that the typewriter is replaced by a computer — a positive change that cuts in half the time necessary to produce legible copy. At the age of seventy-six I find that agreeable.

My end thought is also my beginning thought: it has governed my thinking ever since I first identified it, by chance. The year was 1947, and the resumption of full-scale passenger service, by ship, across the Atlantic. Ocean liners, which had carried hundreds of thousands of troops in jammed quarters during six years of war, were now refitted on a luxury scale. I had a lordly assignment, to sail on the Canadian Pacific's Empress of Scotland, on the first voyage since her restoration — from Montreal to Southampton, and return. I was to write about the kind of people who now enjoyed peacetime travel.

I found myself writing mostly about one person, a man called "Boots." I can't recall his real name. The key is that the image of "Boots" has never left me, a slightly bent Yorkshireman of sixty, who came by his cognomen through occupation and honest toil. All his working life "Boots" had done nothing else but shine shoes — women's shoes, men's shoes, children's shoes. During the war, he did it ashore. Now he was back at sea, his great love, happily shining shoes while the ship rolled and creaked.

I followed "Boots" night after night as he covered the corridors of the Empress of Scotland to pick up and clean the footwear that waited outside many cabin doors. Not once did I think of asking whether he knew tedium. It was plain that "Boots" was as fascinated by the one shoe now in his palm as he must have been tens of thousands of pairs ago. "Look here," he said, pointing to the heel. "You see where the right side is worn much more than the other side. The man who wears this shoe has no fears of life."

How did "Boots" know? He just knew, that's all. Experience had given him this insight, so he could judge the character of an individual — an individual he never met in person — by the way the heel or the sole sloped. "Boots" analyzed every piece of footwear this way. He administered a magnificent shine. He was terribly proud of his work and he was never bored. I look on every story I do with two thoughts: it has never been done before, and while I am doing it, it is the most important story in the world.